"The Having of Wonderful Ideas" and Other Essays on Teaching and Learning

THIRD EDITION

"The Having of Wonderful Ideas" and Other Essays on Teaching and Learning

THIRD EDITION

ELEANOR DUCKWORTH

TEACHERS COLLEGE PRESS

TEACHERS COLLEGE | COLUMBIA UNIVERSITY
NEW YORK AND LONDON

Published by Teachers College Press, 1234 Amsterdam Avenue, New York, NY 10027

Permission Acknowledgments appear on p. x

Library of Congress Cataloging-in-Publication Data

Duckworth, Eleanor Ruth.
    The having of wonderful ideas and other essays on teaching and learning / Eleanor Duckworth.—3rd ed.
    p. cm.
    Includes bibliographical references and index.
    ISBN-13: 978-0-8077-4730-8 (pbk. : alk. paper)
        1. Teaching. 2. Learning, Psychology of. 3. Education. 4. Piaget, Jean; 1896–1980. 5. Teachers—Training of. I. Title.
    LB1025.2.D84 2006
    371.102—dc22   2006022573

ISBN-13: 978-0-8077-4730-8 (paper)

Printed on acid-free paper
Manufactured in the United States of America

For my parents with thanks

Contents

Acknowledgments

I am grateful to Jean Piaget for his remarkable body of work and for his confidence in me. I am equally grateful to Bärbel Inhelder, at whose side and through whose patience I learned, among other things, the practice of critical exploration. There are many others who have, over the years during which this work was done, helped me to learn what I needed to learn, and with enjoyment along the way, among them: Jeanne Bamberger, Magali Bovet, Penny Carver, Mani Denis, Hubert Dyasi, Brenda Engel, Ariane Etienne, Claryce Evans, Christiane Gilliéron, Ann Goldsmith, Joan Green, Ken Haskins, David Hawkins, Mary Ellen Herbert, Lisa Hirsh, Connie Kamii, Evelyn Keller, Catherine Krupnick, Maggie Lampert, Ann Manicom, Debbie Meier, Elliot Mishler, Neil Morrison, Philip Morrison, Phylis Morrison, Elaine Newman, Vito Perrone, Eva Peterson, Mike Savage, Abbie Schirmer, Audrey Schirmer, Boone Schirmer, Peggy Schirmer, Lisa Schneier, Klaus Schultz, Vicky Steinitz, Julie Ince Thompson, Lillian Weber, and Rose-Marie Weber.

I am indebted, in many ways that they know, to Jinny Chalmers, Joanne Cleary, Mary DiSchino, Fern Fisher, Wendy Postlethwaite, and Mary Rizzuto—the moon group.

My students and teaching fellows continue to teach me about teaching, learning, schools, and a grand array of subject matters.

My brothers, Martin and John Duckworth, have never failed to give me support and good cheer when I needed it.

The first and most enduring providers of support and encouragement, whose influence is found throughout these pages, were my parents, Muriel and Jack Duckworth. I dedicate this book to my mother and to the memory of my father.

Grateful acknowledgment for permission to reprint published material:

"The Having of Wonderful Ideas" from *Piaget in the Classroom*, edited by Martin Schwebel. Copyright © 1973 by Basic Books, Inc. Reprinted by permission of Basic Books, a member of Perseus Books, L.L.C.

"The Language and Thought of Piaget, and Some Comments on Learning to Spell" from *The Language Arts in Elementary School: A Forum for Focus*, edited by Martha L. King, Robert Emans, & Patricia J. Ciancolo. Copyright © 1973 by the National Council of Teachers of English. Reprinted with permission.

"Either We're Too Early and They Can't Learn It, or We're Too Late and They Know It Already: The Dilemma of 'Applying Piaget'" from *The Genetic Epistemologist*, Vol. 7, Nos. 3 & 4. Copyright © 1978 by the Jean Piaget Society. Reprinted with permission.

"A Child's-Eye View of Knowing" first appeared in *Reason and Change in Elementary Education*, Omaha, NE: Tri-University Project in Elementary Education, 1968.

"The Virtues of Not Knowing" from *National Elementary Principal*, Vol. 54. Reprinted with permission. Copyright © 1975 by the National Association of Elementary School Principals. All rights reserved.

"Learning with Breadth and Depth" first appeared as the Catherine Molony Memorial Lecture, City College of New York, Copyright © 1979. Reprinted with permission of the Workshop Center for Open Education.

"Understanding Children's Understanding" first appeared in *Building on the Strengths of Children*, edited by Vivian Windley, Miriam Dorn, and Lillian Weber, published by the Dept. of Elementary Education, City College of New York, 1982.

"Structures, Continuity, and Other People's Minds" from *Reunion, Reaffirmation, and Resurgence*, edited by Kathe Jervis. Copyright © 1983, The Miquon School. Reprinted by permission.

"Making Sure That Everybody Gets Home Safely" from *The Connecticut Scholar*, Vol. 7. Copyright © 1985. Reprinted with permission.

"Twenty-Four, Forty-Two, and I Love You: Keeping It Complex" and "Teaching as Research," both from *The Harvard Educational Review*, Vols. 61 & 56, Nos. 1 & 4, Copyright © 1991 and 1986 by the President and Fellows of Harvard College. Reprinted by permission.

"Critical Exploration in the Classroom". Copyright © 2005 from *The New Educator*. Reproduced by permission of Taylor & Francis Group, LLC., www.taylorandfrancis. com. This article was first published in 2004 as "L'Exploration critique dans la salle de classe," in J.-P. Bronckart & M. Gather Thurler (Eds.), *Transformer l'Ecole* [Transforming Schools] (pp. 79–97). Brussels: DeBoeck.

"Design" from *The Poetry of Robert Frost* edited by Edward Connery Lathem. Copyright © 1947, 1969 by Henry Holt and Company. Copyright © 1975 by Lesley Frost Ballantine. Reprinted by permission of Henry Holt and Company, LLC.

"miss rosie" by Lucille Clifton, from *Good Woman: Poems and a Memoir, 1969–1980*. Copyright © 1987 by Lucille Clifton. Reprinted with the permission of BOA Editions, Ltd.

Figures 5.1, 9.3, and 9.4, and related discussion in text from *Learning and the Development of Cognition*, by B. Inhelder, H. Sinclair, & M. Bovet. Copyright © 1974 by the President and Fellows of Harvard College. Included with permission from Presses Universitaires de France.

Introduction

THIS BOOK MAKES assumptions about what education can be. In these essays I assume we want schools in which students come to feel the power of their own minds and their creative capacities. I assume we want students' understanding to be deep, confident, and complex, and their means of expression to be varied and nuanced. I assume we want students to develop a sense of community responsibility, democratic commitment, social justice. And since, as Evans (1981) has said, "Educational practice *is* what teachers do," I assume we want teachers who support students' engagement in their learning, even if this may lead to forms of practice that are unfamiliar to us.

Since this book first appeared, public education has been running in the opposite direction. Teachers have fewer and fewer occasions to support students' own learning engagement with the world—with its cultural traditions, its living beings, its physical regularities, its social structures. A number is accepted as an adequate representation of a student's learning, and as a criterion to determine a student's future within formal education. The fact that the ideas contained in these essays are more at odds with today's educational system than they were 20 years ago makes it all the more important to me to keep those ideas in the public discourse (see also Carini 2001; Hawkins, 2003).

One important emphasis in this collection of essays is that there is a vast array of ways that people come to their understanding—a vast array of perfectly adequate ways. I have also found that, although people come to equivalent understandings in many different ways, they often do not recognize the validity of any way but their own.

In chapter 8, for example, Figures 8.4 and 8.5 show two ways of representing the same event. For many people, only one of those ways makes sense—but for some of them it is one, and for some it is the other. And if only one of those ways makes sense to a person, it is almost impossible for him or her to grasp the sense of the other representation—no matter how it is explained.

Similarly, two ways of figuring out possible arrangements of three objects are outlined in chapter 10. Both ways are perfectly adequate to the problem, but people who solve it one way often have trouble seeing how the other way can make any sense.

The most striking simple example in my experience came from a group discussion about arithmetic division (see Duckworth, 1987). "What does it really mean, 24 divided by 8?" one person asked. A second person responded that if you have 24 things, and you distribute them evenly into 8 piles, you then count how many end up in each pile. Yet another person, astonished, said, no, that's not what it means! It means you have 24 things, and you put them in piles of 8, and you see how many piles you get.

Now clearly it means both of those. But imagine a teacher who believes—as some in that group believed—that it could mean only one of them. Imagine that teacher explaining a division problem to a child who was thinking about it the other way. The teacher, with her own way in mind as the only one possible, would not even notice that the child was thinking differently—adequately and differently. With all the good-will in the world, the discussion would nonetheless come to an impasse. Probably both of them—the teacher and the child—would emerge from that discussion believing that the child was hopeless in arithmetic. Imagine how often such an impasse arises in discussing more complicated matters, and how often learners' ways of understanding are left unrecognized.

Textbooks and standardized tests, as well as many teacher education and curriculum programs, feed into this belief that there is one best way of understanding, and that there is one best, clearest way of explaining this way of understanding. Then we need only decide on the best way to come to understand a given topic, and we can tell teachers to present it to students that way.

This idea that there is one best way of understanding is linked to a pervasive pernicious belief—that the students who do not understand it in our way are not smart enough to understand it at all, that their future in the academy is limited, that they need a different kind of education.

And there is another, related pernicious belief: the idea that intelligence is given at birth in a fixed amount. If people have not been given much of it, we can generously try to do our best with them, but it won't surprise us if they do not manage to understand.

These two ideas support each other quite beautifully: "There is one best way to understand." "Many people are not smart enough to understand." Once we believe those two ideas, a third harmful idea is implied:

"If someone does not understand our way, it is not that there is any problem with our insisting on our way; it is that there is a problem with that learner."

So I find this matter to be critically important. The essays in this book start instead from the premise mentioned above—that there is a vast array of very different adequate ways that people come to their understanding.

Curriculum, assessment, teacher education programs—and all of our teaching—must seek out, acknowledge, and take advantage of the diversity of ways that people might take toward understanding. We cannot plan *"the* logical sequence" through a set of ideas, especially if we want schools to make sense for students whose backgrounds differ from our own. As Lisa Schneier (personal communication, 1997) has said, we must find ways to present subject matter that will enable learners to get at their own thoughts about it. Then we must take those thoughts seriously, and set about helping students to pursue them in greater breadth and depth. In this way we can capture the intelligence of all our students, so we do not lose the one-half, three-quarters, nine-tenths that we lose now.

I need to add to this my conviction that students who succeed in our current one-right-way system are similarly missing out on vast possibilities for learning (see Pettigrew, 2006). The world is far more complex and fascinating than the small piecemeal views that the one-right-way allows.

Part of the work described in these chapters involves giving people an appreciation of their own ways of understanding. Part of it involves giving people experience in figuring out and appreciating other people's ways of coming to understand—ways that are different from their own. Much of the learning described here seems light-hearted, playful. It is. But it is also monumentally serious.

There were two major formative influences as I began my work in education: the work of Jean Piaget and Bärbel Inhelder, and my experience with the Elementary Science Study curriculum development program. These two influences were very powerful.

Piaget's was one of the great minds of the 20th century, and his work, and Inhelder's, are still my most significant source of intellectual stimulation. With Piaget and Inhelder I learned how futile it is to try to change a child's mind by telling her to think something different. It raised the fascinating question of how on earth one can help someone learn, if telling them what you know does not help.

I started to be able to pursue this question when I joined the staff of the Elementary Science Study. My science background was exceedingly limited. The only formal science I had studied since high school was a first-year college biology course. But as a staff member of the Elementary Science Study, where the approach to science education was to engage teachers and children directly with fascinating corners of the material world, my science education took the form of becoming intrigued by phenomena, and struggling to figure them out. I was in the company of people who presented me with such phenomena, who did not insist on explaining to me what they knew, and who talked about what I was doing in ways that never caused me to doubt that what I was engaged in was science. I spent hour after hour exploring materials and phenomena, with my colleagues on hand from time to time to ask how I was getting along and what I was making of things, and to suggest, "Why don't you try it this way?" or "Here, have a look at this." I germinated acorns; I used syringes to move air from one container to another; I explored the effects of different objects as pendulum bobs; I spent a full day with a flashlight battery and bulb by my side, in order to keep trying out ways to arrange a single wire so the bulb would light (I spent about half an hour at the beginning of the morning, went back to it off-and-on all day, and finally succeeded in lighting the bulb in the middle the afternoon; this was but the beginning of many months of explorations with batteries and bulbs). I tried to make liquid mixtures of identical densities—one oil-based and one water-based, so they did not mix with each other. I tried using any long object—a broom, a spoon, a tooth-brush—as a balance; I watched frog eggs develop. I worked hard during these explorations, trying to figure out why something had happened, and to think of what I could do next, to shed more light on it. I was captivated by this world of fascinating phenomena, by its accessibility and its complexity. I was intrigued, also, with what it was like to be learning these things in this way, and with how my colleagues thought about opening the world to children.

These two foundations launched me into the world of education, as an elementary school teacher (too briefly to do it successfully, I am afraid), and in curriculum development, program evaluation, teacher education, and research in the development of ideas. The papers in this volume have been written over almost 4 decades of that work.

The earliest one (chapter 4) was written in 1968, the latest (chapter 11) in 2003. The world of schools has changed many times, in many ways, in the intervening decades. Through these changes, my ideas—of what is important in teaching, of what kinds of research are needed, of what teachers' roles in the organization of schooling can be—have not changed very much. As I work with children, education students, and teachers, the same principles continue to lead to intense involvement of learners with subject matter. My central question has continued to be: How do people learn and what can anyone do to help? *Helping people learn* is my definition of teaching. Telling, explaining, play a very small part in helping people learn. The emphasis in these pages, rather, is on looking at what happens when teachers engage learners directly with the subject matter—as my science colleagues did with me—and then they, the teachers, do the listening while learners explain their own thoughts (see Duckworth, 2001b).

Although the ideas have not essentially changed since the first edition of this book, through the years there has been an evolution in terminology. When I began to see the work I do as a form of research, as well as a way of teaching, I wanted to give it a name. I think in this volume I finally have a name that I am happy with: "critical exploration in the classroom." In these essays, two other names are used to refer to the work. And yet another term—teaching/learning research—was used in a different book (Duckworth, 2001b). The first name I tried appears in chapter 12—teaching-research. Teaching-research for me meant research, the act of which was indistinguishable from the act of teaching: It meant teaching (which involves listening to learners explain) as the best way for us to learn about the development of thoughts. I think this name is apt, but it is undistinguished. There is the large field of teacher-research, and that term covers a vast range of work—almost any research that is done by a teacher. It would take a careful reader to note the difference in spelling, let alone meaning.

The next name I tried was "extended clinical interviewing." Piaget called his method for studying children's thinking "clinical interviewing." I wanted to acknowledge my debt to him and to Inhelder (to whom I had apprenticed in learning to do the research). I added the word "extended," as I explain in chapter 10, because in this work, interviews could be extended in two ways: They could be continued through time, over many different sessions; and they could be carried out with more than one person at once. The drawbacks with this name are that it is a difficult mouthful; that it sounds technical—laboratory-based; and that there is in fact far more to this work than asking questions.

The name "critical exploration" comes from Inhelder. Its origins and my choice to use it are taken up in chapter 11.

The three phrases—teaching-research, extended clinical interviewing, and critical exploration in the classroom—are interchangeable. They are three different names for the same work.

I close this Introduction with a word about chapter 9. Just as school practice has, in the last 20 years, been going counter to the ideas expressed here, so has public practice in the realms of peace and social justice. And just as I think there has never been a greater need to consider ideas about learning and teaching such as the ones in this book, I also think there has never been a greater need to educate children about peace and social justice.

The Having of Wonderful Ideas

KEVIN, STEPHANIE, AND THE MATHEMATICIAN

WITH A FRIEND, I reviewed some classic Piagetian interviews with a few children. One involved the ordering of lengths. I had cut 10 cellophane drinking straws into different lengths and asked the children to put them in order, from smallest to biggest. The first two 7-year-olds did it with no difficulty and little interest. Then came Kevin. Before I said a word about the straws, he picked them up and said to me, "I know what I'm going to do," and proceeded, on his own, to order them by length. He didn't mean, "I know what you're going to ask me to do." He meant, "I have a wonderful idea about what to do with these straws. You'll be surprised by my wonderful idea."

It wasn't easy for him. He needed a good deal of trial and error as he set about developing his system. But he was so pleased with himself when he accomplished his self-set task that when I decided to offer them to him to keep (10 whole drinking straws!), he glowed with joy, showed them to one or two select friends, and stored them away with other treasures in a shoe box.

The having of wonderful ideas is what I consider the essence of intellectual development. And I consider it the essence of pedagogy to give Kevin the occasion to have his wonderful ideas and to let him feel good about himself for having them. To develop this point of view and to indicate where Piaget fits in for me, I need to start with some autobiography, and I apologize for that, but it was a struggle of some years' duration for me to see how Piaget was relevant to schools at all.

I had never heard of Piaget when I first sat in a class of his. It was as a philosopher that Piaget won me, and I went on to spend two years in Geneva as a graduate student and research assistant. Then, some years later,

I began to pay attention to schools, when, as a Ph.D. dropout, I accepted a job developing elementary science curriculum, and found myself in the midst of an exciting circle of educators.

The colleagues I admired most got along very well without any special knowledge of psychology. They trusted their own insights about when and how children were learning, and they were right to: Their insights were excellent. Moreover, they were especially distrustful of Piaget. He had not yet appeared on the cover of *Saturday Review* or the *New York Times Magazine*, and they had their own picture of him: a severe, humorless intellectual confronting a small child with questions that were surely incomprehensible, while the child tried to tell from the look in his eyes what the answer was supposed to be. No wonder the child couldn't think straight. (More than one of these colleagues first started to pay attention to Piaget when they saw a photo of him. He may be Swiss, but he doesn't look like Calvin! Maybe he can talk to children after all.)

I myself didn't know what to think. My colleagues did not seem to be any the worse for not taking Piaget seriously. Nor, I had to admit, did I seem to be any the better. Schools were such complicated places compared with psychology labs that I couldn't find a way to be of any special help. Not only did Piaget seem irrelevant, I was no longer sure that he was right. For a couple of years, I scarcely mentioned him and simply went about the business of trying to be helpful, with no single instance, as I recall, of drawing directly on any of his specific findings.

The lowest point came when one of my colleagues gleefully showed me an essay written in a first grade by 6-year-old Stephanie. The children had been investigating capillary tubes, and were looking at the differences in the height of the water as a function of the diameter of the tube. Stephanie's essay read as follows: I know why it looks like there's more in the skinny tube. Because it's higher. But the other is fatter, so there's the same.

My colleague triumphantly took this statement as proof that 6-year-olds can reason about the compensation of two dimensions. I didn't know what to say. Of course, it should have been simple. Some 6-year-olds *can* reason about compensation. The ages that Piaget mentions are only norms, not universals. Children develop at a variety of speeds, some more slowly and some more quickly. But I was so unsure of myself at that point that this incident shook me badly, and all of that only sounded like a lame excuse.

I do have something else to say about that incident later. For now, I shall simply try to describe my struggle.

Even if I did believe that Piaget was right, how could he be helpful? If the main thing that we take from Piaget is that before certain ages children are unable to understand certain things—conservation, transitivity, spatial coordinates—what do we do about it? Do we try to teach the children these things? Probably not, because on the one hand Piaget leads us to believe that we probably won't be very successful at it; and on the other hand, if there is one thing we have learned from Piaget it is that children can probably be left to their own devices in coming to understand these notions. We don't have to try to furnish them. It took a few months before that was clear to me, but I did conclude that this was not a very good way to make use of Piaget.

An alternative might be to keep in mind the limits on children's abilities to classify, conserve, order, and so forth, when deciding what to teach them at certain ages. However, I found this an inadequate criterion. There was so much else to keep in mind. The most obvious reason, of course, was that any class of children has a great diversity of levels. Tailoring to an average level of development is sure to miss a large proportion of the children. In addition, a Piaget psychologist has no monopoly here. When trying to approximate the abilities of a group of children of a given age, able teachers like my colleagues could make as good approximations as I.

What I found most appealing was that the people with whom I was working judged the merits of any suggestion by how well it worked in classrooms. That is, instead of deciding on a priori grounds what children *ought* to know, or what they *ought* to be able to do at a certain age, they found activities, lessons, points of departure, that would engage children in real classrooms, with real teachers. In their view, it was easy to devise all-embracing schemes of how science (as it was in this instance) could be organized for children, but to make things work pedagogically in classrooms was the difficult part. They started with the difficult part. A theory of intellectual development might have been the basis of a theoretical framework of a curriculum. But in making things work in a classroom, it was but a small part compared with finding ways to interest children, to take into account different children's interests and abilities, to help teachers with no special training in the subject, and so forth. So, the burden of this curriculum effort was classroom trials. The criterion was whether they worked, and their working depended only in part on their being at the right intellectual level for the children. They might be perfectly all right, from the point of view of intellectual demands, and yet fall short in other ways. Most often, it was a complex combination.

As I was struggling to find some framework within which my knowledge of Piaget would be useful. I found, more or less incidentally, that I was starting to be useful myself. As an observer for some of the pilot teaching of this program, and later as a pilot teacher myself, I found that I had a certain skill in being able to watch and listen to children and that I did have some good insights about how they were really seeing the problem. This led to a certain ability to raise questions that made sense to the children or to think of new orientations for the whole activity that might correspond better to their way of seeing things. I don't want to suggest that I was unique in this. Many of the teachers with whom I was working had similar insights, as did many of the mathematicians and scientists among my colleagues, who, from their points of view, could tell when children were seeing things differently from the ways they did. But the question of whether I was unique is not really pertinent. For me, through my experience with Piaget of working closely with one child at a time and trying to figure out what was really in that child's mind, I had gained a wonderful background for being sensitive to children in classrooms. I think that a certain amount of this kind of background would be similarly useful for every teacher.

This sensitivity to children in classrooms continued to be central in my own development. As a framework for thinking about learning, my understanding of Piaget has been invaluable. This understanding, however, has also been deepened by working with teachers and children. I may be able to shed some light on that mutual relationship by referring again to 6-year-old Stephanie's essay on compensation. Few of us, looking at water rise in capillary tubes of different diameters, would bother to wonder whether the quantities are the same. Nobody asked Stephanie to make that comparison and, in fact, it is impossible to tell just by looking. On her own, she felt it was a significant thing to comment upon. I take that as an indication that for her it was a wonderful idea. Not long before, she believed that there was more water in the tube in which the water was higher. She had recently won her own intellectual struggle on that issue, and she wanted to point out her finding to the world for the benefit of those who might be taken in by preliminary appearances.

This incident, once I had figured it out, helped me think about a point that bothered me in one of Piaget's anecdotes. You may recall Piaget's account of a mathematician friend who inspired his studies of the conservation of number. This man told Piaget about an incident from his childhood, where he counted a number of pebbles he had set out in a line. Having counted them from left to right and found there were 10, he decided to see how many there would be if he counted them from right to left. Intrigued to find that there were still 10, he put them in a different arrangement and counted them again. He kept rearranging and counting them until he decided that, no matter what the arrangement, he was always going to find that there were 10. Number is independent of the order of counting.

My problem was this: In Piaget's accounts, if 10 eggs are spread out so they take more space than 10 eggcups, a classic nonconserver will maintain that there are more eggs than eggcups, even if he counts and finds that he comes to 10 in both cases. Counting is not sufficient to convince him that there are enough eggcups for all the eggs. How is it, then, that for the mathematician, counting was sufficient? If he was a nonconserver at the time, counting should not have made any difference. If he was a conserver, he should have known from the start that it would always come out the same.

I think it must be that the whole enterprise was his own wonderful idea. He raised the question for himself and figured out for himself how to try to answer it. In essence, I am saying that he was in a transitional moment, and that Stephanie and Kevin were, too. He was at a point where a certain experience fit into certain thoughts and took him a step forward. A powerful pedagogical point can be made from this. These three instances dramatize it because they deal with children moving ahead with Piaget notions, which are usually difficult to advance on the basis of any one experience. The point has two aspects: First, the right question at the right time can move children to peaks in their thinking that result in significant steps forward and real intellectual excitement; and, second, although it is almost impossible for an adult to know exactly the right time to ask a specific question of a specific child—especially for a teacher who is concerned with 30 or more children—children can raise the right question for themselves if the setting is right. Once the right question is raised, they are moved to tax themselves to the fullest to find an answer. The answers did not come easily in any of these three cases, but the children were prepared to work them through. Having confidence in one's ideas does not mean "I know my ideas are right"; it means "I am willing to try out my ideas."

As I put together experiences like these and continued to think about them, I started developing some ideas about what education could be and about the relationships between education and intellectual development.

HANK

It is a truism that all children in their first and second years make incredible intellectual advances. Piaget has documented these advances from his own point of view, but every parent and every psychologist knows this to be the case. One recurring question is, why does the intellectual development of vast numbers of children then slow down? What happens to children's curiosity and resourcefulness later in their childhood? Why do so few continue to have their own wonderful ideas? I think part of the answer is that intellectual breakthroughs come to be less and less valued. Either they are dismissed as being trivial—as Kevin's or Stephanie's or the mathematician's might have been by some adults—or else they are discouraged as being unacceptable—like discovering how it feels to wear shoes on the wrong feet, or asking questions that are socially embarrassing, or destroying something to see what it's like inside. The effect is to discourage children from exploring their own ideas and to make them feel that they have no important ideas of their own, only silly or evil ones.

But I think there is at least one other part of the answer, too. Wonderful ideas do not spring out of nothing. They build on a foundation of other ideas. The following incident may help to clarify what I mean.

Hank was an energetic and not very scholarly fifth grader. His class had been learning about electric circuits with flashlight batteries, bulbs, and various wires. After the children had developed considerable familiarity with these materials, the teacher made a number of mystery boxes.* Two wires protruded from each box, but inside, unseen, each box had a different way of making contact between the wires. In one box the wires were attached to a battery; in another they were attached to a bulb; in a third, to a certain length of resistance wire; in a fourth box they were not attached at all; and so forth. By trying to complete the circuit on the outside of a box, the children were able to figure out what made the connection inside the box. Like many other children, Hank attached a battery and a bulb to the wire outside the box. Because the bulb lit, he knew at least that the wires inside the box were connected in some way. But, because it was somewhat dimmer than usual, he also knew that the wires inside were not connected directly to each other by a piece of ordinary copper wire. Along with many of the children, he knew that the degree of dimness of the bulb meant that the wires inside were connected either by another bulb of the same kind or by a certain length of resistance wire.

The teacher expected them to go only this far. However, in order to push the children to think a little further, she asked them if they could tell whether it was a bulb or a piece of wire inside the box. She herself thought there was no way to tell. After some thought, Hank had an idea. He undid the battery and bulb that he had already attached on the outside of the box. In their place, using additional copper wire, he attached six batteries in a series. He had already experimented enough to know that six batteries would burn out a bulb, if it was a bulb inside the box. He also knew that once a bulb is burned out, it no longer completes the circuit. He then attached the original battery and bulb again. This time he found that the bulb on the outside of the box did not light. So he reasoned, rightly, that there had been a bulb inside the box and that now it was burned out. If

---

*This activity is from the Elementary Science Study's *Batteries and Bulbs*, 1969.

there had been a wire inside, it would not have burned through and the bulb on the outside would still light.

Note that to carry out that idea, Hank had to take the risk of destroying a light bulb. In fact, he did destroy one. In accepting this idea, the teacher had to accept not only the fact that Hank had a good idea that even she did not have, but also that it was worthwhile to destroy a small piece of property for the sake of following through an idea. These features almost turn the incident into a parable. Without these kinds of acceptance, Hank would not have been able to pursue his idea. Think of how many times this acceptance is not forthcoming in the life of any one child.

But the main point to be made here is that in order to have his idea, Hank had to know a lot about batteries, bulbs, and wires. His previous work and familiarity with those materials were a necessary aspect of this occasion for him to have a wonderful idea. David Hawkins (2000) has said of curriculum development, "You don't want to cover a subject; you want to uncover it" (p. 79). That, it seems to me, is what schools should be about. They can help to uncover parts of the world that children would not otherwise know how to tackle. Wonderful ideas are built on other wonderful ideas. In Piaget's terms, you must reach out to the world with your own intellectual tools and grasp it, assimilate it, yourself. All kinds of things are hidden from us—even though they surround us—unless we know how to reach out for them. Schools and teachers can provide materials and questions in ways that suggest things to be done with them; and children, in the doing, cannot help being inventive.

There are two aspects to providing occasions for wonderful ideas. One is being willing to accept children's ideas. The other is providing a setting that suggests wonderful ideas to children—different ideas to different children—as they are caught up in intellectual problems that are real to them.

WHAT SCHOOLS CAN DO

I had the chance to evaluate an elementary science program in Africa. For the purposes of this discussion it might have been set anywhere. Although the program was by no means a deliberate attempt to apply Piaget's ideas, it was, to my mind, such an application in the best sense. The assumptions that lay behind the work are consistent with the ideas I have just been developing. The program set out to reveal the world to children. The developers sought to familiarize the children with the material wand— that is, with biological phenomena, physical phenomena, and technological phenomena: flashlights, mosquito larvae, clouds, clay. When I speak of familiarity, I mean feeling at home with these things: knowing what to expect of them, what can be done with them, how they react to various circumstances, what you like about them and what you don't like about them, and how they can be changed, avoided, preserved, destroyed, or enhanced.

Certainly the material world is too diverse and too complex for a child to become familiar with all of it in the course of an elementary school career. The best one can do is to make such knowledge, such familiarity, seem interesting and accessible to the child. That is, one can familiarize children with a few phenomena in such a way as to catch their interest, to let them raise and answer their own questions, to let them realize that their ideas are significant so that they have the interest, the ability, and the self-confidence to go on by themselves.

Such a program is a curriculum, so to speak, but a curriculum with a difference. The difference can best be characterized by saying that the un-expected is valued. Instead of expecting teachers and children to do only what was specified in the booklets, it was the intention of the program that children and teachers would have so many unanticipated ideas of their own about the materials that they would never even use the booklets. The purpose of developing booklets at all is that teachers and children start producing and following through their own ideas, if possible getting be-yond needing anybody else's suggestions. Although it is unlikely to be completely realized, this represents the ideal orientation of the program. It is a rather radical view of curriculum development.

It is just as necessary for teachers as for children to feel confidence in their own ideas. It is important for them as people and it is important in order for them to feel free to acknowledge the children's ideas. If teach-ers feel that their class must do things just as the book says, and that their excellence as teachers depends on this, they cannot possibly accept the children's divergence and creations. A teachers' guide must give enough indications, enough suggestions, so that the teacher has ideas to start with and to pursue. But it must also enable the teacher to feel free to move in her own directions when she has other ideas.

For instance, the teachers' guides for this program include many ex-amples of things children are likely to do. The risk is that teachers may see these as things that the children in their classes *must* do. Whether or not the children do them becomes a measure of successful or unsuccessful teaching. Sometimes the writers of the teachers' guides intentionally omit mention of some of the most exciting activities because they almost always happen even if they are not arranged. If the teacher expects them, she will often force them, and they no longer happen with the excitement of won-derful ideas. Often the writers include extreme examples, so extreme that a teacher cannot really expect them to happen in her class. These examples are meant to convey the message that "even if the children do that it's OK! Look, in one class they even did this!" This approach often is more fruitful than the use of more common examples whose message is likely to be "this is what ought to happen in your class."

The teachers' guides dealt with materials that were readily available in or out of schools, and suggested activities that could be done with these materials so that children became interested in them and started asking their own questions. For instance, there are common substances all around us that provide the essential basis of chemistry knowledge. They interact in all sorts of interesting ways, accessible to all of us if only we know how to reach out for them. This is a good instance of a part of the world that is waiting to be uncovered. How can it be uncovered for children in a way that gives them an interest in continuing to find out about it, a way that gives them the occasion to take their own initiatives, and to feel at home in this part of the world?

The teachers' guide suggests starting with salt, ashes, sugar, cassava starch, alum, lemon juice, and water. When mixed together, some of these cause bubbles. Which combinations cause bubbles? How long does the bubbling last? How can it be kept going longer? What other substances cause bubbles? If a combination bubbles, what can be added that will stop the bubbling? Other things change color when they are mixed together, and similar questions can be asked of them.

Written teachers' guides, however, cannot bear the burden alone, if this kind of reaching is totally new. To get such a program started, a great deal of teacher education is necessary as well. Although I shall not try to go into this in any detail, there seem to be three major aspects to such teacher education. First, teachers themselves must learn in the way that the children in their classes will be learning. Almost any one of the units developed in this program is as effective with adults as it is with children. The teachers themselves learn through some of the units and feel what it is like to learn in this way. Second, the teachers work with one or two children at a time so that they can observe them closely enough to realize what is involved for the children. Last, it seems valuable for teachers to see films or live demonstrations of a class of children learning in this way, so that they can begin to think that it really is possible to run their class in such a way. A fourth aspect is of a slightly different nature. Except for the rare teacher who will take this leap all on his or her own on the basis of a single course and some written teachers' guides, most teachers need the support of at least some nearby co-workers who are trying to do the same thing, and with whom they can share notes. An even better help is the presence of an experienced teacher to whom they can go with questions and problems.

AN EVALUATION STUDY

What the children are doing in one of these classrooms may be lively and interesting, but it would be helpful to know what difference the approach makes to them in the long run, to compare in some way the children who were in this program with children who were not, and to see whether in some standard situation they now act differently.

One of my thoughts about ways in which these children might be different was based on the fact that many teachers in this program had told us that their children improved at having ideas of what to do, at raising questions, and at answering their own questions; that is, at having their own ideas and being confident about their own ideas. I wanted to see whether this indeed was the case.

My second thought was more ambitious. If these children had really become more intellectually alert, so that their minds were alive and working not only in school but outside school, they might, over a long enough period of time, make significant headway in their intellectual development, as compared with other children.

In sum, these two aspects would put to the test my notions that the development of intelligence is a matter of having wonderful ideas and feeling confident enough to try them out, and that schools can have an effect on the continuing development of wonderful ideas. The study has been written up elsewhere (Duckworth, 1978), but let me give a summary of it here.

The evaluation had two phases. The procedure developed for the first phase was inspired in part by a physics examination given to students at Cornell University by Philip Morrison. His examination was held in the laboratory. The students were given sets of materials, the same set of materials for each student, but they were given no specific problem. Their problem was to find a problem and then to work on it. For Morrison, the crucial thing is finding the question, just as it was for Kevin, Stephanie, and the mathematician. In this examination, clear differences in the degree of both knowledge and inventiveness were revealed in the problems the students set themselves, and the work they did was only as good as their problems.

In our evaluation study,* we had to modify this procedure somewhat to make it appropriate for children as young as 6 years of age. Our general question was what children with a year or more of experience in this program would do with materials when they were left to their own resources without any teacher at all. We wanted to know whether children who had been in the program had more ideas about what to do with materials than did other children.

---

*Mike Savage was a full collaborator in this work. It couldn't have been done without his insights, support, and logistical maneuverings.

The materials we chose were not, of course, the same as those that children in the program had studied. We chose materials of two sorts: on the one hand, imported materials that none of the children had ever seen before—plastic color filters, geometric pattern blocks, folding mirrors, commercial building sets, for example. On the other hand, we chose some materials that were familiar to all the children whether or not they had been in the program—cigarette foil, match boxes, rubber rings from inner tubes, scraps of wire, wood, and metal, empty spools, and so forth.

From each class we chose a dozen children at random and told them—in their own vernacular—to go into the room and do whatever they wanted with the materials they would find there. We told them that they could move around the room, talk to each other, and work with their friends.

We studied 15 experimental classes and 13 control classes from first to seventh grades. Briefly, and inadequately, summarizing the results of this phase, we found that the children who had been in the program did indeed have more ideas about how to work with the materials. Typically, the children in these classes would take a first look at what was offered, try a few things, and then settle down to work with involvement and concentration. Children sometimes worked alone and sometimes collaborated. They carried materials from table to table, using them in ways we had not anticipated. As time went on, there was no sign that they were running out of ideas. On the contrary, their work became so interesting that we were always disappointed to have to stop them after 40 minutes.

By contrast, the other children had a much smaller range of ideas about what to do with the materials. On the one hand, they tended to copy a few leaders. On the other hand, they tended to leave one piece of work fairly soon and to switch to something else. There were few instances of elaborate work in which a child spent a lot of time and effort to overcome difficulties in what he or she was trying to do. In some of these classes, after 30 to 35 minutes, all the children had run out of ideas and were doing nothing.

We had assessed two things in our evaluation: diversity of ideas in a class, and depth to which the ideas were pursued. The experimental classes were overwhelmingly ahead in each of the two dimensions. This first phase of assessment was actually a substitute for what we really wanted to do. Ideally, we wanted to know whether the experience of these children in the program had the effect of making them more alert, more aware of the possibilities in ordinary things around them, and more questioning and exploring during the time they spent outside school. This would be an intriguing question to try to answer, but we did not have the time to tackle it. The procedure that we did develop, as just described, may have been too close to the school setting to give rise to any valid conclusions about what children are like in the world outside school. However, if you can accept with me, tentatively, the thought that our results might indicate a greater intellectual alertness in general—a tendency to have wonderful ideas—then the next phase takes on a considerable interest.

I am hypothesizing that this alertness is the motor of intellectual development (in Piaget's terms, operational thinking). No doubt there is a continuum: No normal child is completely unalert. But some are far more alert than others. I am also hypothesizing that a child's alertness is not fixed. I believe that, by opening up to children the many fascinating aspects of the ordinary world and by enabling them to feel that their ideas are worthwhile having and following through, their tendency to have wonderful ideas can be affected in significant ways. This program seemed to be doing both those things, and by the time I evaluated it, some children had been in the classes for up to three years. It seemed to me that we might—just might—find that the two or three years of increased alertness that this program fostered had made some difference to the intellectual development of the children.

In the second phase, then, we examined the same children individually, using Piaget problems administered by a trained assistant who spoke the language of the children. A statistical analysis revealed that on five of the six problems we studied, the children in the experimental classes did significantly better than the children in the comparison classes.

I find this a pretty stunning result on the whole. But I want to insist on one particular view of the result. I do not, in any way, want to suggest that the important thing for education to be about is acceleration of Piaget stages (see chapter 3). I want to make a theoretical point. My thesis at the outset of this chapter was that the development of intelligence is a matter of having wonderful ideas. In other words, it is a creative affair. When children are afforded the occasions to be intellectually creative—by being offered matter to be concerned about intellectually and by having their ideas accepted—then not only do they learn about the world, but as a happy side effect their general intellectual ability is stimulated as well.

Another way of putting this is that I think the distinction made between "divergent" and "convergent" thinking (Hudson, 1968) is oversimplified. Even to think a problem through to its most appropriate end point (convergent) one must create various hypotheses to check out (divergent). When Hank came up with a closed end point to the problem, it was the result of a brilliantly imaginative—that is, divergent—thought. We must conceive of the possibilities before we can check them out.

CONCLUSION

I am suggesting that children do not have a built-in pace of intellectual development. I would temper that suggestion by saying that the built-in aspect of the pace is minimal. The having of wonderful ideas, which I consider the essence of intellectual development, would depend instead to an overwhelming extent on the occasions for having them. I have dwelt at some length on how important it is to allow children to accept their own ideas and to work them through. I would like now to consider the intellectual basis for new ideas.

I react strongly against the thought that we need to provide children with only a set of intellectual processes—a dry, contentless set of tools that they can go about applying. I believe that the tools cannot help developing once children have something real to think about; and if they don't have anything real to think about, they won't be applying tools anyway. That is, there really is no such thing as a contentless intellectual tool. If a person has some knowledge at his disposal, he can try to make sense of new experiences and new information related to it. He fits it into what he has. By knowledge I do not mean verbal summaries of somebody else's knowledge. I am not urging textbooks and lectures. I mean a person's own repertoire of thoughts, actions, connections, predictions, and feelings. Some of these may have as their source something read or heard. But the individual has done the work of putting them together for himself or herself, and they give rise to new ways to put them together.

The greater the child's repertoire of actions and thoughts—in Piaget's terms, schemes—the more material he or she has for trying to put things together in his or her own mind. The essence of the African program I described is that children increase the repertoires of actions that they carry out on ordinary things, which in turn gives rise to the need to make more intellectual connections.

Let us consider a child who has had the world of common substances opened to him, as described earlier. He now has a vastly increased repertoire of actions to carry out and of connections to make. He has seen that when you boil away sea water, a salt residue remains. Would some residue remain if he boiled away beer? If he dissolved this residue in water again, would he have beer again—flat beer? He has seen that he can get a colored liquid from flower petals if he crushes them. Could he get that liquid to go into water and make colored water? Could he make colored coconut oil this way? All these questions and the actions they lead to are based on the familiarity the child has gained with the possibilities contained in this world of common substances.

Intelligence cannot develop without matter to think about. Making new connections depends on knowing enough about something in the first place to provide a basis for thinking of other things to do—of other questions to ask—that demand more complex connections in order to make sense. The more ideas about something people already have at their disposal, the more new ideas occur and the more they can coordinate to build still more complicated schemes.

Piaget has speculated that some people reach the level of formal operations in some specific area that they know well—auto mechanics, for example—without reaching formal levels in other areas. That fits into what I am trying to say. In an area you know well, you can think of many possibilities, and working them through demands formal operations. If there is no area in which you are familiar enough with the complexities to work through them, then you are not likely to develop formal operations. Knowing enough about things is one prerequisite for wonderful ideas.

I shall make one closing remark. The wonderful ideas that I refer to need not necessarily look wonderful to the outside world. I see no difference in kind between wonderful ideas that many other people have already had, and wonderful ideas that nobody has yet happened upon. That is, the nature of creative intellectual acts remains the same, whether it is an infant who for the first time makes the connection between seeing things and reaching for them, or Kevin who had the idea of putting straws in order of their length, or a musician who invents a harmonic sequence, or an astronomer who develops a new theory of the creation of the universe. In each case, new connections are being made among things already mastered. The more we help children to have their wonderful ideas and to feel good about themselves for having them, the more likely it is that they will some day happen upon wonderful ideas that no one else has happened upon before.

2

The Language and Thought of Piaget, and Some Comments on Learning to Spell

THE TITLE OF THIS chapter, as many readers will recognize, is an affectionate tribute to Piaget's first book, *The Language and Thought of the Child* (1923/1962a). It is also an acknowledgment of the fact that, in all that has been written about Piaget in the last few years, very little has been said about his views of the role of language in intellectual development. This is not too surprising, because he has concerned himself very little with language and has written very little about it. But it is worthwhile to look at his views on the role of language and to see why he is not more concerned with it than he is.*

The title of his first book, mentioned above, and section titles such as "Grammar and Logic" in his second (*Judgment and Reasoning in the Child*, 1924/1976) would seem to belie the statement that he has not been concerned with language. But these two are among his five "early books," which are quite different from all his later work in style of investigation and even, to some extent, in theoretical orientation. Yet even then his approach was original enough and he continued to subscribe to the main thesis. He did not assume that language and linguistic forms that children use coincide with their thinking. He was trying to look behind the language to the thoughts of which the language may or may not have been an adequate expression. Where language was inadequate, he did not assume that there was a direct parallel with the way that the thinking was inadequate. Rather, he took the language inadequacy as an indication of

---

*After this chapter first appeared, Hermine Sinclair, at the University of Geneva, developed a department of Piaget-based research in the psychology of language. Among the most interesting publications produced by members or former members of that department is *Literacy Before Schooling* (Ferreiro & Teberosky, 1983).

something to look for and proceeded to look for it. Conversely, where language seemed to be adequate, he did not accept it at face value, but, once again, tried to go beyond the language to see whether it meant what it seemed to mean.

What Piaget later found less interesting in these books was that his insights into what children really were capable of doing intellectually were nonetheless based on what they said. In his later work (after 1935) he looked much less at what they said and looked instead at what they did. Through watching the development of sensorimotor intelligence, before the development of language in a small child, he found that the roots of logic are in actions and not in words. He followed the development of this logic of actions through to adolescence, finding at every step of the way that children were able to carry out activities that demand a good deal of intelligence without necessarily using language that reveals this. In sum, his early insight was that language often is a misleading indicator of the level of a child's understanding; a second insight was that there is a good deal of logic in children's actions that is not revealed by their verbal formulations.

In the next sections, I shall use a number of different words in referring to what is behind language: meaning, sense, knowledge, ideas, logic, awareness, feeling, and others. I do not assume that these are all the same thing, but for our purposes we need not define distinctions among them. What they have in common is that they are what is in our minds, if you will accept that phrase, as opposed to what we make explicit through our language.

LANGUAGE AND THINKING

Even a casual observation of ourselves can indicate that each of us, day by day, has at least some thoughts for which we have to look for words, rather than having only those thoughts that come ready-made in words. "I have a feeling that Jack is in that mood again tonight." "What mood?" "Oh well, it's difficult to say." But the speaker surely has an idea of what she means by "that mood"—how she recognizes it, how Jack is likely to act, and how she should act in turn for best results. She might even be able to make those thoughts explicit. But she has them "in mind" even if she never happens to say them.

Again, when we quite easily make thoughts explicit, we might do so in any one of a great variety of ways. In these cases, too, it seems to me that the notion of what we want to say exists in some way, and we then find words with which to say it: "That one is much heavier than mine"; "That one is much heavier than the one I have"; "The one I have isn't nearly as heavy as that one"; or "The one I have is much lighter than that one"; and so on. It seems unlikely that it is in formulating the sentence that the speaker becomes aware of the thought. This is not to deny that there are differences in emphasis among these sentences. A person may be aware of the different possible emphases and form her sentence accordingly—in which case that awareness was there before the sentence was formed; or she may not be sensitive to the emphasis, and, if someone were to point out that the way she said it suggested such and such an emphasis, she would be able to say whether she had intended that or not—in which case, once again, her intention was somehow clear to her independent of the words she used to express herself.

On the other hand, people sometimes use language that goes far beyond their thoughts. Some people can dazzle us with elaborate words when they do not really know what they are talking about. Here is a sentence that I have just produced, with no thought at all in my mind: "The implication of the prognosis indicates that the thrust of our ultimate endeavors obliges us to reconsider all our assumptions and to justify the utilization of the heretofore unconsidered media." As I look at it now, I can find some meaning for most—although not all—of it. But I am working hard to *create* the meaning—it certainly is not given to me by the words. Some people seem to talk this way a lot of the time, with very little thought behind their words.

The poetic aspect of language might be said to share something with each of the two preceding situations. As in the first, when the writer starts, she may have little idea of the form that her words will take. Once she has written, she may look at her writing as a critic, to see whether the emphasis she has given does correspond to her feeling. As in the second, a poet's facility with words sometimes leads her to put them together in ways that go beyond any meaning of which she was aware. Some readers may be able to create for themselves, as they read those words, a meaning of which the writer himself remains unaware.

At other times, words can be so poorly chosen that they mask what is really a good idea. If we think it may be worthwhile, we take time to reflect on a muddled sentence and we sometimes find out that these muddled words do in fact point to an interesting idea, which we can rephrase for ourselves if we wish. This rephrasing corresponds to the real nature of the job of an interpreter. When he is interpreting from one language to another—even simultaneously—he does not do a mechanical input-output job. He listens to a big enough piece to grasp the sense of what is said and then puts that sense into words again, in a different language. He necessarily does a poor job if he is translating a topic he does not understand, even if he has boned up on the vocabulary.

One might say, unkindly, that Piaget has a vested interest in discrediting the view that ideas are only as good as the way they are expressed, because anyone who tries to read him firsthand is quite taken aback by his lack of eloquence and even clarity. Yet what is on his mind—if we go beyond the way he expresses himself—is surely significant.

CONSTRUCTING WHAT WE KNOW

In order to know something or to think about something, then, we do not have to use words. The question for teachers, of course, is how thoughts get into people's minds (or wherever they are) in the first place. Some people believe that, even if we do not always need words to think the thoughts once they are there, it was through words that they got there to begin with. Sometimes, of course, this is true—sometimes we can immediately connect something we are told to what we know already, and the thought becomes our own.

But notice that if we really understand what we have been told, we make new connections for ourselves. We are now the master of these new connections and can express them our own way.

If we cannot make these new connections for ourselves, we do not really grasp what we have been told. In fact this is where we are most likely to hold on to the exact words! If a child is told that water runs downhill, he is much more likely to be able to repeat those same words than he is to be able to *rephrase* them with all the meaning that they represent. He is very unlikely, on the basis of a sentence like that, to be able to draw significant connections—as, for instance, that the outlet from the Great Lakes must be uphill from Quebec City. Piaget's emphasis is that we have to do the work ourselves, making the connections, even if people take pains to point out to us connections they have been able to make.

It is worth looking at two of the most important of Piaget's books, to see what he has to say about the beginning of our thoughts. *The Origins of Intelligence in Children* (1936/1966) and *The Construction of Reality in the Child* (1937/1986) deal with the development of intelligent behavior in infants before the development of language. (See chapter 8 for more on this.) The very fact that he has written two volumes on this topic is an important indication of his position. Infants begin to act in intelligent ways from the day of their birth; that is, they make connections, seek consistencies, and modify their actions in terms of their situation. One might say that they are armed initially with nothing more than their reflexes; a guiding *motivational* rule that might be stated like this, "If I can do it, I will"; and a guiding *intellectual* rule that might be stated, "All else being equal, things will turn out the same." With this equipment, infants proceed to carry out their reflexes in all possible situations, to modify them as necessary, and to figure out which actions in certain situations give rise to more possible things to do. The more they try to do what they can, the better they are able to adapt to the circumstances and the more they start to differentiate and to coordinate what they can do. In this way they come to respond to more aspects of the situation at once. They are making refinements and connections in their actions—"thinking" in their actions—long before there is any use of language.

In their actions, they are constructing what they know about the world, and they are constructing their logic, such as classifying, ordering, conserving. Some things can be grasped, some cannot; some move when they are pushed, some do not; some things fall when you let go of them, others do not. In order to grasp an object, you have to open your fist, put it on the object, and then close your fist—any other order will not work. If a thing swings when you hit it once, it will probably swing when you hit it again. All these insights are independent of language.

What each of them represents is what Piaget calls a "scheme." The totality of your schemes is the totality of what you know. At the prelanguage, presymbolic level, your schemes are what you know how to do.

It is important to realize that what is known, a scheme, is more general than any one instance of carrying it out. Let us say that an infant is reaching for an object that is out of reach, but is resting on a blanket; he manages to get the object by pulling the blanket toward him (a sophisticated connection to make). And let us suppose that, even if that first time was by accident, he realizes that it was a good procedure, and uses it another time on purpose. Now we can say this is a scheme. But the next time he does it, he will not use exactly the same movements. He might reach higher or lower, nearer on the blanket or farther. It might be a coat this time, instead of a blanket, so he would grasp it differently. He might even use the other hand. So it is not simply a motor conditioning. The scheme that is now at his disposition is not simply a matter of superficial movements. It is more like a rule of grammar. Speakers create all sorts of sentences they have never heard, nor even produced themselves before. They have understood the rule of grammar and use it in all sorts of different superficial manifestations. Similarly, once the infant has made the connections, a scheme is at his disposal, and he uses it in all sorts of different superficial manifestations.

Infants do not represent this knowledge to themselves. Lying in a crib, they do not recreate in the mind's eye the actions they might be capable of carrying out. It is when a possibility presents itself to them that they proceed to act appropriately. Not only have they no language, then;

neither have they any other form of representing what is not immediately present.

Piaget describes the development of this ability to represent something by something else in his book *Play, Dreams, and Imitation in Childhood* (1945/1962b). The English translation of his title does not describe its contents well. The book really deals with the development of the child's representational ability. Play, dreams, and imitation are three ways children have of representing what they know of the world—language, of course, being another. In this book, Piaget develops the thesis that children's first internal representation—their first "thinking without actions"—takes the form of internalized imitation.

Imitation, too, has its beginnings in the very first days of life, in primitive forms like circular reactions, imitation of oneself, or involuntary imitation of a sound. But it is relatively late—some time in the first half of the second year—that imitative behavior takes on a really representative function, in the sense that children imitate something on purpose, making connections not made before and using this imitation to stand for something that they know is different from their own actions. Through imitating something a child develops the schemes by which to understand it—very much as Marcel Marceau comes to understand what is involved in tugging on a rope by miming the action. Piaget describes a case where his daughter, at 1 year and 3 months, catches the feet of a toy clown in her clothing. After disentangling it, she hooks her finger into her clothing in the same way and pulls at it in an effort to understand what happened. She is imitating the feet of the clown with her finger; in other words, her finger is representing the feet of the clown.

Much analyzing and coordinating are involved in imitation. Because the child's own body is the first thing available to reproduce with, he or she acts out the analyses and coordinations. Gradually, the child becomes able to internalize these imitations—to carry them out mentally not "in the mind's eye," but "in the mind's body" as it were.

At this age infants also realize that objects have a continuing existence even when they are not present in their own perceptual field. They realize that it is not their looking or holding or chasing that brings the objects into being. They now have a way of evoking things for themselves, even when not in the presence of the objects.

This is the age, too, as all parents know, when children start to use language. Words have always been around them, as part of the situations they have been in. But now that they can use one thing to stand for another, words become available as a useful aspect of the situation to imitate, as a short-cut evocation of it. Thus, language comes into being as one of several ways children develop of representing one thing by another.

Now it should be clear in this case that words do not create the sense or intention or feeling; the words accompany it, or seek to express it, or to refer to it. At this stage the adequacy or inadequacy of the words is not even a close reflection of the adequacy of the sense that is in the child's mind.

It should also be clear that since words are conventions that do not resemble what they stand for, there is no way that a child who is beginning to tune in to language can be sure what a given word or phrase or sentence refers to when she hears it. The child is likely to believe that it refers to what her mind is on at the moment. If she is looking out the window when the neighbor's dog goes by and her mother says "doggie," she might think "doggie" means something going by outside the window; something that comes out of the house next door; anything white and brown; or anything running along the street—depending on what she happens to be noticing.

This is the essence of what Piaget has called "egocentric thought"— what is foremost in the child's thoughts is what she believes others are attending to, also.

As children grow up, they realize that what they are paying attention to is not necessarily what other people are paying attention to. But this is a hard lesson to learn, and nobody ever learns it totally. All of us tend to be absorbed with thoughts that we already have, or have once had; if people start to talk generally in that direction, we tend to interpret what they say as things that we have been thinking. The phenomenon isn't restricted to single words. Whole sentences and paragraphs are misconstrued. We are so intent on what we are thinking that we do not realize that the other person is saying something different. Each of us is familiar with conversations that at some point start to run at cross purposes when the participants have different things in mind. They get straightened out (if indeed they do), with exclamations such as "Oh, I thought you meant—." Often we are so sure of what the other speaker must be saying that we don't hear the clues to the contrary. "Oh, every time you said Chicago, I was thinking Toronto!"

Small children happen to be particularly attached to what they are focused on at the moment. They are very prone to taking in whatever is said and fitting it to what they thought already.

In *The Language and Thought of the Child* (1923/1962a), Piaget notes the extent of this phenomenon in nursery-school-age children and describes situations he set up to look at it more closely. For instance, he would explain to one child how a water tap works. He ascertained how much the child understood. Then that child proceeded to explain it to another child. In general, what he found was that the children explained as if they assumed the other child knew already. The language they used was more in the nature of very sketchy reminders, pointing out a number of highlights and assuming that the connections involved were clear. The child clearly tries to explain (the explanations are full of "You see?" and "And then it comes here, see?"), but he talks as if what is obvious to him as he now is engaged in his explanation is—by that very fact—obvious to everyone else.

Even more impressive is the fact that the child to whom this explanation is being given appears to have equal confidence! The listener constructs his own notion of how the tap works and he interprets the words of the other child so that they fit into what he is thinking! He is sure he understands everything the other child is trying to tell him. Thus, with these two children—one with one view of how a tap works, the other with his own view—lots of words were passed between them, but the words made little headway in conveying any meaning from one child to the other.

There is a clear message for teachers here. Words that people hear— and the younger the child is, the stronger the case—are taken into some thoughts that are already in their minds, and those thoughts may not be the ones the speaker has in mind. A good explainer can anticipate what our interpretations are likely to be—on the basis of what we are likely to know, to be thinking about, or to have noticed already—and can fit the explanation to that, with phrases like, "I don't mean X, I mean Y," or "Look, did you notice this?"

There is a message for listeners, too. A good listener, or a good understander of explanations, is aware that her first interpretation of what is being said may not be the right one, and she keeps making guesses about what other interpretations are possible. This ability is singularly undeveloped in little children but it should be highly developed in good teachers, who try to listen to what children are trying to say to them.

So far we have been dealing with knowledge of how the world works. In summary, each individual has to construct her own knowledge. Sometimes we can be helped by what other people tell us, but we still have to do the work ourselves. Often, we can say things we have been told without understanding what we say.

LOGIC IS DEEPER THAN LANGUAGE

Another aspect of the relation between language and thinking needs to be considered. Language is full of expressions of logical relationships. Some people believe that teaching children careful use of these linguistic forms helps to develop clear ways of thinking. Language reflects levels of classification and subclasses—for instance, some birds are sparrows and all sparrows are birds. It reflects cross-classification—peas are seeds and peas are food, at one and the same time. Language reflects ordering relationships—father, niece, grandfather; big, biggest; more, less. It reflects logical connections—because, even though, if/then.

Since these relationships are all built into language, one might think that children have only to pay attention when they are used in order to understand the relationships. But this is equivalent to assuming that, when a child hears "doggie" as she looks out the window, she knows exactly what "doggie" refers to. On the contrary, the evidence indicates that in this case, also, children think their own thoughts and interpret the language in their own way, which does not necessarily correspond to what the speakers around them have in mind.

One of Piaget's very first questions, in a 1921 article that predated even the first of his books, dealt with the way children use "some" and "all." Later he looked at this question again, when his theoretical position resembled what it is now. He found that, although children had a certain familiarity with what "some" and "all" meant, their understanding of these terms was not what we usually understand by them. In one investigation, children had a collection of red and blue circles, and red squares (no blue squares). One of the questions they were asked was, "Are all the squares red?" Five- and 6-year-olds would generally answer, "No, because there are some red circles, too."

In another investigation, he found that, although children agreed that horses and cows were both animals, they would look at a collection of six horses and two cows and say that there were more horses than animals, because there were only two cows.

In both these cases, the children clearly have some relationships in mind other than the ones that these questions suggest to us.

One of Piaget's collaborators, Christofedes-Papert (1965), repeating this second experiment, asked an additional question. After agreeing that there were six horses and two cows and that they are all animals, the children were asked, "Are there more horses here, or more animals?" "More horses, because there's only two cows." This time the experimenter asked, "What did I ask you?" "You asked me if there are more horses or more cows," "Ah, all right. Now listen to this question. Are there more horses or more animals?" "There are more horses, because there's only two cows." "What did I ask you?" "If there's more horses or more cows," and so on.

The child is making his own comparison between horses and cows. In spite of the experimenter's words, that is the comparison he continues to make. Piaget's interpretation is that he cannot think of horses as both horses and animals at the same time. Whatever the case, the experimenter's words are not getting through to the child. The words themselves cannot put their own meaning into his head.

The same phenomenon is in evidence in other transformations children make in rephrasing things they are told or asked. Sinclair (1967) asked children to give more candies to one doll than to another, which they did, and then asked what she had told them to do. The children said, "Give a lot to that one and a little to that one," which is not necessarily the same meaning but which indicates how the children understood "more" and "less."

This is reminiscent of work done by linguists such as Labov (1970) in studying dialect differences in ghetto children's speech. If the children were asked to repeat a sentence of a form that did not correspond to their grammar (for instance, "I asked Alvin whether he knows how to play basketball"), they repeated the sentence, but with their own grammar ("I asked Alvin do he know how to play basketball"). It was not the words they retained, it was the sense. Then the sense was translated back into words, words that said the same thing but were not the same words.

There is a difference between these children and the children in the Geneva studies. These children do understand exactly the sense of the words they have heard, as intended by the speaker. They have assimilated that sense accurately and have reexpressed it in their own words. The children in the Geneva studies assimilate their own sense, not the speaker's intention, and their rephrasing reveals their own sense. But the similarity between the studies is that the words are so far from being important that they are instantly forgotten and replaced by words that more adequately—from the point of view of the child—express the sense of what the child understood.

Another early concern of Piaget was children's use of conjunctions that express logical relationships. In *Judgement and Reasoning in the Child* (1924/1976) he showed that, even though children could use these conjunctions grammatically, the logic invoked in their use was far from clear. He proposed that children sense some sort of relationship between two propositions and sense that there are certain kinds of words that can be used to indicate such relationships. But the relationships are not clear, and the conjunctions, as a consequence, get all mixed up. He observed this in children's spontaneous use of these conjunctions, so he gave children sentences to complete and found completions like these:

John went away even though . . . he went to the country. (6 years)
It's not yet night even though . . . it's still day. (8 years)

The man fell from his bicycle because . . . he broke his arm. (8 years)

Fernand lost his pen, so . . . he gave it to a kid and he lost it in the park. (9 years)

Fernand lost his pen, so . . . he found it again. (8 years)

I walked an hour more even though . . . I like walking. (6 years)

I did an errand yesterday because . . . I went on my bike. (6 years)

(My translations; cf. English edition, pp. 43, 44, 17, 34, 33, 44–45, 17)

Other research that Piaget points to as supporting his view of the relationship of language and logic is that of Oléron (1957) and of Furth (1966). The general gist of their findings is that deaf children develop the same logical abilities as hearing children, at just about the same ages, without the contribution of a constant verbal bath from wiser adults.

A large-scale and subtle study by Sinclair (1967) also looked at relationships between language level and intellectual level. Her expectation at the outset was that children who did better in Piaget situations would have a better language level, and she hypothesized that this more sophisticated language would be what accounted for their more sophisticated thinking. The two Piaget situations she studied were conservation (the classic pouring-of-liquids experiment) and serial ordering (putting ten sticks in order of length). She did, in fact, find that children who succeeded in these tasks had more sophisticated language abilities, in a number of different ways. But then she proceeded to teach the less advanced children the language of the more advanced, believing that this would help them in their cognitive tasks. She found, first of all, that it was extremely difficult to teach them the language patterns. Their language seemed to be limited by their level of understanding. Nonetheless, she did make some headway with most of the children. Yet she found that, even with more sophisticated language, they did not, on the whole, do better than they had before on the intellectual tasks. Contrary to her original hypothesis, she concluded that language development is *dependent* on the level of thinking rather than being responsible for the level of thinking.

The pedagogical implications here seem to be fairly clear-cut: Teaching linguistic formulas is not likely to lead to clear logical thinking; it is by thinking that people get better at thinking. If the logic is there, a person will be able to find words adequate to represent it. If it is not there, having the words will not help.

This point may be clarified by referring once again to the development of intelligence at a preverbal age. Earlier in this chapter we considered the totality of one's schemes to be the totality of what one knows. For infants, schemes are what they know how to do. For older children or for adults, schemes are, in addition, the thoughts in their minds, their ways of putting things together and making sense of the world. Coordinating thoughts is as big a job as coordinating actions in an intelligent way. Think of trying to develop in a baby the scheme of pulling the blanket to get the toy that is on it, by holding her arms and maneuvering her through it. If the infant is just about ready to make the connection for herself, she may "get it" when shown in this way. But if she doesn't see the connection, it won't become her scheme. The next time around, it still will not be part of her repertoire. Similarly, an older child will not be able to internalize and to make some logical connection that somebody makes for her—even many times—if that connection is far beyond her.

Drilling children in sentences of the "if/then" format is not likely to develop in them the notion of logical implication, contrary to Bereiter and Engelmann's (1966) expectations. Some of Piaget's collaborators gave children a collection of different sorts of dolls and asked them to make subgroups corresponding to certain descriptions. One of the descriptions was "If it is red, then it is big," and for this the children would take only red, big dolls. They "heard" those words to mean "It is red and it is big," and they would accept no nonred dolls in the collection, even if the experimenter suggested it. It is doubtful that Bereiter and Engelmann's preschoolers would do any differently, despite their drillings.

BUILDING NEW CONNECTIONS

Thoughts are our way of connecting things up for ourselves. If others tell us about the connections they have made, we can only understand them only to the extent that we do the work of making these connections ourselves. Making connections must be a personal elaboration, and sometimes a person is simply not capable of making the connections that someone is trying to point out.

Often, of course, we do use words in our thinking, especially if we are trying to elaborate something new. Through trying to make things explicit for ourselves, we can see our own loose ends and we can see where we must make still other connections. Similarly, words from somebody else can point out loose ends in the way we have put our thoughts together. They can also point to connections that someone else has made, so that we may be able to make the same connections when the way has been suggested. This they do as any other representation does. A Calder wire sculpture can draw our attention to the soulful fatness of a cow. A museum waterflow model can indicate something about river currents. A film can make us stop and reconsider some of our beliefs about people. A ballet can lead us to new insights into the nature of madness. Painting, pantomime, model building, mathematical symbols—to the extent that these have at least some aspect of recreating, reconstructing, or representing something other than what they themselves are—represent, for the person who creates them, something of her understanding. It is no clearer in these cases than in the case of language that what they evoke in the beholder is the same understanding or knowledge or feeling as that which the producer had in mind. They call on the beholder to make her own connections, in order for the representation to make sense to her.

In passing, notice how Piaget's very methodology reflects his views of language. Piaget and his researchers engage in a rather loose discussion with a child. The researcher has a number of key questions in mind, to be brought up in a standard order. But the phrasing of the questions and ensuing discussions with the child depend on the child's reactions. Piaget is criticized by many psychologists for not having a standardized format—a fixed set of questions, phrased in a fixed way, so that exactly the same words are used with each child. The point of this standardization is to guarantee that each child is dealt with in the same way. But from Piaget's point of view, standardizing the words has little to do with standardizing the problem for children. The words are only a way to get the thinking going. There is no guarantee that the same words will cue in the same way for every child. It is important to vary the words used until they make contact with the child's thinking. Reaching the child is what has to be standard. Sticking rigidly to a fixed formula can almost guarantee a *lack* of standardization.

LEARNING TO SPELL

The argument that we have been advancing in this chapter so far is that there is no need to give children "language tools" in order to facilitate clear thinking, intelligence, or greater knowledge. Their own use of language will always be adequate for their own thinking.

However, there is no denying that linguistic style and "correct" language have an important place in communicating with others. Children may be able to say things in their own way and make themselves understood, yet their way may be neither elegant nor "standard" and some people will hold it against them. They may be able to write things with "standard" grammar and even with elegance, but with idiosyncratic spelling, and again some people will hold it against them. There is ample justification for this. Part of the reason for standardizing grammar and spelling is precisely so that we do not notice them and can give all our attention to what is said, rather than to distracting aspects of how it is said.

But there is a conflict for teachers here. To the extent that children are acting intelligently, they will be paying attention to the sense of what they hear and read, and not to the detail. Somehow, we must turn their attention to the detail. This would seem to imply that they have to turn off their intelligence while they do this. Indeed, that is the way "correct" grammar and spelling have most often been taught.

Teachers' attitudes to conventions like this might be characterized as "running scared"—in the sense that, since there is only one right way, explorations of other ways must be avoided at all costs. But why not encourage explorations in these matters, just as teachers encourage exploration in other areas? For one thing, running scared doesn't seem to work. If seeing or hearing something the right way often enough did work, why do children keep making mistakes? Most words that they misspell are words they have already seen dozens of times. Yet no matter how often they see words spelled correctly—and rarely do they see them spelled any other way—the correct spelling does not seem to get imprinted.

On the other hand, think of how confusing it is. Let's take a prereader, who is learning not spelling, but his letters. He has happily learned the shape of a C, for instance, and draws it—but backward. "No!" he's told, "That's not a C; a C is like this." An hour later, in another prereading exercise dealing with shapes, he is expected to realize that a square is still a square when it is sitting on its point looking like a diamond! How can he make sense out of all that? A backward C looks much more like itself than does a square sitting on its point. He is meant to be intelligent when he deals with squares, moving them around and looking at them in all sorts of ways, but he is severely restrained from being intelligent in dealing with letters.

Even in learning conventions, "right ways," why not give children the chance to be intelligent? With letters, that would seem to be as simple as encouraging them to explore their shapes, just as they explore any other shapes—"Yes, you're right, that's a C" (a C would still be a C even if it's lying on its back)—while at the same time pointing out that, in writing, you draw it in one position only.

In grammar, surely the same thing can be done. As linguists have made amply clear, a sentence like "Larry never got none" represents just as much knowledge of grammar as the standard "Larry didn't get any." It's just a different grammar. It can be accepted on its own terms, while at the same time other ways of saying the same thing are explored, including "Larry got none," "Larry never got any," or "Larry didn't get none." Instead of running scared of anything but the standard form, teachers can encourage the search for all possible forms that say the same thing. And the standard can be pointed out along the way.

This does seem a bit scary. By way of reassurance, let me describe an approach to spelling that has been developed in a school in Montreal, a French-speaking school called L'Ecole Nouvelle Querbes. This approach was elaborated by Albert Morf, a psychologist of the University of Montreal, formerly of Piaget's Center in Geneva. It was developed for the classroom by first-grade teachers Hélène Pothier, Denise Gaudet, and Cécile Laliberté. The approach is slightly more appropriate to French than to English, but aspects of this approach could certainly be adapted to English.

The reading program starts with writing—not handwriting, but writing to say something. A child suggests a word she wants to be able to write. Then the class together breaks it up into component sounds. *Cousin*, for example (I shall use the French version of the word), is broken down into *K OO Z IN*. The teacher then presents all possible ways of spelling each of those sounds: *C* or *K*; *OU* or *OO*; *S* or *Z*; *EIN, AIN*, or *IN*. (In this respect, the method is somewhat more difficult in English. In French, the "possible ways" are more regular.) The children proceed to produce all possible ways of spelling the word. "Yes, that's one way. Any more?" The more ways they get, the better. They write them on the board, and if a child has a way that is not yet on the board, he or she adds it to what is there. When all possible ways have been produced, the teacher tells them the way that is conventionally used.

Note that instead of feeling stupid for creating an unconventional spelling, the children feel clever. And they know that whoever may be dumb, in making spelling such an arbitrary exercise, it's not they! They also know, just as well as any other child, that there is only one correct way to write any given word, and this way is underlined in their notebooks, among all the possible ways. Moreover, as time goes on they develop greater and greater ability to guess, for themselves, which is likely to be the conventional way.

At the same time, the emphasis in general is on their saying what they have to say through writing. By the time they have built up a collection of how to write all the sounds, they can write anything adequately enough for someone to be able to read what they have said. The spelling may be unusual but it is always readable, and the writing is accepted for what it says.

In this process there is, for one thing, a proper sense of values: Writing is what it is all about. The first requirement of spelling is that writing be readable afterward, and the writing of these children always is. Then, to make it easier for readers, a single conventional spelling is learned. The expressive writing of these children is remarkable and becomes better through the six years of elementary school. But this is not the main point.

In other schools of various sorts children do equally remarkable writing. The point is that these children really learn to spell, withal. They learn to spell not by avoiding wrong spellings in a panic, but by actively seeking out every possible wrong spelling! When the children start reading, they notice the spellings of new words that they read. Since they realize that any number of other spellings might have done the communications job just as well, they sit up and take notice. "Gee, is that how they spell that?"

Note too that using a dictionary to check up on a spelling is possible only to the extent that you are able to generate possible spellings in advance. You can't get anywhere with a dictionary if you don't know how to start. These children know how to start.

Finally, just as when they see a written word they know that somebody has made an active choice about how to spell it, so when they see a written text they know that somebody—some fallible person somewhere—has made an active choice about how to write it. When one child reads out loud what she has written, the other children are active listeners. Sometimes their reaction is immediate acceptance—"*Oh, c'est beau.*" But other times they make suggestions about how else the original author might have said the same thing, and she sometimes decides to say it another way. They are, in budding form, aware of the thesis of this chapter—that the words themselves aren't the substance; they are one possible way of trying to express the substance, and they needn't be taken at face value.

3

Either We're Too Early and They Can't Learn It, or We're Too Late and They Know It Already: The Dilemma of "Applying Piaget"

SOME HISTORY

PROBABLY THE LARGEST single area of research inspired by Piaget's work has been the study of the genesis of an idea or an "intellectual structure" to see whether its development in the child was really as late as Piaget said it was. Skepticism was understandable. After all, his first discoveries were stunning. A 5-year-old who can count to 29 does not realize that if you take eight eggs out of eight cups and put them in a small pile, there are still as many eggs as eggcups. A child who battles daily with brothers and sisters to get a "fair" share of everything does not realize that if juice is poured from one glass to another of a different shape, the quantity doesn't change.

Even Piaget was skeptical at first. It was with epileptic children that he made his astonishing discovery that "number" is not a natural intuition: The ability to recite numbers in order does not necessarily have anything more to do with quantifying the number of objects, than does the ability to recite a nursery rhyme. The situation Piaget first designed to study this phenomenon has come to be known as "the merchant and the pennies." He, the adult, started with a number of objects, The child started with the same number of pennies. The child "bought" the objects from the adult—one object per penny. After five or six purchases, Piaget stopped, covering his remaining objects and the pennies he had received, and asked the child how many pennies he (Piaget) now had. All the child had to do was to count the number of objects he had acquired through one-to-one exchange. But he did not do this. And when it was suggested that he count his own objects, he did not see how that could tell him anything about the number of pennies Piaget was hiding.

This early experiment, which soon gave rise to the classic egg and egg-cup form, produced results that astonished Piaget as much as it did his early readers. In fact, at first he believed that it was specific to epileptics—that he had discovered a new diagnostic tool for epilepsy! As Thomas Kuhn (1962) has made amply clear, and as the later body of Piaget's own work shows over and over again, all of us, from children to scientists, have difficulty accepting data that go against our firmly held beliefs. We have to restructure too much of our intellectual framework to assimilate such surprises. It is far less costly, at least for a time, to keep the framework and deny the fact. Hence, the early skepticism about Piaget's findings and the lengthy attempts by American psychologists to see if they were really true. And, yes, they turned out to be true: "The children in my home town might be a little speedier than the children in Geneva, but I have to admit that they do, at some age, act just as Piaget said."

Efforts then turned to trying to see how to teach children the truth about such matters. "Learning experiments" replaced "replication experiments." Piaget's own view was that such development took time and could not be hastened. Simply telling children the truth about something could not make them understand it. This attitude was even more of a shock to the common sense derived from decades of acceptance of behavioral or stimulus-response psychology. One would think that if we can shape pigeons to play pingpong, we can shape children to conserve number. Surely we have only to devise the proper situations, focus the children's attention on the pertinent factors, elicit and reinforce the correct responses, and the job will be done.

Experiments based on Piaget's work have entered a new phase and are still going on. Convinced behaviorists remain convinced. They can now look at the facts and agree that most children are nonconservers when they enter school. The facts now, after four decades [this chapter was written in 1978], have found common acceptance among psychologists concerned with child development or learning. But these notions can still be accepted by behaviorists without changing their theoretical framework by acknowledging that, on the whole, children in preschool years are simply not put into situations where the correct notions would develop. They still need not restructure their framework if they can show that, with the right training, these ideas can be made accessible to children.

This debate is not over. An instructive example is the interchange between Siegfried Engelmann (1971), on the one hand, and Constance Kamii and Louise Derman (1971), on the other. This particular exchange is not recent, but the issues it highlights remain.

Engelmann, a behaviorist, undertook to teach a number of kinder-gartners some notions that usually develop much later—among them the idea of specific gravity as an explanation for the floating or sinking of objects. He then allowed Kamii and Derman to assess from a Piaget per-spective the extent to which they thought the notions had been learned. Among the rules Engelmann taught the children, the principal one was: "An object floats because it is lighter than a piece of water the same size; an object sinks because it is heavier than a piece of water the same size." Kamii and Derman describe fascinating instances of conflicts between the rules the children were taught and their own intuitions—their common sense. In addition to the rules, they often gave other explanations typical of children their age: "because it's heavy," "because it's little," "because it has cracks in it," "because I pushed it," "because it has air inside," or, simply, "I really don't know why."

In other instances, the rules seemed to come between the children and their intuitions in ways that led to nonsense not normally encountered in children their age. One child hefted a large candle in one hand and a birthday cake candle in the other, but having seen that they both floated, maintained "they weigh the same." Another child said that a tiny piece of aluminum foil that sank weighed more than a large sheet that rested on the surface. Clearly, these children were trying to apply the rules rather than coming to terms with the objects. A typical 6-year-old's reaction to the aluminum foil, for example, might be to say that the tiny piece sank because it was too tiny, and the large piece floated because it was flat.

In another part of the Kamii and Derman assessment, no longer deal-ing with floating and sinking, the children were asked why the water level rose in a glass when an object was immersed in it. Two of four replied, "Because it is heavier than a piece of water the same size." The other two children, who tended generally to remain true to their intuitions, answered that the object pushed the water out of the way. In general, confronted with a result they did not expect, the rule-bound children hesitated briefly, and then searched their memory for a learned rule that might apply, whether it really made sense to them or not.

Engelmann's interpretation did not, of course, accord with Kamii and Derman's. Engelmann concluded that with more time the job could be better done; the rules could be better designed to cover a wider variety of situations and could be taught to elicit what I presume he would call a higher criterion of performance. Kamii and Derman's interpretation seems more persuasive: The children had learned a verbal overlay, but their deep-seated notions had not evolved.

Behaviorists are not the only psychologists to have undertaken learn-ing experiments based on Piaget's findings. Learning research of a differ-ent character was stimulated by *The Process of Education* (1960), a report

by Jerome Bruner of the landmark Woods Hole conference. This conference was the point of departure for much of the curriculum reform of the
1960s. Piaget's long-time collaborator, Bärbel Inhelder, participated in the
conference, and, according to Bruner, was asked to suggest ways in which
the child could be moved along faster through the various stages of intellectual development in mathematics and physics. Inhelder (personal communication, April 16, 1978) reports that in fact there were lengthy debates
at the conference on that point. Physicists and psychologists, including
Bruner, generally reproached the Genevan researchers for their observa-
tional passivity. In effect, they said, "You've done nothing but document
the child's unaided development; you don't intervene. Surely each of the
notions you have studied is composed of other simpler notions. Surely
it is sufficient to decompose each of the complex notions into its simpler
parts, to teach the simpler parts, and to aid the construction of the whole
notion in this way," the parallels with physics are clear. The world of physics is infinitely manipulable. If one knows the constituent mechanisms,
one can unmake and remake a process in innumerable ways, taking it
apart and putting it together as one wishes. In contrast, the biologists, on
the whole, understood Inhelder's point that a child's thinking was not as
manipulable as a physical phenomenon. Biological organisms have their
own interrelated rhythms and structures. Inhelder observed that, among
the physicists, only Francis Friedman understood that a child's thinking
responded with the integrity of a biological organism and not like the separate components of a physical mechanism. Friedman's influence, tragi-
cally cut short by his death in 1962, was nonetheless seminal in the early
thinking of the staff of the Elementary Science Study—the one U.S. program of the 1960s curriculum reform movement most consistent with the
work of Piaget and Inhelder in psychology.

Bruner and psychologists of a similar bent certainly differed from
Engelmann in their attitudes toward learning. For them, learning was not
a matter of acquiring verbal rules; understanding remained central. But
they too assumed that understanding could be engineered, molded by an
outsider. A great number of learning experiments derived from Piaget's
findings were undertaken on this basis.

For educators, the Woods Hole conference was important in bringing
Piaget to the fore, since *The Process of Education* was widely distributed,
and Piaget was the one psychologist discussed. Clearly, his work had
great significance for education. But what was it? Almost without exception, educators followed the learning research and sought ways to speed
the development of key ideas that, at their natural pace, develop slowly.
It was the prevalence of these attempts that gave rise to the supposed
dilemma of my title, a dilemma that besets current thinking about the ap-
plications of Piaget's work to education.

GENEVAN LEARNING RESEARCH

An essential part of this story is that in the mid-1950s "learning research" played a central role in Piaget's own Center for Genetic Epistemology. In 1957–1958, it was the main theme of the center. Four volumes were published on the research of that year (Apostel, Jonckheere, & Matalon, 1959; Goustard, Greco, Matalon, & Piaget, 1959; Greco & Piaget, 1959; Morf, Smedslund, Vinh-Bang, & Wohlwill, 1959). None of these books has been translated, and more's the pity. Even now, 60 years later, they still make surprising and provocative contributions to the discussion.

The research was largely undertaken to find the extent to which children's level of understanding sets limits on what they are able to "read" from the environment and, conversely, to see the extent to which encounters with selected data from the environment affect the child's level of understanding. Of the seven research articles in these four volumes, the most exemplary for this discussion is that of Greco in Greco and Piaget's *Apprentissage et Connaissance* (1959). The problem he chose to study was taken from Piaget's *The Child's Conception of Movement and Speed* (1946/1970): three colored beads, black, white, and red, threaded on a stick, are inserted in a tube, from left to right. If red goes in first, which color is at the right-hand end? If red goes in first, which color is at the right-hand end after the tube is rotated 180°? Which color is at the right-hand end if the tube is rotated 180° *two* times? For those of us who do not have to do the experiment to know in advance, our answer to the last question is based on the following reasoning: One rotation results in the opposite order; two rotations result in the opposite of the opposite, which amounts to the original order. The same reasoning allows us to generalize: Any odd number of rotations will result in the opposite order; any even number of rotations will result in the original order.

This seems simple enough. Most of us would be surprised that children would have any difficulty understanding it, but Piaget's research had shown that they did. Beyond that, most of us would not suspect that "understanding" had much of a role to play in finding the rule. It would seem a simple enough generalization for children to draw for themselves, if they were shown enough examples. This is what Greco wanted to investigate.

He carried out the research with 4- and 5-year-olds who did not at the outset understand the relationship between the number of rotations and the positions of the beads. Various techniques, corresponding to a number of different forms of analysis, were used. Single rotations caused little difficulty. If the rule was not immediately seen, it was easily generalized from a few examples: When you turn, it comes out the opposite. But two rotations were another story, and often the child's rule for one rotation suffered along the way.

Some children needed as many as eight different sessions before they were able to predict consistently what would happen in these two different cases. The data are not "seen" for a long time. For example, in one session, Chal (5 years, 10 months) predicts incorrectly four times in a row, when black has entered first, and the tube has been rotated twice. "Why do you always say red?" she is asked. "Because before/[in a series of single rotations] when you turned it, it changed color." "And now?" "Not always," Greco notes that she has just witnessed 14 double rotations in a row (some with black going in first, some with red); but all she has seen is that it doesn't "always" change color (Greco, 1959, p. 117).

Since the data are so simple, all the children finally do manage to get the rule. But for many of them, the rule for double rotation remains just that—a rule. They see no sense in it. The one rule they understand is that when the tube is turned once, the color changes. The double rotation is learned only as an exception to this rule; for some reason, when you turn it twice, it doesn't change. It is not a matter of changing twice, and thus coming back to the original position. It is, for some inexplicable reason, a matter of not changing at all. The rule is formulated and remembered without understanding.

Other children do come to understand, but their understanding is clearly the result of their own struggle to make sense of the data. Dar (5 years, 5 months) makes six wrong predictions in seven items of double rotation. He himself counts his mistakes on his fingers, and he declares, "I still made six mistakes." "You haven't got it yet?" "No, because when you turn once, I know it changes color; but when you turn two times, it's the same color, so I don't get it." At the next session, the whole series is answered correctly, and Dar exclaims: "Oh yeah, when you turn two times it's the same color!" At the end of the session, Greco asks him why. "Because the black that came there [to the left end] comes back here [to the right end] when you turn it the second time" (p. 129).

His words are precisely the same in the two cases. "When you turn two times it's the same color." But the first time he doesn't "get it"; he doesn't think it ought to be that way, so he doesn't give in to it. He sees the generalization, but he keeps predicting the way it *ought* to be, much like the skeptics' reactions to Piaget's early results.

The children who don't have Dar's insight, and who are perhaps more willing than he is to accept a rule they don't understand, finally gave in to it as an exception to the rule they do understand. They seem to be defeated by the evidence. The difference between those children and children like Dar is clear. Here is an "explanation" from a child who simply gave in to the rule: "When you turn it two or three times [it was never turned more than twice] it stays just the same" (p. 137). Here are some other explanations from children who, like Dar, understood the reason: "It doesn't stay the same all the time, it changes, and then it changes again" (p. 137). "When you do two turns, it changes sides twice; at every turn the black changes sides" (p. 137). In a subsequent posttest, where the number of rotations was increased to three, four, and five, the children like Dar did significantly better than the children who gave in to the rule without understanding it. They did not, however, do as well as those who had known, without needing the learning experience, that a double rotation amounted to the same thing as no rotation.

It is possible, then, for a child's understanding of this kind of necessary relationship to evolve in especially devised situations more quickly than it would spontaneously. But it is not the pressure of data that gives rise to the understanding. It is, on the contrary, the child's own struggle to make sense of the data.

Greco underlines this point by devising four experiments where various kinds of direct help were given to the children—either perceptual clues to help follow the movements of the appropriate end of the tube or a direct statement of the rule during the course of the learning sessions ("See, every time it turns, it changes color; you just have to say, 'red, black' like that" (p. 143). In no case did this outside help, characteristic of the Engelmann type of behaviorist research, speed up the learning process. In those cases where the verbal rule was given, the children conscientiously applied the verbal alternation, "black, red, black, red," but they did so without seeing the relationship between the rotations and the colors. Sometimes when the rotations were stopped the children added a term to their alternating verbal series, so it would turn out the way they thought it should. The only accepted part of the rule was the part they understood to begin with: "When it turns it changes color."

Of the situation with perceptual clues, Greco says, "The failure of these methods . . . shows that the discovery of the rule could not be the product of perceptual learning. . . . It is the discovery of the law which makes possible the correct use of visual tracking" (p. 142).

Piaget's summary of these four volumes of research includes the following statements: "In the first place, it is incontestable that a certain amount of learning of logical structures can take place" (1959, p. 16). Some children did learn that the result of two rotations is necessarily the opposite of the result of one rotation. "However, in the second place, this learning of logical structures remains very limited" (p. 16). That is, it took a long time and was neither universal nor generalizable. "In sum the learning of logical structures . . . consists of the construction of new coordinations" (p. 16). Here the effect of the second rotation had to be coordinated with the result of the first.

This research was clearly the basis for Inhelder's insistence at Woods Hole that there are limits to the engineering one can do with children's understanding. It is nonetheless of some historical interest that Piaget agrees that "a certain amount of learning of logical structures can take place." Well after the Woods Hole conference, Piaget was understood, by most American educators at least, to believe that children's logical construction could not be "accelerated" at all.

The misunderstanding of Piaget's own position probably arises from his reaction to what he called, in the early 1960s, "the American question," referring no doubt to the debate at the Woods Hole conference: If it is true that children's levels of understanding develop so slowly, what can we do to speed them up? It was Piaget's good-natured mocking of this question that perhaps led to the misconception that he believed nothing could be done to speed them up. But in fact that was not what he meant to convey. He simply meant to question the reason for doing so. A few years later he pointed out that for him the question was not how fast we can help intelligence grow, but how far we can help it grow.

According to Inhelder, the Woods Hole debate played a role in stimulating another body of learning research. It is much better known to the American audience, since it has been translated into English (Inhelder, Sinclair, & Bovet, 1974), and it is perhaps the most interesting learning research done to date. A dozen years after Woods Hole, Inhelder took up the challenge of the physicists and psychologists and tried to break up a notion into simpler constituent parts to see how children managed to recombine them. But the research took on quite a different character from that which the conference participants might have imagined. The attempt was to put into relief the conflicts that were engendered when any single child based a judgment on one or another of two different ways of thinking. (Examples can be found in chapters 5 and 9 of this book.) It was an effort not simply to see whether specific experiences could make logical understanding easier, as Greco's research did, but to see what goes on when a child passes to a new level of understanding. What conflicts led children to see the inadequacies of their own notions and to modify those notions in order to resolve the conflicts?

Again, it is clear from this research that children's understanding is not infinitely malleable. At certain levels, the children do not even see the conflicts in their own thinking. Conflicting notions are simply compartmentalized, and no need is felt to reconcile them. Only if children recognized and were bothered by a conflict did they sometimes manage to construct a more adequate notion to coordinate the two conflicting ones.

Two points from Piaget's preface to the Inhelder, Sinclair, and Bovet study shed light on this discussion. The first is that, for him, the interest

of these experiments does not lie in whether the acquisition of certain notions can be accelerated, but rather in what research like this can tell us
about the process involved in passing from one level of understanding to
another. What he found significant is that in every case where acceleration takes place, it results from a conflict arising in the child's own mind.
It is the child's own effort to resolve a conflict that takes him or her on
to another level. Piaget's second point concerns the effects that outside
stimulation might have on the child's initiative. He questions whether,
when some notions are facilitated by learning experiments, they will serve
as points of departure for new, spontaneous constructions, or whether the
child will then tend to depend on outside provocation, rather than his or
her own initiative, in pursuing the relationships among ideas.

This seems to be a critical question for educators. Indeed, in his preface, Piaget puts it directly to educators, not to psychologists. Early in the
preface he speaks of the "psychologist" and the "subject"; but in raising
this question, he abruptly switches to the "teacher" and the "pupil." His
question brings us squarely into the realm of the dilemma posed in the
title of this chapter, and it adds another dimension.

BREADTH AND DEPTH

It is clear that the dilemma of the title is a false one. The problem lies in
the wrong assumptions about what the "it" of education ought to be, as if
all knowledge or all intellectual preparation consisted of logical structures
and conceptual frameworks. On the contrary, Piaget's work suggests that
this is the one area of intellectual preparation that educators need worry
least about; left to their own rhythm and given the opportunity, children
tend to develop the basic frameworks as naturally as walking.

On the other hand, there are clearly enormous differences among people in what they make of their basic frameworks. By age 7 the naturalist
Gerald Durrell was intimately acquainted with the ways of every bug and
amphibian in his back yard. A 15-year-old of my acquaintance, skeptical
about whether 300 raffle tickets selling from 1¢ to $3.00 would leave much
profit beyond the price of the tennis racquet that was offered as the prize,
reinvented, as she sauntered down the street, Gauss's formula for finding
the sum of numbers from 1 to n. My 11-year-old country neighbor has
the mechanics of my lawnmower and rototiller down pat. And, from the
other extreme, a group of adults I once worked with, intelligent but un-
trained in science, spent seven sessions experimenting with floating and
sinking before it occurred to one of them that floating might depend on a
relationship between weight and volume (Duckworth, 2001a). Contrary

to Inhelder and Piaget's own suggestion (1958), logical structures alone did not lead to a grasp of this phenomenon. What is it that affects what individuals actually do with their basic frameworks? This, surely, is the critical question for educators.

I once had what struck me as a great insight, derived from Piaget's work: "All the rest of the world passes us by unless we think of thinking about it in that way." What brings us to think of thinking about parts of the world in new ways? The question applies at all levels. Nobody until Einstein thought of thinking about space and time as interdependent variables, though once he had done so, other physicists were able to think that way too. Nobody until Freud thought of thinking about the power of the unconscious in human activity. Nobody until Piaget, for that matter, thought of thinking about how children thought about conservation problems. Until he did, that whole put of the world passed all of us by.

It was actually in the context of sensorimotor intelligence—the practical intelligence that infants construct before the development of language—that I was struck by this image. I thought of a baby girl lying in her crib with the whole of the universe, or at least some part of it, around her. But, for lack of knowing what to do to this universe, all of it passes her by except for the little that responds to what she knows how to do. She has only to push, and this part of the world will swing; she has only to shake and that part of the world will jingle; she has only to let go, and some other part of the world will fall down and bang on the floor. But since she has not yet come to invent these actions (which, for infants, is a better way of saying that she has not yet thought of thinking about the world in these ways), all of that entertainment passes her by.

I was thinking, of course, of Piaget's own studies of infants. *The Origins of Intelligence in Children* (1936/1966) is the only one of his books in which he studies the child's practical use of what he or she already knows. This research is so closely related to my theme that I would like to quote in full one short example of how one kind of action that a child knows how to effect gives rise to a new action (a new scheme, in Piaget's terminology), providing the infant access to another part of the universe.

> For Laurent, the scheme of hitting came into being in the following way. At 4 months, 7 days, he looks at a letter opener tangled in the strings of a doll hung in front of him. He tries to grasp [a scheme he already knows] the doll or the letter opener but each time, his attempts only result in his knocking the objects [so they swing out of his reach]. He then looks at them with interest and starts over again.
>
> The next day, same reaction. He still doesn't hit intentionally, but after trying to grasp the letter opener, and failing each time, he then only sketches out his grasping gesture, and so simply keeps knocking one end

of the object. The next day Laurent tries to grasp a doll hanging in front of him; but he only manages to make it swing, and not to hold onto it. Then he shakes his whole body, waving his arms [another scheme he already knows]. But in so doing he hits the doll by accident; then he does it again on purpose, a number of times . . . At 4 months, 15 days, with another doll hung in front of him, Laurent tries to grasp it, then shakes himself to make it swing, knocks it accidentally, and then tries simply to hit it. Now the scheme is almost differentiated from the preceding ones, but it does not yet have an independence of its own. At 4 months, 18 days, Laurent hits my hands without trying to grasp them, but he started by simply waving his arms around, and only afterwards went on to hit my hands. The next day, finally, Laurent immediately hits a doll hung in front of him. The scheme is now completely differentiated. Two days later he hits some hanging rattles, making them swing over and over again. Starting at 5 months, 2 days, Laurent hits objects with one hand while holding them in the other. (Piaget, 1936/1966, Obs. 103; my translation)

It is this level of analytic description that is the fascination of *The Origins* of *Intelligence.* A new procedure is developed from old ones, and leads to yet other new ones. Note that Laurent's knowledge is broadened, in the sense that he can conceive of (which means that he can act on) the world in more varied ways; it is deepened, in the sense that he can know more aspects of one given object or situation. His repertoire is greater; he sees the pertinence of his repertoire to any one situation. More situations now make sense; any one situation makes sense in a greater number of ways.

In the companion volume, *The Construction of Reality in the Child* (1937/1986), Piaget analyzes the way various schemes are coordinated into structures, forming the framework of a child's understanding of space, time, causality, and the permanent existence of objects. It is this level of analysis that he pursues in all his subsequent work, and in all of his work with older children. Never again has he looked at the detail of how one child's actions or thoughts evolve.

Piaget's emphasis on structures has been very fruitful for epistemology, which is his field of interest. But for educators it is the detail of a single child's broadening and deepening knowledge that is the important thing. The lesson we can take from *The Origins of Intelligence* is that knowledge is always based on other knowledge—a refinement and a reintegration of the knowledge one already has. How does this work with older children? How does a child or an adult mobilize capacities? Whatever the state of development of his or her notions at a given moment, the child may or may not even think of bringing them into play. That is why the dilemma of the title is so much beside the point. The real question for educators should be when and how does anyone think of bringing ideas into play?

GOING BEYOND THE DILEMMA

Some Genevan research addresses this question. This work of Inhelder and her collaborators with children from 4 to 12 years of age is strikingly similar to Piaget's observations of infants years ago. Children are called on to put their knowledge to use in a practical situation, where "the knowledge is not already organized in a way that can be applied as is, but . . . must be created (or recreated) . . . during the solution procedures" (see Ackermann-Valladao, 1981).

Blanchet (1977), in a paper dealing with the methodology of this kind of research, writes, "A good experimental situation . . . Must permit the child to establish plans to reach a distant goal, while leaving him wide freedom to follow his own routing" (p. 37). I am struck by the fact that Blanchet's statement could as easily be said of all the best curriculum programs I know. The opening phrase might just as well be "a good learning situation."

What Inhelder and her collaborators look for is what a child notices about a situation, what the child does, how the first acts develop, how the results of these acts modify what is noticed, and how all that is noticed becomes integrated into a broader and deeper understanding of the situation as a whole. It is worth developing one example.

The researchers (Blanchet et al., 1976) spent two years analyzing a videotape of a 6-year-old boy, Didier, as he worked with a set of five Russian dolls of the kind that can be separated at their middles to nest inside one another. Videotape was a relatively recent technology in Genevan research and it was used here to full advantage. Every gesture, expression, hesitation, swift action, and glance was taken into account as an indicator of the thought that might be guiding Didier's actions. It is significant, also, that the analysis was done by a group. It would be only too easy for one individual to become caught up with a single possible interpretation of the various indicators. When several observers are doing the analysis, they are more likely to "think of thinking about" the situation in a variety of ways, and to be obliged to confront their various ideas to see which seems most appropriate.

The dolls are first presented to Didier with each one assembled as a separate doll. He is given no specific problem. "You can play with these however you want. Do what you want." He starts immediately by trying to nest them, but he starts with the big ones first. He opens the biggest, and goes to put the next one inside it. But he stops, looks at the smallest, and then slowly reverses his procedure, and starts from the smallest.

Starting from the smallest, he succeeds easily. But he is still perplexed because the dolls cannot be nested from biggest to smallest, as open boxes can be. What is it about these things that is so like a set of different-sized open boxes, and yet so different? This becomes the question that keeps him going. Twice more he tries to nest them from biggest to smallest, as if trying to understand why it won't work. Each time, he ends up nesting them from smallest to biggest.

The general idea of "doing the opposite," which first appears here in the smallest-to-biggest, biggest-to-smallest contrast, is carried out in other ways. At one point, he groups the dolls into big ones and little ones, and then he inverts their positions, by crossing his hands, picking up two, uncrossing his hands again, and putting them down on the "opposite" side. When the smallest doll falls over by accident, he places it on its head, and then nests them all again, but putting each one *upside* down into the next.

He starts working with the bases separately. He places each one upside down, which is one way of doing the opposite; and at the same time he places them, at last, from biggest to smallest. This time he no longer has a nest. He has a tower. Rapidly, he does the same thing with the heads—turns them over, and works from biggest to smallest. But this time, to his surprise, he doesn't get a tower. He gets a nest again. As a next step—and the observers believe he is still trying to make a tower—he changes two things. He places the heads right side up and works from smallest to biggest, which gives him another nesting, the other side up.

At this point his universe has become rather complex. He has two procedures—from biggest to smallest and from smallest to biggest, and two positions—right side up and upside down. These also must be coordinated with the fact that, in one case, upside-down means that the opening is up, while in the other case, upside down means that the opening is down. Given this complexity, which now has produced two surprising results (his actions have twice created nests rather than towers), Didier takes apart his two constructions and tranquilly goes back to his very first procedure. He redoes the complete nesting of the dolls, then takes the nest apart, builds his tower with the bases, and, finally, with no false moves, builds the tower with the heads.

Two themes emerge in the numerous studies undertaken to date by this group, and both find support in the example of Didier. The first is the constant presence of alternation between trying to achieve a certain result and trying to understand the situation. At the outset, Didier did not seem to concern himself with understanding the relationships among these dolls. He seemed satisfied with his understanding of things that could be nested and set out simply to achieve this result. It was when he found to his surprise that one of his ways of nesting things—biggest to smallest—didn't work that he started to be interested in understanding what was special about these particular nestable objects. In the course of exploring them, he simply happened to build a tower with the bases, just as Laurent happened to set the letter opener swinging. Building a tower with the heads then became another task—a new result to be achieved. But it coexisted with the goal of understanding their characteristics: Witness the fact that in the case of both of his unsuccessful attempts to build a tower with the heads, he saw his procedure through to the end, as if he were interested in seeing what its outcome would be. His last nesting sequence was carried out for reasons very different from the first nesting sequence. It was not a goal in itself this time: It was a consolidation of what he understood, subordinated to the last remaining goal of constructing a tower with the heads.

This hypothesis is explored in a number of excellent studies (Ackermann-Valladao, 1977; Karmiloff-Smith & Inhelder, 1975; Kilcher & Robert, 1977; Montangéro, 1977; Robert, 1978; Robert & Sinclair, 1974). One of these studies, published in English, has the suggestive title "If You Want to Get Ahead, Get a Theory" (Karmiloff-Smith & Inhelder, 1975), and it sheds light directly on the Greco study—the difference between simply succeeding in a task and understanding what is going on. Children from 4 to 9 were asked to balance a variety of boards across a narrow bar. Some of the boards were plain, some were visibly weighted at one end, some were invisibly weighted at one end. A child does not need much of a theory to succeed in balancing a board; trial-and-error and readjustments suffice. But, then, each case is seen by the child as separate: Understanding is no better at the end than it was at the beginning. From the moment any theory arises—and the first one usually is that to balance a board you should put it in the middle—each particular result can be seen both as an instance of a practical success or failure *and* as a confirmation or invalidation of one's theory. Balancing a board by putting it near one end (when it is weighted) is a practical success, but it is an invalidation of the "to balance it put it in the middle" theory. It is only if a child *has* a theory that a result can contribute to the development of his understanding; he can pay attention to results that contradict his theory and try to figure out some other theory that would take them into account.

The simple fact of a success or a failure does nothing for his understanding—just as it did nothing for the understanding of Greco's children—unless the child has some guiding idea that he is testing as he tries to achieve his practical aim. Until he thinks of thinking about the role of the distribution of the weight, the data provided by the successes and failures simply pass him by.

This brings us to the second theme of the Inhelder group's work. In a given situation, what is it that sets us reaching for elements that are already part of our knowledge, and which elements? What determines whether the infant Laurent will hit an object, reach for it, suck it, drop it, or shake it? What determines whether an adult will think of putting weight in relation to volume?

The hypothesis of Inhelder and her associates is that our knowledge has three lines of access. One is perceptual: Something about the way things look connects to something about how things looked before. Another is action: Something about what we do calls up what we have done before. The third is conceptual: An idea, a word, or a formula is the link. In any given situation, it is the interplay among these three that determines our understanding of it and what we do with it, not our conceptual knowledge alone and still less our logical structures.

> These three types of knowledge each gives rise to a very different accounting of the situation, since they break it up and put it back together again according to different units and transformations. The problem then becomes one of coordinating these forms of knowledge to allow for a real understanding of the situation. We believe that no one of these modes of knowledge alone allows for a complete understanding of the problem. . . . One could even define different depths of understanding by the number of modes brought into play. A real understanding could be characterized by the free passage of information from one type of knowledge to another, of any given element of the problem. (Blanchet et al., 1976, p. 5)

Depending on the situation, either its perceptual aspects, the actions it can give rise to, or the ideas, words, and formulas it evokes may have relatively greater importance. None of the three is, a priori, more valid. Words and formulas are useful summaries of a collection of relationships; on the other hand, their apparent simplicity is misleading. They leave out a lot, and they are slippery. Attaching them to the other access routes keeps them honest.

In Didier's case, the perceptual aspect was important at the very beginning: The dolls looked like nestable things. Then an idea, "the opposite," guided his approach to the dolls for most of the session. More than once he actually said he was trying to do *"le contraire."* But it is unlikely that he was even aware of the various senses of "opposite" that came into play—biggest to smallest or smallest to biggest, upside down or right side up. "Opposite" really took on meaning in this specific situation only through his actions and their effects on the dolls. Similarly, after Didier had built a tower with the bases of the dolls, he set out to do "the same thing" with their heads. But did "the same thing" mean "build another tower" or "work from big to small" or "turn them over?" Until he actually went to work with the heads, he seemed to think that it meant all three of these actions.

It is much too easy for all of us to think we understand a situation simply because we can apply to it a word or a formula. If notions like "the opposite" and "the same thing" are slippery, how much more so, for most of us, are "air pressure" or "cultural deprivation." It is all too easy to get carried away into worlds of our own invention that may or may not have any connection to the full complexity of real situations.

Furthermore, when we have learned something only in the form of a word or a formula, we may not even recognize situations where this knowledge is pertinent. Marion Walter (personal communication, October 24, 1972) gave a rather stunning example of this, arising from a teaching methods course she gave for adult students who all had degrees in mathematics. The students were working with geoboards. Each student had a board with a 5-by-5 array of nails and a number of rubber bands with which to make various shapes on the nails (Figure 3.1). Taking a small square of four nails as the unit of measurement, one student had set herself the problem of calculating the area of a triangle constructed on a base of three nails in the bottom row, having as an apex the first nail of the top row. Having calculated the area of that triangle, she moved the apex over one nail. To her great surprise, she found that the new triangle had the same area as the first. She then moved the apex over two more nails. Amazement—it was still the same area and it remained the same area for all triangles on that base with apexes in the top row. Excited by her discovery, she announced it to the whole group. After considerable discussion, one member of the group realized that her discovery was none other than a "fact" that they had all "known" since elementary school: that the area of a triangle is half the base times the height. There was a sense in which they did already know it. But since the formula had been without adequate ties to how things look, or what one can do with them, the knowledge was not evoked by a pertinent situation.

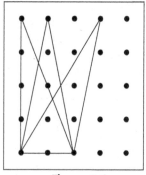

Figure 3.1

BEYOND THE FALSE DILEMMA

The study of Didier seems almost sufficient in itself as a response to the dilemma of my chapter title. One of the "basic logical structures" to which that dilemma has been applied is precisely the structure of seriation—systematic ordering of objects according to size or some other variable. Note that one does not even know whether Didier has developed that structure. Nothing in this situation enables us to say whether he would be able to order objects whose size differences were not so striking, or whose baseline was not already given by the fact that they stand up on the table. Furthermore, that is quite beside the point. It is neither too early nor too late for him to be engaged in these activities, which call on him to make use of whatever knowledge he has in a new situation.

I would like to linger a bit on this point, because another current interpretation of Piaget (mentioned in chapter 1) is that one should diagnose children's intellectual levels and tailor individual instruction accordingly. This has always seemed to me an impractical aim. To begin with, in any one class we can assume there are 30 children. A minimum number of Piaget notions that are pertinent to teaching at any age would surely include number, length, area, volume, causality, time, spatial coordinates, and proportions. This is only a beginning, but let's say modestly that a dozen tasks might serve to diagnose a child's intellectual level. That adds up to 360 tests for one class of children. And, of course, tests should be carried out periodically to assess progress during the year—let's say 360 tests, four times a year. Even with a full-time school psychologist assigned to each teacher, this pace could probably not be maintained.

But, again, this problem is significant only if our emphasis is on developing specific notions. If our emphasis is on broadening and deepening the child's use of the notions he or she has, such diagnoses lose much of their interest. The only diagnosis necessary is to observe what the children in fact do during their learning. This is not a diagnosis of notions: It is an appreciation of the variety of ideas children have about the situation, and the depth to which they pursue their ideas.

What one can assume, without any diagnostic tests at all, is that in any one group of 30 children—no matter how much one has tried to homogenize them—there will be enormous variations in levels of understanding and in breadth and depth of knowledge already developed. Certainly we would want each child to have the occasion to work at his or her own level. The solution for the teacher, however, is not to tailor narrow exercises for individual children, but rather to offer situations in which children at various levels, whatever their intellectual structures, can come to know parts of the world in new ways. It is not an easy job, but how much more interesting a human enterprise it is. And how much more to the point it is to think of a child's education as knowing and learning about how the world works than to attempt to resolve the dilemma in the title.

I return to Blanchet's thumbnail characterization of a good experimental situation in order to propose it again as a criterion for a good learning situation: It "must permit the child to establish plans to reach a distant goal, while leaving him wide freedom to follow his own routing." If we can create situations like this, then differences among children are by definition taken into account—without our having to diagnose in advance each child's level in a dozen domains. We can also be sure that children will take their own individual notions further as they strive to make sense of any situation, without our having to be obsessed with relating a particular activity to any one of the notions highlighted by Piaget.

Finally, I would like to refer again to the two themes brought out in the current Genevan research: the interplay between the child's attempt at a practical result and his or her efforts to understand, and the interplay among the various access routes to knowledge—perceptions, actions, and words or formulas. Both these themes suggest that practical situations, which are the ones that correspond most to children's natural activity, not only are sufficient, but also are the best kinds of learning situations. In the course of trying to solve practical problems, children spend time reorganizing their levels of understanding; in real situations, children develop multiple access routes to their knowledge. Learning in school need not, and should not, be different from children's natural forms of learning about the world. We need only broaden and deepen their scope by opening up parts of the world that children may not, on their own, have thought of thinking about.

4

A Child's-Eye View
of Knowing

CONCEPTS

GIVEN MY BACKGROUND, if there is anything I'm supposed to know it's what a concept is. But the fact is that I don't. I have generally dealt with that fact by never using the word, but there have been some exceptions. A notable one was the time I was a member of a team working on the evaluation of the African Primary Science Program referred to in the first chapter.

Here is what we were doing. This program consists of a number of studies that take four to eight weeks to teach. The studies are not necessarily tied together in an ordered curriculum. That is, one study does not build toward a later study, nor depend on any particular earlier one. What we evaluators set out to do, as a first step, was to examine each of these self-contained studies, in order to find what were the chief concepts in each one that the children were meant to learn. Then we proposed to proceed to try to evaluate the extent to which the children had in fact learned them. Some of us had reservations about this procedure, and for me it included the focus on "concepts." But we had to make a start somehow, and I was in fact a bit curious about where the use of the term might lead me.

As I used it, I noticed some things. For one thing, I noticed a reason why I had never wanted to use it, why I had never found it fruitful. Concepts, on the whole, are stated nouns, which one "has" or "hasn't." Children are said to have, or not to have, as the case may be, concepts such as "commutativity" (in multiplying numbers), "a square," "kinship," "energy," "shape," "the subject of a sentence," "justice."

Now this kind of statement of what a child knows, or is meant to know, seems very limited to me, and I would like to suggest an alternative way of looking at what children know, which I think is more useful. I first want to make just one small attempt to show why I think that dealing in concepts-qua-nouns is barren—an example where someone can "have" one of these things, and not be able to do much with it. From my sample list of noun-concepts, mentioned above, let's take "commutativity of multiplication." I should think one could be said to "have commutativity" if one knew that 47×22 would give the same number as 22×47; and in fact, given any two numbers multiplying the first by the second would give the same number as multiplying the second by the first. Yet it is not hard to imagine that someone might very well "know" that, and yet never think of simplifying his life by turning around a problem like 47×22 into 22×47. (It is clearly easier to multiply 47 by 2 twice than to multiply 22 by two different numbers.) My point is that he could quite legitimately be considered to "have commutativity," if that is the way we have chosen to state what he knows; but if that is all we pay attention to, we're missing something. What he "has" is likely to be useful to him only when we ask him, "Does $47 \times 22 = 22 \times 47$?"

So this was the first thing I realized in that working group: "Concept" usually seemed to imply a noun, and when I'm trying to state things I would like children to know, I usually can't state them as nouns.

I continued to work in the group, and to use the word with my colleagues, as we tried to analyze what the children were meant to learn when they used the materials developed by this project. But as we proceeded, it became clear that in point of fact, there were many things we wanted children to learn in this program that could not be summed up in a noun. Let me show specifically how that became clear.

We had broken into pairs, each pair to examine carefully one of the studies in order to find what were the central things that the study hoped to teach. I was working with Bill Walton on a study of which he was co-author, called *Making Things Look Bigger* (African Primary Science Program, 1970). It is concerned with making and using a simple magnifier and a simple microscope. Walton had managed to design a magnifier made of cardboard, water, and a matchbox, and a more powerful and flexible microscope of cardboard, water, a sliver of wood, cigarette foil, and a piece of thread. Each child is given a booklet, in the back of which are two pages of cardboard printed with cutout designs. The child cuts the cardboard, folds on the dotted lines, and assembles the various pieces as directed. He makes a pinhole to look through. For a lens he uses a drop of water. A piece of cigarette foil is used as a mirror to direct the light. It is an elegant instrument.

In the unit, Walton included some effort to show how a simple microscope works: What is the function of the pinhole, of using a bigger drop of water, of getting one's eye close, of moving the lens up and down, of turning the little mirror? But much more important than that, what he really cared about was that children should learn that all around them there is a world of tiny things they have never seen before, or even thought of trying to see; that it is fun to see these things; that they can make a tool to look at these things out of simple, unmysterious materials; that if they share with their friends the things they see, everybody is likely to end up seeing more; that they can follow printed directions to some purpose.

It really did not matter much whether the children learned how the microscope worked; nor whether they learned about the internal structure of unicellular animals; nor whether they learned about the optics of a water drop. Another study of the microscope might have these as major aims, and they would be perfectly legitimate. But they were not the major aims of this one.

Now *Making Things Look Bigger* is no doubt an extreme case. The majority of classroom work would state aims that could much more easily be referred to as concepts. But many people do believe that the kind of goals that Walton aimed at are important. Many curriculum projects, education departments, teachers, and school reform programs list among their educational aims general statements about developing the students' interests in learning, and their ability to continue learning on their own. As a case in point, here are the stated goals of this African Primary Science Program, subscribed to by everyone in any way connected with the program—ministry officials, scientists, the funding agency, teachers, and so forth:

1. to give the children a firsthand knowledge of the material world;
2. to develop an interest in further exploration of the material world;
3. to give them confidence in their ability to find out about the material world on their own;
4. to help them know how to make discriminating use of secondary sources—colleagues, books, radio, experts.

Walton's aims can readily be seen to fall within the realm of these stated goals, so it was certainly legitimate for us to be concerned with them. But you can appreciate that it was difficult to list them as concepts to be learned—very difficult to sum them up as nouns!

BELIEFS

It occurred to me, though, that they could be stated as sentences, and as such, they did represent beliefs that we wished the children to develop.

Each one of Walton's aims could be broken down into sentences that children might say to themselves (whence the title of this chapter), for example, "Sometimes I miss things when I look; it's a good thing there are other people to check with." And then it occurred to me that these beliefs were all things to be learned, and in fact had all the same characteristics of the more limited set that we had been referring to as concepts. Here are characteristics that I think hold true of anything that anybody believes:

A. An opposing belief is conceivable, and would give rise to different actions, in a situation where the belief is pertinent.
B. You may have learned a belief by being told, or you may have concluded it yourself from evidence that you have been told about, or you may have developed the belief from your own personal evidence.
C. A belief can be confirmed or disconfirmed by further evidence (yet evidence that may be confirming or disconfirming to one person may be irrelevant to another).
D. A verbal statement of the belief may not really mean that the belief is held:
    i. You may enunciate it because you think it is expected of you, even though you know you don't believe it.
    ii. Or you may think you believe it although you really don't—it conflicts with some other belief that really determines how you act.

Here are some examples of four different kinds of beliefs, all of which I think share these characteristics. They correspond to the four stated goals of the African Primary Science Program, because I think that those four goals could be generalized to characterize most of what we would like children to learn.

1. Beliefs that have to do with knowledge of the world I am going to call "the-way-things-are" beliefs. An example would be, "A lens that is more curved magnifies more than a lens that is less curved."
2. Beliefs that have to do with interest in a given pursuit I shall call "it's-fun" beliefs. An example would be, "It's fun to read poems by Randall Jarrell."
3. Beliefs that have to do with being able to do something I shall call "I-can" beliefs. As an example, "I can figure out how much wallpaper I need to paper a room."
4. Beliefs that have to do with sharing one's knowledge, and

knowing when to call upon other resources, I shall call "peo-
ple-can-help" beliefs. As my example, I shall take, "My grandfather is the best source of information there is on what Montreal was like in 1910."

I shall now attempt to show that there is really no difference in kind
among these, with respect to the four characteristics of beliefs listed earlier.

1. *"A lens that is more curved magnifies more than a lens that is less curved."*
   A. It is very easy to think of a situation that puts this belief to the
      test. You want to magnify as much as possible, and you have
      two lenses to choose from. One is a small sphere and the other
      is a piece of glass thicker than the sphere with only a slight
      curvature at top and bottom (see Figure 4.1). If you hold that
      greater curvature magnifies more, you will choose the small
      round one; if you hold that thickness magnifies more, you will
      choose the other.
   B. Someone may have told you that the greater the curvature of
      the lens, the more it magnifies. Or someone may have shown
      you a group of lenses and told you what you could see through
      each of them, on the basis of which you generalized the rule for
      yourself; or you may have looked through a lot of lenses and
      reached that conclusion on your own.
   C. Confirming and disconfirming evidence is easy to think of. I
      won't bother here. But I would like to show how the same evi-
      dence might lead one person to believe one thing while every-
      one else believes something else. Let us say that you have four
      lenses, all of the same diameter. In cross-section, however, they
      range from being thin and scarcely curved to being thick and
      very curved (see Figure 4.2). In fact, the thickest, most curved
      of these lenses would magnify most, and the thinnest, least
      curved would magnify least. If you believe curvature is the
      factor, then looking through these four lenses could be seen as
      confirming it. Someone else, who believes thickness is the fac-
      tor, could take this evidence to confirm his belief. If this were
      the only evidence anyone had thought of offering, you might
      be the only one who believed that thickness was irrelevant.

Figure 4.1   **Figure 4.2**

D. (i) You may have been taught to say that more curved lenses magnify more, having been shown the evidence from the above four lenses (see Figure 4.2). But you may have noticed that the thickness also changes, and you may say to yourself, or to a confidant: "I'll say it's the curvature, because they want me to, but I really believe it's the thickness."

OR (ii) Given the above evidence, you may say and think you believe it's the curvature, without ever noticing that you were basing your choice on the thickness, and that the thickness was only incidentally correlated with the curvature. Even to yourself or to a confidant you would say that curvature was the factor. But confronted with the choice under 1A, you would choose the thick one.

2. *"I like to read poems by Randall Jarrell."*
   A. I happen to believe this statement, but many people could very well not believe it. Whether one believes it can determine whether one chooses to spend time reading Jarrell's poems, or indeed to spend money buying books of them.
   B. You may believe this because someone you trust has told you that poems by Randall Jarrell are a delight; or someone may have told you that a poem by Randall Jarrell can really let you know what it feels like to be a chipmunk, and that appeals to you; or you may have read lots of poems by Randall Jarrell, and taken pleasure in the reading.
   C. Confirming evidence could be meeting more people who tell you that it is interesting to read these poems; or learning the additional fact that one of his poems can even let you know what it feels like to be a mermaid; or reading more of his poems and enjoying it.

   Disconfirming evidence could be meeting people who say it is boring; or learning the additional fact that his poems can make you realize how frightening it is to be a bat when an owl is on the hunt, and you have a dread of being frightened by nighttime things; or reading his poems and being bored.

   Note once again that evidence that is ostensibly the same can be confirming for one person and not for another. Although we both talked to the same person, I may trust his judgment and you may not. Although we both read the same poem, you may have seized the lilt of the rhythm and I may not.
   D. (i) Everybody around you is saying that it is interesting to read poetry by Randall Jarrell, so you decide you had better say the

same thing, even though you don't like it at all. To a confidant, you would confess it.

OR (ii) You had so expected to enjoy reading these poems that you didn't notice that in fact you had to force yourself through them. You keep saying—and believing—that you enjoyed them, but you never manage to find the time to read any more of them.

Let me point out here in passing that most of us would say, and think we believe, that microscopes are inherently interesting to look through. But how many of us have made a $100 dollar investment in a good small microscope to have around the house! In order to really believe this, we need to have overcome the initial difficulties and taken pleasure in seeing things. And the role of a teacher is clear—to make sure that the microscope we have in our hands is adequate, and to encourage us while we develop our technique to the point where we enjoy it.

In talking about the importance of "it's-fun" beliefs, my emphasis is on adding to children's repertoires of things that they are interested in doing; I am not trying to advocate a "learning must be fun" position.

3. *"I can figure out how much wallpaper I need to paper a room."*
   A. If you have a room to paper, whether or not you believe this can affect whether you do the calculations yourself, or whether you find somebody else to do them.
   B. You may have been told this: "Yes, you can do it; go ahead." Or you may have developed this confidence by having done such calculations before. Or you might have seen someone else do it, and decided that you could do it too.
   C. You might try and find you had succeeded; or you might try and find that you had failed. Whereas the former is likely to be confirming, and the latter is likely to be disconfirming, neither one is necessarily so. In the former case, you might say, "I was only able to do it this time because the wallpaper roll was just the right width; I could never do it again." In the latter case, you might say, "I made that one silly mistake in multiplication; I really could have hit it right if I'd concentrated."
   D. (i) You could say you can do it, so other people will believe it without really thinking that you can.

      OR (ii) You might think you believe it, without realizing that when you hired someone else to do the job it was not for want of time but for want of confidence.

4. *"My grandfather is the best source of information there is on what Montreal was like in 1910."* (This example comes to mind because of a social studies project carried out in 1966 in the same elementary school as the spelling project described in chapter 2, L'Ecole Nouvelle Querbes in Montreal. It was a study of what Montreal was like from 1900 to 1920, based in large part on children's interviews of people who had lived there at that time. This was supplemented by newspapers, magazines, schoolbooks, family photographs, toys, clothes, and tools of that time. Along with learning what Montreal used to be like, the children learned a good deal about the kinds of sources available to historians, and how dependable they are.

A. If you want to know what Montreal was like in olden days, your belief in this matter will affect whether you go to ask your grandfather.

B. Your mother may have told you, "There's nobody like your grandfather for telling you what Montreal was like in 1910." Or your cousin might have told you lots of things that your grandfather once told him about Montreal in 1910. Or your grandfather may already have told you more things about old-time Montreal than anyone else ever did.

C. Confirming evidence would be talking to someone else who tells you how much your grandfather knows; or finding that after talking with your grandfather you know lots more things about old Montreal than any of your friends have been able to find out. You might even find that he knows more about how they used to make soap than is written in a book you have found on soap-making in old Montreal.

Disconfirming evidence would be finding after you talked with him that you still didn't know much about the topic; or finding that what he said about the collapse of the Quebec bridge was contradicted by three different newspapers of the day and by your grandmother.

On the other hand, your grandfather might tell exactly the same tales to both you and your brother, tales that are contradicted by other people; your brother might decide that your grandfather really didn't know so much, but you might have such faith in your grandfather that you prefer to discredit all the other sources.

D. (i) You might decide to say that your grandfather was the best source, in order to humor him, because you know he likes to believe he is; but you really believe your teacher is a better source.

OR (ii) You might think you believe that your grandfather is the best source, without being aware that you never really believed what he said until you had found it corroborated in a book.

EDUCATIONAL GOALS

Now let me point out why I think it is important to consider all these kinds of beliefs as essentially the same. As I said earlier, many people subscribe to goals of the it's-fun (interest) and I-can (self-confidence) types, but when it comes to detail, almost never does one see a concern with anything other than the-way-things-are beliefs. Lesson-by-lesson objectives are almost without exception of this type, despite the fact that general goals very often mention things like interest, confidence, and resourcefulness. This is, of course, because it is difficult to produce a noticeable change in any of these in the course of one 50-minute lesson. But notice that as a result all the effort is put into attaining the objectives stated for the lesson.

Sometimes a curriculum might be conceived, say, as a two-month unit, with no lesson-by-lesson outline, and with goals stated for the study as a whole, including all the kinds we have been discussing. Still, when it comes to evaluation, attention turns without a second thought to the beliefs that have traditionally been tested—the-way-things-are beliefs—and the degree of success of the study is judged on the basis of such tests. As a consequence, the other goals—although stated and no doubt believed in—do not get their share of the teacher's concern and effort.

Now there are many reasons for this neglect in the detail of the other stated goals—historical reasons, technical reasons, administrative reasons. But I think as important as any is the fact that things like interest and confidence are generally considered vague and imprecise "affective" aspects of a child's education, and as such different in kind from "knowledge." One acknowledges their importance, but one doesn't know what else to do with them. One hopes, perhaps, that if we are good at teaching knowledge, the others will necessarily develop, too.

This is why I think it is important to see that they are not different in kind. If we state as teachers, or administrators, or psychologists, that our goals include the awakening of interest and the development of confidence and how to make discriminating use of resources, then we must think about teaching these beliefs just as carefully as we think about teaching the-way-things-are beliefs. All of these have to be learned, and all of them can be confirmed and disconfirmed in various ways with varying degrees of validity. And they are all quite specific. You can take pleasure in the romantic imagery of Shelley without appreciating the critical wit of Alexander Pope. You can believe in your ability to solve quadratic equations without believing in your ability to prove Euclidean theorems. You may be able to see through a pseudo-scientific television commercial without being able to sift reporting from opinion in a newspaper article.

Another thing I think this analysis can reveal is that teaching some of these beliefs can get in the way of teaching others. This increases the urgency of our being aware of all of them. We must decide to what extent we are willing to let one suffer in favor of another. In *Making Things Look Bigger,* learning more about the physics of magnifiers may mean learning less about what fun it is to use them. We have to decide, then, that a class in which every child takes a magnifier home with him at night and runs back for it if he forgets it, but nobody knows that the apparent size is a function of distance, would score, say, 95 out of 100, whereas the inverse case (all know the rule but nobody looks unless they're told to) would score 5. Notice how awareness of the relative importance of these two beliefs would influence the way a teacher dealt with teaching this study. And notice how testing the first class on their knowledge of the physics of a magnifier would totally overlook the fact that they are developing a whole new sense of something that is worthwhile doing.

Another of the science studies deals with finding the optimal germinating conditions for different kinds of seeds. One of the beliefs that this study sets out to develop is "I can learn about seeds by experimenting with them." Another is "I can save time learning about seeds by finding out what experiments the others have done." Now in a certain sense, these two are in conflict. On the one hand, students are learning to depend on what they do themselves, and on the other hand they are learning to depend on other people's reported results. We want, then, to be aware of this conflict, and to include in addition beliefs of the following sort: "Some people are more dependable experimenters than others."

It seems to me that this broader view of what we want children to learn can shed some light on questions of instructional strategy. One of the main beliefs in a number of the African Primary Science units is "I can think of how to find answers to questions." One such unit is called *Ask the Ant Lion* (African Primary Science Program, circa 1967). An ant lion is a small creature, slightly larger than an ant, that digs interesting little holes in the ground in which it catches ants for food. Children set about finding out about ant lions by watching them, finding questions to ask, and figuring out ways to answer their questions. What question the children find an answer to is not very important. What is important is that they realize that answers can be found through their own investigations. In this case, then, if the teacher says, "Oh, I see you're not getting it; what ant lions do is catch prey with their pincers," the aim of the work is lost. The belief to be developed was not "Ant lions catch their prey with their pincers," but "I can find out how ant lions catch their prey." In this case, not telling how ant lions catch their prey is not just a cute teaching gimmick. It is an essential.

In another case, however, there is every justification for telling the children what you want them to know. To take *Making Things Look Bigger* again, at one point it is necessary for children to know that if they add a drop of water to the pinhole they are looking through, they will be able to see more clearly. In this case, the major aim is not "I can think of how to make things look still clearer." It is simply "Things will took clearer if I add a drop of water." Having children try to guess how to make things look clearer is then of relatively slight importance.

Once again, it seems to me, being aware of the various kinds of beliefs we want to develop can help us in our decisions about how to go about our job.

Before leaving this part of the chapter, I would like to acknowledge the difficulties involved in trying to evaluate the development of these various kinds of beliefs. The only obvious thing is that pencil-and-paper tests won't do it. My own effort to evaluate this particular program was described briefly in chapter 1 in the section entitled "An Evaluation Study."

TEACHER EDUCATION

The last part of this chapter introduces some thoughts about teacher education. First, I think it is very important for teachers to have a chance to watch themselves learn. A colleague (Ed Prenowitz) and I once spent two hours a day, for four weeks, with a group of teachers studying circuits made with flashlight batteries of different sizes, light bulbs, magnets, and wires of different resistances. An enormous amount can be learned about electricity with nothing more than these materials, as witnessed by the fact that at the end of the four weeks we were all aware of enough questions that remained to occupy us for at least that long again. But the interesting thing was that at the same time we paid attention to how the teachers were learning. This was not done in a self-conscious way, but from time to time aspects of their learning leapt into prominence. Several times they came to an obstacle in their work, and had to step sideways to solve an accessory problem before proceeding, only to find after solving it that "Of course, we 'knew' that a week ago!"

In another instance, two different problems appealed to two different groups, and they went to work independently. After two or three days' work, having reached a degree of closure on their own problems, they re-ported to each other, and found that, through totally different routes, they had reached an understanding of the very same phenomenon.

At one point, we had come to a dead end in trying to understand what the teachers were calling "resistance." From the start, they had been us-ing the word as a cover-all explanatory term for almost any situation they didn't understand. ("Air pressure" is often put to the same use, by both children and grown-ups.) When they got to the point of wanting to get behind the shield of that word, it was clear that they could not get away from the ill-understood, conflicting senses in which they had been using it. So we outlawed its use. For a couple of days, the teachers were forced to talk about what they were doing and seeing without falling back on it. When they finally developed a real feeling for a specific phenomenon that enabled them to make predictions that worked, and that then could be re-ferred to by a name of its own, they thoroughly understood the havoc that is created by substituting impressive-sounding words for clear statements of what you are talking about. (Maybe this can be taken as another reason for preferring sentences to nouns.)

On another occasion I was trying out an idea with a single teacher. I had been working on the development of a study of pendulums. The apparatus was a support from which are suspended two threads with hooks on the end. The length of each thread could be adjusted by a screw arrangement at the top. A variety of bobs was available to hang on the hooks. Various factors could be studied, then, by comparing the swings of these two threads, which could be put at different lengths, or hung with different bobs, or pulled back different amounts.

A pair of us was teaching the first pilot class of this study, and so far all we had used as bobs were glass marbles, all the same size, and steel balls, of the same size as the glass but a different weight. Children had explored the effects of different lengths, different weights, and different ways to set the pendulums in motion. Now I wanted to raise the follow-ing question: Suppose you want to make one pendulum half the length of another. Where do you measure the length? Do you take half the length of the string, down to the hook? Or do you take half the whole length, right down to the bottom of the bob? Or do you take half of something else? None of these "halves" come out to be the same.

To raise this question, it occurred to me that the children could com-pare a small round bob with a long cylinder, and see which lengths have to be lined up in order to get these two to swing at the same rhythm.

Now the problem with this is that one has to pay attention to a pos-sible difference in weight between the two bobs. But—and I am sorry to announce this, because if you don't know it it's so much nicer to find it out through playing with pendulums—in point of fact you don't have to pay attention to a difference in weight. Two pendulums of the same length will swing at the same rhythm no matter what their weights.

The children in the pilot class were already on their way to realizing that. But I wanted to try out my idea of marble versus cylinder on somebody before I tried it in the class, so I prevailed on a teacher who happened to be there, and he cheerfully agreed to serve my purpose. To bring him up to the level of the class, I gave him a crash program that consisted of comparing a marble ball on one string with a steel ball of the same size on the other string. After a few predictions, trials, and adjustments, he realized to his surprise that the two would swing together if they were at the same length.

So now I was ready. I gave him a cylinder to substitute for one of the balls, and asked him how he would make a cylinder and a ball swing together. To my amazement, before he even started to think about whether to line up the hooks or to line up the bottoms of the bobs, or look for some other point to line up, he said, "Let's see now, are they the same weight?"

What an insight that gave both of us into the trials of teaching and learning! I reacted by crying, "But you just *did* weight!" To which of course he reacted by being shaken and embarrassed. When we both came back to our senses, we realized the two remarkably important lessons we had learned. He as a learner seemed to have learned something quite straightforward, but this one stripped-down instance had not been sufficient for him to learn solidly that "weight doesn't make any difference." Learning is messy. On the other hand, I, as a teacher, had the impression that I had taught something quite straightforward. And my reaction to the inadequacy of my teaching was to embarrass *him*. We both, fortunately, learned both these lessons well.

Learning about the physical world is perhaps ideal for watching yourself learn. You can assess yourself so well: Can you or can't you predict what will happen now? And so many networks can be found in which ideas recross and reinform each other. I have a tendency to think that even if the teacher is not going to teach science, pursuing a study of this sort can play an important role in revealing the intricacies of learning in general (see Duckworth, 1983).

The other main suggestion I have is that prospective teachers spend a significant amount of time in a one-to-one teaching situation. Once again, this is in the interest of learning more about learning. The pendulum example can serve as an instance here, too, I think. I think that the lesson I learned from that as a teacher could not have been as stark in a classroom. I probably would have thought I had missed something that had influenced the student in the meantime. It is surely rare to learn so much as a teacher from one 15-minute tutoring session. But 10 sessions, say, of watching the same person develop mastery in some small area could not but be revealing of what learning is like.

As an extension of this, I think it is also enormously revealing to tutor independently a number of different individuals in the same topic. This can bring into very sharp focus the manifold ways in which people can come to essentially the same mastery. This, by the way, takes on some aspects of psychological research. What in fact is in common about the many different ways of learning that can reach the same end? How might other pendulum-naive adults react in the specific situation I described? There is no reason every prospective teacher could not do some research of this sort.

There is another aspect of one-to-one teaching that might be important, too, as Claryce Evans (personal communication, April 3, 1965) has pointed out. So far I have discussed the role of tutoring in shedding light on the nature of learning. It can also shed light on at least one aspect of the nature of teaching: the importance of keeping the pressure off. In tutoring, you simply can't force, or the situation disintegrates. Needless to say, one also hopes to learn how not to force. It's not easy for a teacher to let go of a plan of how things are expected to proceed.

Since Evans brought this to my attention, I came to recognize in retrospect a tutoring situation in which I was forcing a 9-year-old, in the context of some research in mathematics learning. This was a long time ago, when I was still a rather bad psychologist. The problem for the day had been decided in advance and typed on a card. It had even been tailored for this particular child, in response to the direction in which he had gone in the previous lesson. He read the card, and set to work on a problem that was related, suggested by the problem on the card, but not in fact the problem given. I kept trying to get him back to our determined problem of the day. "Yes, but," I kept saying, "that's not what you're trying to do." This situation proved less tragic than it might have, because this boy was unusually determined and articulate. He finally got me off the hook by exclaiming, "Yes it is. Yes it is. It's what *I'm* trying to do."

5

The Virtues of
Not Knowing

KNOWING THE ANSWER

I WAS ASKED TO WRITE a paper called "The Nonpassive Virtues." At the time I thought I understood what it meant, but when I sat down to write, I realized that I had no idea what the passive virtues of the intellect would be. In matters of intelligence, with what could nonpassive virtues be contrasted?

It occurred to me, then, that of all the virtues related to intellectual functioning, the most passive is the virtue of knowing the right answer. Knowing the right answer requires no decisions, carries no risks, and makes no demands. It is automatic. It is thoughtless.

Moreover, and most to the point in this context, knowing the right answer is overrated. It is a virtue—there is no debate about that—but in conventional views of intelligence it tends to be given far too much weight.

In most classrooms, it is the quick, right answer that is appreciated. Knowledge of the answer ahead of time is, on the whole, more valued than ways of figuring it out.

Similarly, most tests of intellectual ability seek to establish what children have already mastered. Whether the tests are concerned with verbal ability, mathematical ability, general reasoning, or whatever, the task they demand of the child is to fill in the blank and move on to the next. True, intelligence tests require that certain things be figured out, but the figuring out doesn't count. If the figuring out leads to the right answer, then of course the right answer counts. But no tester will ever know and no score will ever reveal whether the right answer was a triumph of imagination and intellectual daring, or whether the child knew the right answer all along. In addition, the more time the child spends on figuring things out on the test, the less time there is for filling in the right answers; that is, the more you actually *think* to get the right answers on an intelligence test, the less intelligent the score will look.

I would like to give some attention to what is involved when the right answer is not already known.

TWO EXAMPLES

In chapter 3, I referred to Inhelder, Sinclair, and Bovet's work (1974), which tries to shed light on what happens when a child takes himself from one level of understanding to another. My first example comes from that work. The researchers would meet with a child several times over a period of one to three weeks (depending on the experiment), each time presenting him or her with situations in which the contradictions in his or her own thoughts would be brought into relief. In this way they could witness the child's attempts to put his or her ideas together in different and more satisfactory ways. In no way, however, did their procedure seek to teach children "the right answer." They sought instead to give children the opportunity to explore their ideas and to try to make more sense of them.

Among the most fascinating aspects of the book are the lengthy accounts of children grappling with their own nonunderstanding—occasions when the children knew that something was not quite right and tried to do something about it.

One of the experiments deals with the realization that an amount of liquid remains the same quantity even though it is made to look different, for example when it is poured into a glass of a different shape. The apparatus Inhelder and her colleagues used is shown in Figure 5.1. Small valves allow the liquid to run from upper glasses to lower ones. The glasses A, A', C, and C' are all the same. In the middle layer, glasses of different dimensions are used: B (the same as A and C), N (narrow—as shown), and W (wide—the same height, but wider than B). The flasks F and F' were used to fill the top glasses. (In the following description, translations are mine from the original French. Cf. pp. 56, 57 in the English edition.)

In his first session, A and A' are filled to the same level, and Jac, a boy nearly 6 years old, correctly predicts that the quantities and levels of the liquids in C and C' will be the same. As the liquids flow, he remarks spontaneously, "Gee, that's high there [in N]. But I poured with the same bottle [F]. I poured all of it." During the second part, a real conflict is born. A and A' are again filled to the same level. A is emptied into B, and then Jac is told to run the same amount from A' into N. "How can I do that?" he asks. "If I stop at the same place [that is, the same levels in B and N], I won't have the same amount to drink at the end [in C]. Look, I left a bit up

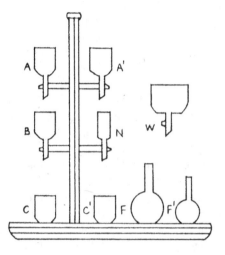

Figure 5.1

there [A']. To get the same at the end, I have to pour all of it. But then that doesn't go up the same." He pours it all into N, and remarks, without any prompting from the investigator, "It looks like too much, doesn't it?"

The wider glass, W, is then substituted for B, and Jac is asked to do the same thing again. He is visibly perplexed, "That's really funny. If I don't leave that little bit up there, I never get the same thing here [indicating the level in W and N]. In that one it's so big, and in the skinny one . . . But that *has* to be just as much water: It's all there. I know! It only *looks* like there's more! In the skinny glass, the water is squeezed in, so it has to go up. In the big one it's spread out!"

To begin the second session, the glasses B and N are behind a screen when the liquid is poured into them—equal amounts from A and A', Jac predicts how high the level will be, and then the screen is removed. He seems delighted to see his predictions confirmed. "I know, it's like last time! There's always the same amount to drink; it just looks like there's more. The water just goes into the glass different."

Next, A is filled from F and A' from F', so there are different quantities to begin with, but the levels are the same once they have flowed into B and N. Jac is bemused for a moment when he sees them in B and N. "How come? I poured the little bottle in there [A'] and now it's the same. Oh, I know! It's still the same! You'll see at the end . . . Wait! I know, all the time it's still less on that side [the right hand side]. There wasn't any more in the middle. There can't be!"

"Gee!" "How can I do it?" "That's really funny." "How come?" "Wait—wait!" "Oh, I know!" Surprise, puzzlement, struggle, excitement, anticipation, and dawning certainty—those are the matter of intelligent thought. As virtues, they stand by themselves—even if they do not, on some specific occasion, lead to the right answer. In the long run, they are what count.

The second example comes from a classroom. I once watched a class of 10-year-olds while they learned about pendulums. In the class, there was a boy named Alec who would be any teacher's joy. He was full of ideas, articulate about them, and thoughtful and industrious about following them through. During the course of the pendulum study, Alec, working in his usual thorough and competent way (with a partner in tow), pursued many questions that nobody else had the interest or the patience to work through. The rest of the class occasionally took an interest in what he had been doing, but usually he and his partner went their own way.

After a number of weeks, the class watched some film loops in which a pendulum dropped sand as it moved, thus leaving a record of its travels. One question the students considered was, when a pendulum is swinging back and forth, does it slow down at each end of its swing, or does it maintain the same speed and simply change direction? Alec, who was something of a mathematician by inclination, finding merit more readily in deduction than in experience, quickly maintained that the pendulum did not slow down at the ends, "because there's no reason for it to." The other children tended to agree, because the first opinion came from Alec. The teacher said nothing, but continued playing the loop in which the sand was falling into a row of straws.

After a while, one child said, "I don't get it. Why isn't it the same all along the straws, then?" There was silence again as they continued to watch. Another child said, "There's more at the ends; it piles up at the ends." Other remarks came: "How come it isn't higher in the middle—because it goes back and forth over the middle!" "It probably goes fast over the middle—fast over the middle and slows down at the ends." "Besides, how can it stop without slowing down?"

Gradually, the comments added up—always directed, at least implicitly, to Alec's idea. At last one child dared to commit himself: "It has to be slowing down at the ends." And one by one, each child committed himself to an opinion that was the opposite of Alec's. Alec, who was used to being the only one to hold to a given opinion, was unconvinced for a long time by their reasons, long enough so that almost every child in the class, independently, summoned the intellectual courage to maintain a position that was the opposite of Alec's—and even to argue with him. Finally, Alec was convinced by their reasons, and quietly changed his mind.

The class played out in public view virtues concerned with courage, caution, confidence, and risk. (See, for a comparison, Howard Gruber's account of Charles Darwin's courage, in *Darwin On Man*, 1981.) The courage to submit an idea of one's own to someone else's scrutiny is a virtue in itself—unrelated to the rightness of the idea. Alec's idea was wrong, but it was his customary willingness to propose it and defend it that paved the way for a more accurate idea. The other children were right, but they would never have arrived at that right idea if they had not taken the risk—both within themselves and in public—to question Alec's idea.

There was an epilogue, too. The next and last time the teacher visited that class, Alec put forth another idea during public discussion, again with easy confidence that it would work. It didn't. It was discarded and the class looked for others. On neither of those occasions did Alec suffer, either in his own eyes or in the eyes of anyone else. He had never been arrogant when his theories worked out well, so he felt no disgrace when an idea failed. There was neither false modesty nor defeat when he said to the teacher as she left that day for the last time, "You know, I've learned one thing in this class—I don't always have such great ideas." Alec was used to defending a theory that he judged sound. What was new for him was the honest recognition that some of his thoughts might bear a closer look before deserving his commitment to them—and they might even benefit from the scrutiny of other children.

In both of these examples, problems were set for the children, and we saw what was involved in trying to resolve them. Another whole domain of virtues we have not even mentioned is that of sitting alone, noticing something new, wondering about it, framing a question for oneself to answer, and sensing some contradiction in one's own ideas—in other words, all of those virtues that are involved when no one else is present to stimulate thoughts or act as prompter.

CONCLUSION

The virtues involved in not knowing are the ones that really count in the long run. What you do about what you don't know is, in the final analysis, what determines what you *will* know.

It is, moreover, quite possible to help children develop these virtues. Providing occasions such as those described here, accepting surprise, puzzlement, excitement, patience, caution, honest attempts, and wrong outcomes as legitimate and important elements of learning, easily leads to their further development. And helping children to come honestly to terms with their own ideas is not difficult to do. There was nothing particularly subtle in the roles of the adults in these examples.

The only difficulty is that teachers are rarely encouraged to do that—largely because standardized tests play such a powerful role in determining what teachers pay attention to. Standardized tests can never, even at their best, tell us anything other than whether a given fact, notion, or ability is already within a child's repertoire. As a result, teachers are encouraged to go for right answers, as soon and as often as possible, and whatever happens along the way is treated as incidental.

It would make a significant difference to the cause of intelligent thought in general, and to the number of right answers that are ultimately known, if teachers were encouraged to focus on the virtues involved in not knowing, so that those virtues would get as much attention in classrooms from day to day as the virtue of knowing the right answer.

6

Learning with
Breadth and Depth

I F IDEAS DEVELOP ON their own so slowly, what can we do to speed
them up? In chapter 3, we pointed out that Piaget referred to this as
"the American question." For him the question is not how fast you go
but how far you go. He delighted in the results of a study of kittens carried
out by Howard Gruber. Studying his own children, Piaget had concluded
that they were about a year old before they realized that an object had its
own continuing existence and location even when out of their reach and
out of their sight. Gruber found that kittens go through all the same steps
that children do, but instead of taking a year, they take six weeks (Gruber, Girgus, & Banuazizi, 1971). Piaget cheerfully pointed out that you can
scarcely say that kittens are better off for having cut almost a year off the
time. After all, they don't get much further.

How could it be that going fast does not mean going far? A useful
metaphor might be the construction of a tower—all the more appropriate
given that Piaget thinks of the development of intelligence as continual
construction. Building a tower with one brick on top of another is a pretty
speedy business. But the tower will soon reach its limits, compared with
one built on a broad base or a deep foundation—which of course takes a
longer time to construct.

What is the intellectual equivalent of building in breadth and depth?
I think it is a matter of making connections: Breadth could be thought of
as the widely different spheres of experience that can be related to one
another; depth could be thought of as the many different kinds of connections that can be made among different facets of our experience. I am not
sure whether intellectual breadth and depth can be separated from each
other, except in talking about them. In this chapter I shall not try to keep
them separate, but instead try to show how learning with breadth and
depth is a different matter from learning with speed.

PRODUCTIVE WRONG IDEAS

If a child spends time exploring all the possibilities of a given notion, it may mean that she holds onto it longer, and moves onto the next stage less quickly; but by the time she does move on, she will have a far better foundation—the idea will serve her far better, will stand up in the face of surprises. Let me develop a hypothetical example to show what I mean, based on the notion of the conservation of area.

Imagine two identical pieces of paper; you cut one in half and rearrange the pieces so the shape is different from the original one, while preserving the same area, as in the example in Figure 6.1. One might think that it would be to anyone's advantage to realize early in life that a change in shape does not affect area; that no matter how a shape is transformed, its area is conserved. But I can imagine a child not managing to settle that question as soon as others because she raises for herself the question of the perimeter. In fact the perimeter *does* change, and thinking about the relationship between those two is complicated work. One child might, then, take longer than another to come to the conclusion that area is conserved, independent of shape, but her understanding will be the better for it. Most children (and adults) who arrive smartly at the notion that area is independent of shape do not think about the perimeter and are likely to become confounded if it is brought up. Having thought about perimeter on her own, she has complicated the job of thinking about area, but once she has straightened it out, her understanding is far deeper than that of someone who has never noticed this difference between area and perimeter.

Figure 6.1

Exploring ideas can only be to the good, even if it takes time. Wrong ideas, moreover, can only be productive. Any wrong idea that is corrected provides far more depth than if one never had a wrong idea to begin with. You master the idea much more thoroughly if you have considered alternatives, tried to work it out in cases where it didn't work, and figured out why it was that it didn't work, all of which takes time. After this hypothetical introduction, here are some examples where making the mistakes and correcting them reveal and give rise to a far better grasp of the phenomenon than there would have been if no mistakes were made at all.

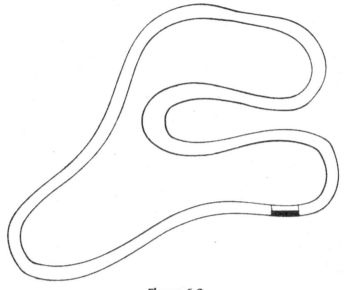

Figure 6.2

One experiment involves an odd-shaped lake like the one in Figure 6.2 with a road around it, and a bi-colored car on the road, one side black and one side white. Let's say the white side is next to the water to start with; the question is, after the car drives around a corner, or around several corners, which color will be beside the water? Six-year-olds, after one or two mistaken predictions, usually come to be quite sure that it will always be the white. Eight-year-olds, on the other hand, can be very perplexed, and not quite get it straight, no matter how often they see the white side come out next to the water. They keep predicting that this time the black side will be next to the water.

Now one might be tempted to think that 6-year-olds know more than 8-year-olds. They, after all, do not make mistakes. But I think it is the greater breadth and depth of the 8-year-olds' insight that leads to their perplexity. Eight-year-olds are often just at the point of organizing space into some interrelated whole: Your left is opposite my right; something that you can see from your point of view may be hidden from my point of view; if a car in front of me is facing right, I see its right side, and if it turns 180°, I'll see its left side. With all these shifting, relative relationships, what is it about the lake that makes that relationship an absolute? No matter how many curves there are in the road, the same side is always next to the water. If a car turns 180°, I thought I would see its other side; well, how is it that the *same* side is next to the water? What is it that stays the same and what is it that changes, after all? The 6-year-old, who has no idea of the systematic changes involved in some spatial relationships, has no difficulty seeing the constant in the lake problem; it is because the 8-year-old is trying to make sense of the lake in a far broader context that the right answer is not so immediate. The dawning organization of something new throws into confusion something that had been simple before. But when, a few months later, the 8- or 9-year-old does start to understand that the same side must always stay next to the lake, his or her understanding is far deeper than that of the 6-year-old; it is set in the context of an understanding of spatial relationships as a whole.

Here is another example, where what appears to be less facility really indicates greater understanding. I was working with two children, who happened to be brother and sister, and they were making all possible arrangements of three colors. After each of them had found all six possibilities, I added a fourth color, and they tried again. The sister, who was younger, rapidly produced a dozen, and was still going. The older brother stopped at four, and declared that that's all there were. But look at what he had done. With three colors, he had made the arrangement shown in Figure 6.3. Now, into what he had already, he inserted the fourth color, in each of the possible positions as shown in Figure 6.4. It was *because* of his sense of system—his sense (which can only be called mathematical) that there was a fixed and necessary number of placements—that he stopped there: The new color was in each possible position, within a system that had all of the other colors already in each possible position. It is true that his thinking left out one step, but nonetheless his was a far deeper understanding of permutations than his sister's facile but random generation of yet more arrangements that looked different.

R	B	Y	
R	Y	B	
B	R	Y	
B	Y	R	
Y	R	B	
Y	B	R	

Figure 6.3

G	R	B	Y
R	G	Y	B
B	R	G	Y
B	Y	R	G

Figure 6.4

WAYS OF MEASURING—PRODUCTIVE AND UNPRODUCTIVE

Getting closer to everyday concerns in the classroom, think of measurement. It can seem very straightforward—count the number of units that apply to some quantity and there it is, measured: so many foot-long rulers in a table, plus a number of inches; so many minutes in the running of a mile, plus a number of seconds. But take this example, for which I am indebted to Strauss, Stavy, and Orpag (1981): You've measured the temperature of one glass of water—100°; you add to it another glass of water, which is also 100°. What will the temperature be now? Most of our measurement experience would lead us to say 200°! And that is what a lot of children do in fact say—having easily understood how to add measurements together, but never having wondered *when* or *whether* to add measurements together.

Let me, by contrast, give some examples of invention of ways of measuring, which might seem tedious and inefficient, but which are thoroughly understood by their inventors. The first one deserves a better accounting than I can undertake here. In a class studying (once again) pendulums, children had explored coupled pendulums, set up like the example in Figure 6.5. If everything is symmetrical when you start one bob, then after a few swings the other bob starts to move; gradually bob A's movement diminishes and bob B's movement increases, until A is stopped and B is swinging widely. Then the movement passes back to A, and so on. Suppose, however, that everything is not symmetrical—the stick is tilted, or one string is longer than the other, or one bob weighs more than the other. In that case, the bob that starts swinging does pass some of its movement on to the other, but it does not come to a halt itself; the halts are asymmetric—they belong only to the bob that was at rest when the other started swinging.

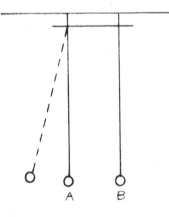

Figure 6.5

That is a long introduction. The point is that in this class, a time came when the children were interested in comparing the weights of the wooden bobs and the steel bobs. Scales were available, and most of the children went to them. But Elliott, who happened to be the least scholarly child in the class, had a different idea. He set up a coupled pendulum, hung a steel bob on one string, and then added wooden bobs to the other, trying the coupled motion each time he added a bob—until, at four wooden bobs, the halts were alternating symmetrically from string to string. So he knew the four on one string must weigh the same as the one on the other. This astonishingly imaginative grasp of what it means to compare weights of things should be contrasted with the following tale.

In a different pendulum class, junior high school students had just previously been taught the equilibrium formula that applies to balances: Distance times weight on one side must equal distance times weight on the other. The only weighing mechanism available to them now was a strip of pegboard, supported in the center (Figure 6.6). When the students became interested in weighing the bobs, they hung a wooden bob on one end, and then a steel bob on the other side, not on the end, but placed so as to make the pegboard horizontal, announcing, "There, they weigh the same. We learned that just last week, they weigh the same." It seemed clear that that formula had been hastily learned, and remained quite unexplored.

Figure 6.6

The next example comes from work done with Jeanne Bamberger and Magdalene Lampert at the Massachusetts Institute of Technology (Bamberger, Duckworth, & Lampert, 1981). We were working with a group of Cambridge teachers, helping them examine their own ways of knowing in order to understand better children's ways of knowing. During a musical exploration, they were building tunes, and at one point they wanted to know whether a tune they had built had sections that were the same length. They didn't know how to think about that. They tried to use a wristwatch but couldn't tell from this whether the first half of the tune was the same length as the second half. This led us to invent time-measuring machines. We took a recorded tune, as the standard event, and they were to construct time machines (without using a stopwatch) to tell whether some other piece of music, which we were subsequently going to play, was as long as that first piece, or longer, or shorter. They all made what we called tune-specific time-measuring machines; that is, they did not set out to find some unit that would be repeated a number of times, but instead tried to make something that measured just the length of the standard piece: water dripping out of a cup, down to a line that indicated the end of the piece; or a candle burning down just to the end of the piece.

One team made a ramp of two pieces of metal, each about 4 feet long. To their dismay, the ball rolled off the 8 feet of ramp before the music stopped. They changed the slope; the ball still rolled off. They made a pathway on the floor at the end out of tongue depressors so that the ball could keep rolling along the floor, but now the ball stopped too soon. They changed the slope—very steep, or barely any slope at all—but no matter what they did with the slope, the ball stopped too soon. They finally concluded that they would have to make the ball do something else after the roll down the ramp; otherwise they would simply have to abandon the ramp idea. So they moved the ramp up onto a long table, set it up with barely any slope at all, and arranged it so the ball could drop off at the end. Now what could they have it do when it dropped off? Casting about for available material, they took a pan from one of the pan balances, and suspended it at the end of the ramp, so the ball would fall into it (Figure 6.7). As the recorded tune started, the ball started rolling slowly down

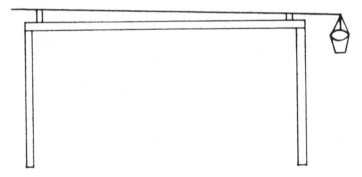

Figure 6.7

the ramp, fell into the pan at the end, thus setting it swinging, and at 32 swings of the pan the tune was ended. A single-purpose time machine it was, but a perfectly dependable one—it was a roll down the ramp followed by 32 swings of the pan, every time. The tune that was to be compared with it, moreover, turned out to be a roll down the ramp followed by 37 swings of the pan; so their machine was shown to be adequate to its time-measuring task.

These stories can be thought of as comic relief. In a sense, they are. But the comedy of the coupled pendulum and the ball on the ramp is very different from the comedy of the 200° water and the misuse of the pegboard balance. The latter two are sad tales of too rapid assumption of understanding. The other two are the rather appealing consequences of avoiding such facile rapidity. How to measure can be taught rapidly, but when it is, the inadequacies are stunning. It is quite different from the breadth and depth of understanding involved in messily constructing your own ways of measuring, knowing what they mean, how they are applicable or not applicable, and how they inform each new situation.

RAISING QUESTIONS ABOUT SIMPLE ANSWERS

Readers may think that any adult must of course know what time measurement is about, and that the only challenge in the work of these teachers was the technological one of getting some machine to work dependably. But it is worth reflecting on how you would know, without having some other ready-made timer, whether a candle burns with the same speed during its first quarter-inch and during its last quarter-inch. How do we know that a sweep second hand takes the same time for each one of its sweeps? How, back there in history, did anyone conclude that some event always takes the same amount of time, and so could be used to measure the time of other events? Without a standard unit, how did they establish a standard unit? This group of teachers gave those questions a lot of thought. And here is a question that gave them pause for a long time: One of them had heard that between five and seven in the evening, demands on electricity are such that electric clocks always run slower. Is that true? If it were, how would we ever know? If it is not, why isn't it? Wouldn't any time piece, in fact, keep going slower and slower as the battery wears out, or as the spring unwinds? As teachers, I think one major role is to undo rapid assumptions of understanding, to slow down closure, in the interests of breadth and depth, which attach our knowledge to the world in which we are called upon to use it. There may, for some given situation, be one right answer, even one that is quite easily reached. But I think a teacher's job is to raise questions about even such a simple right answer, to push it to its limits, to see where it holds up and where it does not hold up. One right answer unconnected to other answers, unexplored, not pushed to its limits, necessarily means a less adequate grasp of our experience. Every time we push an idea to its limits, we find out how it relates to areas that might have seemed to have nothing to do with it. By virtue of that search, our understanding of the world is deepened and broadened.

I would like to develop this thought in the context of the adult thinking of this same group of teachers. Having started with music and proceeding to measure time, they came to the study of ramps, and the main interest of this study was that they pushed the limits of what seemed to be ordinary, even obvious, thoughts about time, speed, and space.

The tune-specific time-measurement machines developed in the direction of a search for units of time measurement—calibrating the candle as it burned, counting the water drips, looking for natural phenomena that keep a steady rhythm. The search applied to ramps, too: Could a ball rolling down a ramp give rise to units of time? This led to another question, as a preliminary: What does the speed of a ball do as it rolls down a ramp? Does it remain constant? Increase? Decrease and then increase? Increase and then remain constant?

One group, watching a ball in order to make an initial guess about the answer, noticed a spot on it. The spot came up faster and faster as the ball rolled, until by the last part of the ramp its occurrences were no longer distinguishable—it looked like a blurred continuous line. This supported the idea that the ball was going faster and faster as it rolled down the ramp, but this group wanted to do a better job of it than that. It occurred to one of them that if the dot left a mark as it rolled they would be able to see better what the speed of the ball was doing. A bit of experimenting and they found a substance they could mark the dot with that would leave a spot each time it hit a long sheet of computer printout paper that was stretched down the ramp. The reader might want to predict what the spots did. We have since discovered that about half the adults we ask predict that the dots will get closer together, a few predict they will get farther apart, and the rest predict they will remain at a constant distance. The roll of computer paper with the spots left by the ball looked like the graph in Figure 6.8 (see next page). The reaction of at least one member of the group was to take a piece of string and measure the distances, saying something to the effect of, "Gee, those dots don't get closer together as noticeably as I had thought they would!"

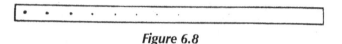

Figure 6.8

That turned out to be just the beginning of many perplexities in this consideration of speed-space-time relationships. Another group, also trying to establish what the speed of a ball does as the ball rolls down a ramp, produced the graph shown in Figure 6.9.

Figure 6.9

I am not going to say here how the second graph came about. My purposes are better served if readers put themselves to the task—because in this case the answer to the ball-ramp problem is really beside the point; what I would rather do is make vivid how much harder it is to think coherently about space-speed-time phenomena than it is to enunciate formulas.

At a subsequent seminar, the teachers who had been absent when the two graphs were produced were given the job of interpreting them—trying to establish how each had been made, and what each of them said about the speed of the balls rolling down the ramps.

Here are a couple of the inferences made by the teachers who had been absent. One person thought the spots on the first graph looked as if the ball had left its own mark as it rolled; but then, she went on to say, it would have to have been rolling at the same speed all the way, so it couldn't have been rolling down a ramp. The second graph was thought not to have been made by the ball itself. This inference was made not on the basis of the distances between the marks, but because the marks looked as if they were drawn by a hand-held felt marker. One generally accepted thought was that marks were made indicating where the ball was after equal time intervals.

The discussion of these two graphs went on for two hours. The members of the group who had been present to generate them got caught up in considering what interpretations were possible in addition to those they knew to be the case. Does the first graph say anything about speed? Is anything to be learned by superimposing the first graph on the second? What picture would you get if you made both graphs at once, of one ball rolling down a ramp? What does the speed of the ball do in the second graph, anyway? The point of this work was to build a construction of space-time-speed ideas not rapidly, but solidly, and to know what the relationships are, after all, that are summed up in that easy high school formula. At the end of those two hours (which, remember, followed a number of other hours of experimental work and thought), no matter how I pushed the conclusions into paradoxical or counter-intuitive extremes, the teachers resisted. No one could be seduced by what sounded like a sensible thought if it did not fit into the idea-structure, that they had created, in all of its breadth and depth.

TIME FOR CONFUSION

One other topic that this group of teachers worked on was the moon. All of us know that the earth turns upon itself, the moon goes around the earth, and while both these things are going on, the earth is also going around the sun. All of us also see the sky get light and dark again every day, see the sun pass overhead, often see the moon, sometimes full and sometimes not. But how many of us can make a connection between these two kinds of experiences? On a given afternoon in Massachusetts, for example, at 5:00, the moon was slightly less than half, and it was visible quite high in the sky. Now, in a model of sun, earth, and moon, could you place them in the relative positions to indicate where they would be in order for the sky to look like that? Almost nobody I've run into can do that. Those two kinds of knowledge about the moon are, for the most part, quite separate. Bringing them together, moreover, is a difficult job, which makes this a marvelous subject through which to study one's ways of making sense of one's experience, and especially to realize how a simple formal model can have almost no connection with the experience it is meant to describe.

It takes months of watching and finding some order in the motions before one can know, when looking at the moon, in what direction it will move from there; where it will be an hour later, or 24 hours later; how the crescent will be tipped 2 hours from now; whether it has yet reached its highest point of the night; whether, tomorrow it will be visible in the daytime. Does the moon pass every day straight overhead? Does the moon ever pass straight overhead? Does it depend on where you are on the earth? If, right now, from here, it was up at a 70° angle from me, at what angle would it be if I climbed up to the top of that building? If I were sitting down, at what angle would it be? Or if I walked down the block toward it?

Figure 6.10   **Figure 6.11**

One friend claimed he had seen the moon like the drawing in Figure 6.10. How was it possible, he asked, for the round earth to have cast a crescent-shaped shadow on the moon? He could understand seeing the moon itself like a crescent, as in Figure 6.11, but he could not understand what he claimed to have seen. It is a good question for moon-watchers, and I put it to the readers, with what seem to me three possible explanations: Either he did not see the moon shaped that way; or there are circumstances under which a sphere (the earth, in this case) can cast a crescent-shaped shadow; or the crescent that is missing from the side of the moon is not the shadow of the earth.

Another friend confessed how perplexed she had been when she realized that people standing on the moon looked up to see the earth. Surely, from the moon, one should look down at the earth if, from the earth, one looks up at the moon? Figuring out that puzzle for herself was a source of considerable joy.

In our seminar, moon questions took us into sun-earth questions that were no less difficult. How, with models of earth and sun, do you represent the sun coming up over the horizon? What is the horizon, anyway? If the sun is, for you, on the horizon, where is it for everybody else? If the sun is straight overhead at noon (and *is* it straight overhead at noon?), is it straight underfoot at midnight? If the sun's rays go out in all directions, past the earth, can we see them? Does that mean that the part that is in darkness on earth is smaller than the part that is in light?

One of the teachers, Joanne Cleary, drew on the blackboard this picture of the earth in the midst of the sun's rays (Figure 6.12), and was trying to articulate her thoughts about it. Another member of the group was asking her to be more precise. Did she mean *exactly* half the earth was in darkness? Did it get suddenly black at the dividing line, or was there some gray stripe? The one who was trying to articulate her thoughts grew angry, and gave up the attempt. She said later that she knew the questions were necessary at some point, but she had not been ready to be more precise. She was struggling to make sense of a morass of observations and models, an idea was just starting to take shape, and, she said, "I needed time for my confusion."

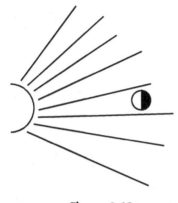

Figure 6.12

That phrase has become a touchstone for me. There is, of course, no particular reason to build broad and deep knowledge about ramps, pendulums, or the moon. I choose them, both in my teaching and in discussion here, to stand for any complex knowledge. Teachers are often, and understandably, impatient for their students to develop clear and adequate ideas. But putting ideas in relation to each other is not a simple job. It is confusing; and that confusion *does* take time. All of us need time for our confusion if we are to build the breadth and depth that give significance to our knowledge.

7

Understanding
Children's Understanding

"GIVING CHILDREN REASON"

IT HAS SEEMED TO ME for some time that teaching *about* Piaget, through lectures and reading, is not an adequate way to make his work helpful to teachers. I could draw on any number of examples where I myself have tried to teach about Piaget's notions to little avail, but I believe the best example for the purpose here comes from a time when I was teaching elementary school science methods, and a colleague was teaching a course on Piaget to the same students. In the course on Piaget, the students had been learning about the differences between concrete and formal operations, including the fact that before they reach the stage of formal operations children have difficulty dissociating factors. As part of their work for my course, one pair of students was watching 10-year-olds exploring two pendulums to see what factors related to the rhythms of their swings. The children decided to change the length of one of the pendulums, and wanted to do a good experiment to determine what difference that made. But one of them realized that in changing the length she would be changing the weight, too, because she would be adding string, and the string weighs something. If my students had never heard of Piaget, they probably would have marveled at the children's subtle experimental thinking. However, what they reported back to me was that this example shows that children at the age of 10 are indeed incapable of dissociating factors!

What teachers are taught about Piaget usually does not actively interfere with their understanding of children, as it did in this example. But there is no doubt that it is notoriously unhelpful. I do not mean to say that Piaget's work is any less helpful to teachers than anybody else's. It is just that Piaget is the most frustrating case, because it does seem as if his work *should* be helpful, yet it barely is.

My own thinking about this problem relates to the work referred to briefly in chapter 6, carried out with Jeanne Bamberger and Magdalene Lampert over a period of two years at the Massachusetts Institute of Technology (Bamberger, Duckworth, & Lampert, 1981). We worked with 16 elementary school teachers: 7 for a two-year period, and 9 others who joined them in the second year.* They met for a three-hour seminar once a week. We were convinced that no amount of theory can affect children in schools except as it becomes a fundamental part of a teacher's thinking. Taking into account the context in which the matter is of importance to them, we set out to find ways to develop teachers' understanding of the nature of learning, in all its complexities and ambiguities, rather than to give a simplified presentation of basic theoretical elements. As one onlooker (Barbara Nelson) said of the work we did, "You aren't teaching teachers *about* Piaget, you're teaching them to *be* Piaget," by which she meant, teaching them to probe children's thinking, to appreciate how they are making sense of a situation, to understand their understanding.

As suggested in chapter 6, a major element of the work of this project was to have the teachers examine their own ways of knowing by exploring together some sets of phenomena such as time measurement, or nonconventional musical notation, or the relative motions of moon, sun, and earth as these can be understood from watching apparent motion in the sky. In each case, we encouraged the teachers to take their own knowledge seriously, to be willing to pay attention to their confusion, to make an effort to understand each other's ways of understanding the phenomena, to take the risk of offering ideas of which they were not sure.

To their great credit, they did make these efforts and take these risks (see chapter 8, pp. 106–110, for one example). For our purposes in this chapter I would like simply to quote some parts of a discussion that took place after an exciting session in which, working in base 5, the teachers had come to a far deeper understanding than they had ever had before of the arithmetic operations they worked with every day. One teacher said, "Well I got really excited when Fern put that formula on the board, because it related to what I had done. . . . So when she put it on the, board—it took me a few minutes to figure out, why is that, what is it, you know, how did she get that answer, and . . . Mary and I were talking and it came about that I began to understand that what I had done in my way was in fact her numeral representation of it all. So that was very exciting." Fern replied, "When you were up there and when you were doing your

*The participating teachers were Jaqueline Apsler, Jinny Chalmers, Joanne Cleary, Mary DiSchino, Fern Fisher, Corinne Gaile, Mary Gale, Carol Hamilton, Fran Hiller, Rosalind O'Sullivan, Wendy Ann Postlethwaite, Lucy Rathjens, Mary Rizzuto, Pat Tabors, Susan Wheelwright, and Risa Whitehead.

columns, . . . it made me realize how, when people develop their own structures for doing things they're going to look different. . . . [Mine] was just one structure, and it happened to be dramatic, but . . . I didn't understand what you were doing right away, and then when I did, I realized it was like the same thing I was doing, but it looked different, and that step of just realizing people are understanding based on their own structure, whatever it is, is easy to forget."

The following reaction to this session was perhaps the most significant from the point of view of this chapter. "The thing I get from, when I'm working with someone else, is trying to understand how they understand something, and seeing how we can get to the same answer. Like if I come up with an answer and my partner comes up with another answer and we got to it different ways, I try to figure out how my partner got to that way. . . . The biggest thing isn't getting hooked on [base 5] and understanding [base 5]; the biggest thing is understanding how someone else is understanding something—like exercising my understanding of understanding" (Mary Rizzuto).

After some months, we asked the teachers to take note of instances in their classrooms where a child said or did something that puzzled them—something indicating that the child's understanding was not the same as theirs. They were by then relatively free about acknowledging when they themselves did not understand something about the moon or about mathematics or whatever we had been working on together, and they had developed a level of confidence in each other that really was an essential element of this work. As Lampert (1981) pointed out, the situation is compounded: For a teacher, looking honestly at what a child really understands can be a self-evaluative act; it can be seen as a measure of the teacher's own competence as a teacher. Once again, the teachers were prepared to take this risk with each other. When they brought examples from their classes, everyone joined in trying to understand what the child's understanding might be.

We also brought children to the seminar, and worked with them while the teachers watched. The teachers again tried to understand each child's individual way of thinking about something. (There is an extended example later in this chapter.)

On one level, then, the teachers learned both to question and to trust their own experience as learners; as a result, on another level, in their work with children they started to develop the capacity to see the sense of a child's question, a "cute" remark, or a "wrong" answer.

The following incident helped to focus the teachers' understanding of this agenda. The teachers were asked to watch and comment on a videotape of two boys engaged in a simple game. The two boys were seated at a table with a screen between them so they could not see one another. One boy had in front of him a pattern made of pattern blocks. The first boy had a similar set of blocks to work with and was to build the other boy's pattern by following his instructions. The attempt went far askew. The boys almost totally lost touch with one another—unknown, of course, to the boys themselves, since neither of them could see what the other had in front of him.

In discussing what they had seen, the teachers spoke generally of a "communication problem"; they also tended to see the boy who had the job of building the pattern from the other's instructions as rather dull, "unable to follow directions." In contrast, the instruction-giver was seen as having "well-developed verbal skills," and as being "orderly and clear" in his instructions. The teachers' analyses stopped there. They seemed to see no further way of understanding or probing for the specific events that led to the misunderstanding between the two boys.

Lampert intervened at that point to suggest that at one moment she thought she heard the boy who was giving instructions tell the other boy to take a "green square," whereas there were no green squares; all the squares were orange, and the only green things were triangles. That small, misleading instruction had, in fact, been the starting point of the second boy's difficulties, and understandably so: He had put a green thing—a triangle—where the other had put an orange square. From then on, all the instructions had been ambiguous, but the boys had no way of knowing that. Indeed, considering the circumstances, the boy following instructions had been remarkably inventive in trying to reconcile later instructions with what he had, quite reasonably, put before him.

When the teachers viewed the videotape again, to see if Lampert's remark was in fact the case, they were astonished. The whole situation as they had initially seen it was reversed. They could now see exactly why the second boy made the moves he did. He no longer looked dull, and he had, in fact, "followed instructions."

Joanne Cleary said of Lampert's remark, "She gave him reason." She referred, of course, to the second boy, the pattern-builder, to whom Lampert had been able to "give reason"—reason for behavior that had previously been seen merely as inattentiveness or perhaps inability to follow instructions. To "give a child reason" became the motto, the aim, of much of the teachers' subsequent work. This was the challenge they put to themselves every time a child did or said something whose meaning was not immediately obvious. That is, the teachers sought to understand the way in which what a child says or does could be construed to make sense—they sought to give him reason.

"BEING" PIAGET

As I have tried to make clear, we attempted no systematic presentation of Piaget's theory or findings in this project. We did not apply his stage designation in protocol analysis, or in interpreting individual children in the teachers' classes. Our one explicit use of Piaget was to demonstrate clinical interviews of children working on classic Piaget problems, and I would like now to give an account of one of these sessions, which took place some time after the above incident.

Piaget's problems were not intended, and cannot well be used, to pinpoint any one child's level. Piaget's goal was to trace the development of a notion, and to do this he based his conclusions on a whole set of protocols. However, it is the good fortune of educators that his clinical method, and the problems he posed to children, are wonderful probes for revealing a child's thinking in ways at once richer and less precise than the assignation of a substage.

The first time I did such clinical interviews in this group, the teachers' reactions were, from one point of view, similar to the reactions of other groups who have watched such demonstrations: They were impressed with the children's involvement and spontaneity, and their willingness to think hard about difficult problems. They noticed that the emphasis was on what the children were thinking, not on its rightness or wrongness. They noticed the effort put into finding a way to ask a question that does not at the same time tell its answer. They noticed that the adult is often silent and that the silence is productive. They saw examples of how weak data is in the face of a strong conviction, and how children "really do" think things as Piaget has described. But, at the same time, it was clear that there was also something that hadn't worked with this group.

On reflection afterward, the staff realized that this demonstration was out of step with the usual pace of the seminar. There was a sense of an embarrassment of riches—far too much to take in and give its due. Four different children had worked with five different problems in contrast to our usual mode of spending sometimes two or three hours on one problem or one child's work. This group of teachers was accustomed to taking an experience apart, considering it from every angle, and raising questions about its various kinds of significance.

The second time we invited children to the seminar we took a different approach. Two children worked at the same time on just one problem, and I undertook to stop at the end of this one problem in order to discuss with the group what had happened, before going on to anything else. This time, in fact, we never got to a second problem. There was so much already that the teachers wanted to pursue.

The problem was a classic one from *The Child's Conception of Geometry* (Piaget, Inhelder, & Szeminska, 1948/1981) known as "The Islands." In its classic form, the child is presented with a solid wooden block, 4" high and 3" × 3" cross-section (see Figure 7.1); a pile of small (1") wooden cubes; and a blue board (meant to be a lake) on which there are three patches of cardboard (meant to be islands)—one 4" × 3", one 3" × 2", and one 2" × 2". The child is told that the solid block is an apartment building; that everyone has to leave that building; and that with the small cubes the child is to build a new building to accommodate the occupants on one of the islands. The base of the new building is to cover the entire island, but it can't go off into the water. *The new building has to have just as much room in it as the original one.*

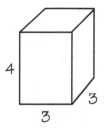

Figure 7.1

Piaget outlines, of course, three stages, each with two substages. It is not necessary here to repeat his outline. Consistent with our approach, I used the problem to explore the thinking of these two children, as far as possible. This entailed keeping in mind the basic question inherent in the task and a variety of possible responses, and—most important—engaging in an interesting intellectual discussion with the children.

In our version, the model was oil-based clay. Each child had his own "lake" and one "island," Timmy's being 4" × 3" and Sandy's 3" × 2" (Figure 7.2).

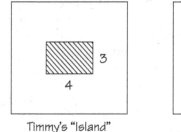
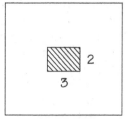

Timmy's "Island"   Sandy's "Island"

Figure 7.2

Sandy built his building one layer higher than the model—five layers on a 3″ × 2″ base (Figure 7.3)—then moved the model over beside his building and took off a layer, so they would be the same height. He recognized that he now had less room in it, but couldn't immediately see what to do about that without building out into the water. Timmy suggested building it higher; Sandy thought it was a good idea, and added two layers.

Figure 7.3   Figure 7.4

Timmy also stopped when his building was the same height as the model (Figure 7.4) and, while acknowledging that his had a little more room in it (note that it is on a larger base) neither of the boys could see what to do about it other than cutting out a patch of cardboard to make an island the same size base as the model, and starting again.

"What if you took off some like that?" I asked, removing just three cubes, that is, part of one layer (see Figure 7.5). "It would goof up the whole thing," said Timmy. "It's just a little smaller, that's all," said Sandy. I responded to Timmy's "goofing up" objection by removing the rest of the layer (see Figure 7.6). Neither of them found that an acceptable solution. After repeated suggestions from them—to cut a new base or to add more clay to the model—I said, "All you can do is take more blocks off or put more blocks on." Timmy said, "You'd have to get thinner blocks."

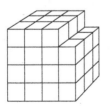

Figure 7.5   Figure 7.6

I then made a suggestion—to see how the children reacted to it. I turned the *model* on its side so that it was on a base identical to Timmy's (see Figure 7.7). With surprise and pleasure, the boys responded that the two buildings were now "equal." "So that, you think, is equal, do you?" I asked. "Yeah," said Timmy. Sandy nodded, I turned the model upright again (see Figure 7.8). "Now what do you think?" Timmy answered, "Now you have to put more on." Timmy explained this for a while, but did not in fact do it, and then I asked, "Has one of them got more room in it than the other?"

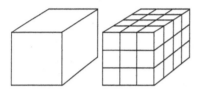

Figure 7.7

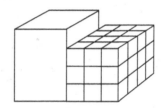

Figure 7.8

TIMMY: Yup.
DUCKWORTH: Which one?
TIMMY: This one right now. *(The model.)*
DUCKWORTH: Why do you say that?
TIMMY: No, I think they have the equal amount of . . . *(mumbles)*
DUCKWORTH: Pardon?
TIMMY: Because this one's bigger *(the model)* and this one's wider *(the one he built).*

He then proceeded to measure (with his fingers, not with a block) to see by how much the one is "bigger" (higher), and by how much the other is wider.

TIMMY: The same width up and the side. *(That is, the model is taller by the same amount as his building is wider.)*
DUCKWORTH: The same width? Is it?
TIMMY: Yup, I just measured it, and they both came out the same way.

His procedure convinced Sandy, to whose building attention then turned.

After an initial tendency to want Sandy's building to be the same height as the model again, they settled on having one extra layer (Figure

7.3). This time Sandy measured with the blocks, to show that one layer was missing in width, and thus, one layer needed to be added on top.

Their solutions, then, were a three-layered building on Timmy's 4" × 3" base (correct), and a five-layered building on Sandy's 3" × 2" base (one layer too short). I probed some more, made some counter suggestions; they stayed with their solutions, and I stopped there.

My interpretation was that both boys were drawn to judge the overall amount of space by the most salient dimension, the height; that they were able to think how to remedy it in one case (Sandy's, when they had to build higher) but not in the other (Timmy's, when they had to take off a layer); that they then saw that a greater size in one dimension (height, say) could be compensated for by a smaller size in another (width, say); that in both cases they judged that it needed not only to be higher (or wider) but *the same amount* higher (or wider); that this worked in one case (Timmy's) but not the other (Sandy's)—indicating that "the same amount" applied to a single dimension, and not to a two-dimensional slice; that there was no tendency to think of the original solid block as composed of units whose number could be calculated.

Piaget's interest in this problem concerns the epistemology of the notion of volume. Of the kind of work Sandy and Timmy did, for example, he says:

> In all these trends, there is growth in the articulation of Euclidean intuitions of volume. It is through that increasing articulation that notions of volume lose their topological character and come to conform with Euclidean notions of length and area which are elaborated at this level. However, although these articulations pave the way for operational handling of the various relations together with their logical multiplication, they are insufficient to enable children to effect those reversible compositions which mark the operational level proper. Thus these responses are intermediate in character, and this fact appears most clearly in the answers, given to our questions about conservation. (Piaget, Inhelder, & Szeminska, 1948/1981, p. 369)

Now this takes some effort to understand; moreover, it takes a far broader context—references are made to notions that have been studied and subsequently discussed through two entire volumes (Piaget & Inhelder 1948/1967; Piaget et al, 1948/1981). It is not a criticism of Piaget to point out that the quoted discussion is not easy to grasp if one has not read the rest of the volume, and if one is not concerned with those epistemological issues. But the fortunate thing is that this kind of work with children has other values that are directly useful to teachers as they work with children. The main thing—common to Piaget's interests, as well—is the focus on how children are making sense of the situation in their own way. We can all appreciate, and even he awed by, watching this happen, without putting our emphasis on Piaget's interpretation of what is meant by "in their own way."

That points to a second difference between Piaget's own writing and other uses of his problems. In reading Piaget's protocols it is difficult to be "awed" by children's intellectual work. Indeed, it is very difficult to read them at all—to follow the steps in what the children do and say—and certainly to come to our own conclusions about what they mean. And most importantly, it is simply not possible at all to read into Piaget's brief protocols what is actually entailed for the child as he or she does the work—the surprise, puzzlement, dogged pursuit, resistance or susceptibility to suggestion, doubts, conviction, and so on, all of which give us an appreciation of a mind at work. It was all of these aspects of the session with the children, not to mention gestures, facial expressions, and eye movements, that contributed to the teachers' understanding of Timmy's and Sandy's thinking.

Piaget's contributions here are, on the one hand, having located what are essentially crucial intellectual issues for children, and finding ways to put the issues in a form that catches their interest; and on the other hand, developing the "clinical interview" technique in which the adult role is to find out as much as possible about what the child believes about an issue. Both these aspects are what gave the session with Timmy and Sandy its significance.

I had stopped at the end of what is thought of as one part of the classic technique, and the children left temporarily. It is clear that the teachers did seize the basic nature of the question. They discussed at length what had happened, and came up with three further questions they wanted the children to think about and respond to. Despite the fact that none of the teachers had read any of Piaget's books, all three of these questions turned out to be ones that Piaget had asked in other parts of his exploration of children's notions of volume—evidence enough that the teachers had seized the crux of the problem (and were, in their invention of further questions, "being" Piaget):

> "What would happen if you took the model away and asked the kids if the two [Timmy's and Sandy's buildings] have the same number of rooms?"
> "I would just like to see them build a copy of the model, without talking about islands."

"What if you asked them: If you only had this many blocks [the
blocks in Timmy's building] could you build that one [Sandy's]?"

The children returned, and these three questions were then pursued,
very productively. In answer to the first question, Timmy replied, "If both
our buildings fit that building, the clay building, then both of ours would
be the same." Sandy agreed. (The question came back later, however.)

The most intriguing episode of all arose when they were asked to reproduce the model. For each of them, it was a problem to make the base,
although each resolved that problem without undue perplexity. (One held
the model up just off the table, and built a base of blocks under it—as if
he were constructing with the blocks the patch of cardboard similar to
the other islands.) Once the base was established, both proceeded easily.
Sandy finished his first, and Timmy was left without enough blocks to
finish. He had two complete layers, and five blocks on the third layer; he
needed four more to complete that layer, and nine for the top layer (see
Figure 7.9). I asked him how many blocks he needed.

Figure 7.9

TIMMY: About ten.
DUCKWORTH: How did you figure that?
TIMMY *(counts, then announces):* Nine more.

Sandy was persuaded (with difficulty) to lend Timmy nine blocks from
his own building. As Timmy added them to his, it became clear that there
weren't enough. Timmy was dumbfounded.

DUCKWORTH: Odd, eh? How many more do you need now?
TIMMY *(counts):* Four.

The nine blocks were given back to Sandy, and I tried to move on to
another question, but Timmy was still totally taken up with the mystery
of the nine blocks.

TIMMY: I counted wrong.

DUCKWORTH: How did you count wrong?

TIMMY: I didn't have these on when I counted. (*He takes off the five of the third layer.*)

DUCKWORTH: What happened?

TIMMY: You musta took some.

DUCKWORTH: How many now do you think you need?

TIMMY (*counts four missing from third layer, five present in third layer, and three more, it's unclear from where*): Twelve.

DUCKWORTH: How'd you get twelve?

TIMMY: I went one, two, three, four, five (*the five present*), six, seven, eight, nine (*the four missing*) . . . I still need nine!

SANDY: Timmy, if you get four more blocks, and then another nine there, it would probably be just like mine.

Sandy grew surer and surer of this; he figured out that that would make 13 and tried several times to explain it to Timmy. For much of the time, Timmy was still trying to count. For example:

TIMMY: Wait a sec, one, two, three, I have four here, right? I mean five, I count one more layer one, two, three, four, five—

SANDY: But you said—

TIMMY: Wait—five, six, seven, eight, nine, ten. Wait a minute I have five here, and then I need five more on the top and then I need s-, s-, and then I need five more, six, seven, eight, nine— oh, wow!

Sandy finally managed to explain his way of going about it; he took 13 blocks from his building and added them to Timmy's while Timmy counted. When they had all been added, Timmy brought over the clay model, to check that this building was just like it. "Yup," he said. He gave no sense of understanding Sandy's reasoning; he seemed, rather, to be worn out. I left it there.

They went on then to calculating the number of blocks that were in each building, and although that was full of interest, our purposes here are better served by looking at the teachers' discussion of "the 13 problem." The first teacher to bring it up said:

TEACHER 1: He didn't have a good system for counting—he would count the ones he had, and then say these were the ones he needed.

Another teacher responded that she thought he did have one part of a very good system:

> TEACHER 2: But that makes—if you have five and those five are raised and you know you need another layer, then you need at least those five. Right? You know what I mean?
> TEACHER 1: Yeah, I'm with you.
> TEACHER 2: All right—so I thought—that was a strategy that would have worked, if he had extended the bottom layer—I mean if he had doubled, then, the spaces.
> TEACHER 1: . . . doubled the bottom.
> TEACHER 2: . . . you know . . . then he'd drop that and forget that he needed to move that up. It wasn't until the end that I could see that counting strategy.

Teacher 3 and Teacher 4 said they thought he asked for nine because he knew he needed one more layer; Teacher 3 thought he then forgot about the four missing in layer three; Teacher 4 thought he simply didn't know how to take them into account.

> TEACHER 5 (*in disagreement*): Sandy would say "You need four more for this layer," and Timmy would say, "No, I need five more for this layer"—so he was talking about different layers.
> TEACHER 6: When I was watching him count, he seemed to be counting the four empty spaces and then the five that were up—and it was as if . . . he knew he had to reach a fourth layer, and in order to reach a fourth layer, he had to count more on the five that were up, and he also was realizing that if he counted four more in the spaces he would have a flat layer and I think he was confusing like the flat layer with the top layer.
> TEACHER 7: I felt like he understood that he had to go up another layer and so he counted five on top and then somehow when he counted the four he was filling in the spaces but then he couldn't also fill in the spaces again.

One teacher had the impression that Timmy knew that one layer consisted of nine blocks, and referred to the way he had built his 3″ x 3″ base. Others disagreed on that point, and cited other evidence.

> TEACHER 6: I'm not sure he realized—I'm not sure *I* realized—that the five that were up and the four that were spaces, together

form one layer. Because they're not—I mean, I don't think he
was seeing the five and the four as part of a whole layer. Some
were up and some were down.

These excerpts show at least four different interpretations the teachers
made of what *most* people would simply think of as a "mistake."

This discussion would do credit to a graduate seminar in cognitive
research. The questions were good ones and the evidence invoked in support of possible answers was good also: Did Timmy know that part of
what he needed was a complete layer? Did he know that adding together
the number present and number absent made a whole layer? Did he know
there were nine in a layer? Even more subtle are the three interpretations
of how Timmy might have come to add together some blocks that were
present and some blocks that were absent in trying to determine how
many he needed (Teachers 2, 6, 7).

"AND IN THE VERY PROCESS . . ."

But the teachers did not see this as an exercise in psychology. Rather it
was as *teachers* that they wanted to make sense of what the children were
doing. It was as *teachers* that they realized that the better they could judge
how children were seeing a problem, the better they could decide what
would be appropriate to do next.

Jinny Chalmers wrote about this session in the following way:

As always the task is to be really invested in understanding what
a child is thinking. And in the very process of unearthing that,
learning, growing, changing is going on. I feel closer to being able
to do that after watching [the work with the children, above] than
ever before. I feel closer to changing the vested interest in my objectives—or at least believing that the process alone is valuable. I
guess for the first time clearly I saw children learning—the process
of learning without the answers fully intact. Ah, so many times
around on this issue.

Chalmers' reflections shed light on Lampert's observation cited early
in this chapter: A teacher tends to feel that what the child understands is in
the last analysis *her* responsibility. She writes here of "changing the vested
interest in *my objectives*"—by which she meant she could free herself from
feeling that it was up to her to see that the children came out with the
"right answer"; she could then relax and try to attend to what the children
really do think.

That freedom seemed to be exceedingly important to her. It went hand-in-hand with another interesting relationship referred to in this quotation. To the extent that one carries on a conversation with a child, as a way of trying to understand a child's understanding, the child's understanding increases "in the very process." The questions the interlocutor asks, in an attempt to clarify for herself what the child is thinking, oblige the child to think a little further also. This kind of question was a constant thread throughout the work of this project. It can be seen in the work with Timmy and Sandy, but it was also all through the sessions with the teachers themselves: What do you mean? How did you do that? Why do you say that? How does that fit with what she just said? I don't really get that; could you explain it another way? Could you give an example? How did you figure that? In every case, those questions are primarily a way for the interlocutor to try to understand what the other is understanding. Yet in every case, also, they engage the other's thoughts and take them a step further.

Mary Rizzuto, late in the second year, said that she no longer thought of her class as one adult and many children. She said instead, "We're all learners." Child to child, teacher to child, or child to teacher, a frequent refrain was, "I don't really get that; what did you mean?" I saw something of this in her class of 8-year-olds. She had read to the children a story about invasions from outer space, and they were engrossed in a discussion of it, including whether there really is life in outer space. In the midst of the discussion, one boy asked, "Does all water have germs in it?" Rizzuto was puzzled, as, I must say, was I, and made a couple of guesses about what he meant. Did he mean both cold and hot? Did he mean both lake and sea? Did he mean both outdoors and indoors? He didn't really answer, but just repeated his question; Rizzuto, not knowing what the question meant, didn't know how to answer it. It seemed wholly unrelated to the discussion underway but she suspected that it might be more related than it seemed, and she stayed with it. Through a series of insights and questions that I did not record, she established what he was thinking about. He "knew," from some authoritative source, that there was ice on Mars. He also "knew" that when the sun shone on that ice, it would melt, at least somewhat. That would mean that there was water on Mars; and if all water had germs in it, then there would be germs in that water on Mars, and since germs are alive, that would mean there was life in outer space.

From an answer given in a science workbook to a method devised for doing long division, or a question about why words are spelled as they are, time and time again the teachers managed to "give the child reason," and in doing so, to find ways to go further.

8

Structures, Continuity, and Other People's Minds

THIS CHAPTER IS bipartite: part of it about infants and part of it about adults. I am hoping the themes from these two age groups, taken together, will shed light on the work of teachers of school-age children.

STRUCTURES FOR TAKING IN THE WORLD

In chapters 2 and 3, I pointed out that Piaget's work on infants is presented in his three books on the sensorimotor period: *The Origins of Intelligence in Children* (1936/1966), *The Construction of Reality in the Child* (1937/1986), and *Play, Dreams, and Imitation in Childhood* (1945/1962b). In these three books Piaget followed the development of individual minds, those of his own three children. His detailed observations enable us to see more clearly than in any of his other work the critical importance of the child's own means of organizing what he or she knows and does.

To understand what Piaget says about infancy we have to understand something about the way he sees the relationship between biological organisms and intellectual structures. He points out that a biological organism is organized to function and that the organization (or structure) and the functioning are interdependent. A digestive system is organized to digest food, and it cannot maintain this organization unless it digests. Physiologically, the organism takes in parts of the world—milk, say—and transforms that milk into the organism itself. Piaget used to say that when a rabbit eats cabbage, the cabbage becomes rabbit, the rabbit doesn't become cabbage. Assimilation is an obvious word to use, in this physiological sense. The basic fact is of an organized structure set up to function, needing to function in order to maintain its structure, and needing parts of the world in order to function.

This basic fact is, in Piaget's view, a psychological fact as well. Children are born with other capacities, less essential for immediate survival than the digestive system, which are the basis for psychological development in that the child has some control over them and takes an interest in them. Like the digestive and respiratory systems, they need to function in order to maintain themselves, and they need parts of the outside world in order to function. Babies are born with eyes, hands, and mouths, but eyes cannot work unless there is light to look at; the grasping reflex cannot work unless there is something to grasp; sucking cannot work unless there is something to suck. Infants take in, incorporate, those parts of the world that enable them to do what they are organized to do. In a quite literal sense, this, too, is assimilation.

When infants modify their own organization in order to be able to incorporate yet more of the world, they are accommodating. The only food infants can take in at first is milk. Later they manage to change their own structures, to be able to take in more forms of nourishment. Similarly, they accommodate their mouth movements to a series of different objects, thus becoming able to enlarge the range of things they can suck. The greater the flexibility of the structures for taking things in, the better.

Along with this more or less outsider's view of what infancy is about, Piaget also proposes an insider's view—that is, a view of what the experience is like for the infant. It takes considerable effort for an adult to think oneself into that frame of mind.

It is important for us as teachers to attempt that insider's view because it is critical to be able to make connections between children's meaning and our own. The second part of this chapter will continue to develop that point: the importance of teachers' capacity to appreciate what a given experience means to another person.

All our thinking throughout life bears the mark of the origins of infant thinking, and those origins shed light, in particular, on the thinking of school-age children. According to this insider's view, as an infant at birth you are not conscious of being yourself, or conscious of being an infant, or conscious of being an individual surrounded by a world. There are sensations and feelings and awarenesses but it is unclear what you are the cause of, and what is simply happening to you. There isn't a you, and there isn't a world. There is just awareness. If a hand comes in front of your face you don't know that it is part of you. You don't even know that it is an object. There is change in your visual sense, change in your whole body feeling, but you don't know that it is your body and you don't know that it is your visual sense. As an adult, it is hard to think yourself into that frame of mind. It is even harder to think yourself into the infant's frame of mind as she "tries" to, or gives signs that she "wants" to do such and such. In

Piaget's view, the basic motivational element is simply that if she can do it, she will. But what does it feel like for the baby?

The story I would like to tell is the case of one of Piaget's children, Lucienne, and the development of the coordination of her grasping and vision, that is, of being able to reach for things that she sees. The major theme of this story is that Lucienne organizes her own experience. But I would also like to make another point in passing: One of the greatest and most frequent distortions of Piaget's thought is the idea that the stages he described are discontinuous—you flip into another stage by some magic that is usually considered maturational, although it is sometimes considered experiential; either way, if you live long enough, you flip into the next stage. The story, reconstructed here, however, as is true of all of the accounts in the three books on infancy, provides remarkable detail of the continuity of each accomplishment with the ones before and after.

Piaget divides the sensorimotor stage into six substages. The account I am going to give takes place primarily within the second of those substages, although it starts with the first, the reflexes. (Reflexes are essentially what the baby is furnished with for the first few weeks.) The second substage lasts for a few months.

The development we will be following starts with and grows from visual, grasping, and sucking reflexes, so we will start with examples of each of those in turn. Then we will follow Lucienne as she coordinates those three kinds of reflexes. All the observations come from *The Origins of Intelligence*; most of them will be referred to by number. A few are without observation number, and will be referred to by page. (All references given are to the English edition, but the translations are mine from the original French.)

Piaget gives an example of a baby boy, about a week old, being moved away from a window. The baby keeps turning his head toward the window, keeps the light within his field of vision (p. 62) (not knowing, of course, that it was a window and not knowing that it was his head he was turning, much less that it was his eyes; simply continuing to do what he had to do to keep the feeling that went with his eyes' functioning). At 16 days, his daughter Jacqueline's eyes cannot yet follow a match flame that comes within 20 centimeters of them. She changes her expression at seeing the flame and then moves her head a little as if she is trying to get that light source back again, but she does not follow it. At 24 days, in the same conditions, she can follow it perfectly well (Obs. 28).

As for grasping, in the first few hours after Lucienne's birth, when Piaget puts his finger in her hand, she grasps it with her fingers—without her thumb—and then lets go right away (p. 89). At 12 days, his son Laurent manifests some interest in grasping: Piaget puts his finger in Laurent's palm when he is crying, and he stops crying and grasps it, interested in this grasping action that he is able to do (p. 89). (He does not, of course, realize that it is somebody's finger that enables him to do it, nor that it is he who is doing it; he does what he does to preserve the feeling.*) Piaget points out that in their first few weeks infants are continuously moving their arms around, moving their hands slowly, opening and closing their hands and fingers (p. 89). Those are the kinds of things that they are organized to be able to do, and therefore they do them.

In Observations 1 through 10 Piaget details his children's first sucking activity, and how they gradually accommodate their reflex activity to the nipple and to other objects that happen to touch their lips. Later he describes how Lucienne manages to provide herself with her own hand to suck. "At 1 month and 25 days, and again the next day, her hands keep just barely touching her mouth. But I notice, again, her inability to keep her thumb between her lips for very long, or above all to find it again if it slips out" (Obs. 23). She does not know how to keep her thumb in her mouth (not knowing, of course, that there are a thumb and a mouth, nor that they are hers). "A few days later, at 2 months and 2 days, I made the following two observations: At six o'clock, after her meal, her hands are moving in the air around her mouth and she sucks alternately her fingers, mainly her index finger, or the back of her hand, or her wrist. When her hand escapes from her mouth it tends to come back and the coordination is reestablished" (Obs. 23). (Note that she still does not know it is her hand that has escaped; she simply keeps doing what she has been doing. She does not know what she is doing, nor that "she" is doing something, but she tries to recover the feelings she had. The closest experience of my own that I can draw on, to help myself understand this, has been trying to get back into a comfortable position I had moved out of in some state of semi-sleep; I don't know what the position was, but I know I'm not in it now, and I move about in various ways until I recognize that I am back in it again. When the baby's thumb gets out of her mouth, she manages somehow to find the position again, and back it goes into her mouth.) "At 8 o'clock she is awake and she is again sucking her fingers. Her hand remains immobile for long periods and then when it slips away, one sees simultaneously that her mouth tries to find and grasp something, while at the same time her hand comes back" (Obs. 23). These are the beginnings of her coordinating her hand with her mouth.

At about this time, this is what is happening with the infant's hand itself. The specific observations are of Laurent, but Piaget attributes "the same vague reactions" (Obs. 54) to Lucienne. The hand still encounters

---

*Given this emphasis, in infancy, on how things feel, I was later entranced to encounter and read Suzanne Langer's *Mind: An Essay on Human Feeling* (1967).

things only by chance, but once something touches the palm, the baby grasps it tightly. By now, when the hand is touched somewhere else, not necessarily the palm, the infant responds to that also, moving the hand about. When moving it about leads to its being touched in the palm, then the baby has provided herself with something to grasp (Obs. 52).

By 2½ months, Lucienne's grasping things becomes systematic and develops into other schemes: She scratches things, picks them up and lets them go, rubs them. Whenever her hand touches anything—her blanket, her clothes—she tries to get her hand around it and pick it up (Obs. 54).

There is an important development when she starts watching her hands doing these things. "At 2 months, 27 days, she looks at her right hand which holds a doll, but she does not know how to keep it in her visual field" (Obs. 60). When it is there she looks at it, but if it wanders out of her sight, she does not know how to find it again. She looks at her empty hands too, when she can, opening and closing, moving about; but she does not know how to hold them in her visual field. "At 3 months and 3 days she attentively watches her right hand which is clutching her cover; she lets go of the cover and picks it up again, all the while attentively watching. When her hand loses contact with the cover, she looks at the cover but her hand does not follow her looking. The hand then finds the cover again of its own accord, uncoordinated with her looking" (Obs. 60). The active hand is something interesting for her to look at, so she looks at it while it is in view; but she has no idea that the two things she feels herself doing—looking and grasping—have anything to do with one another.

During the fourth month, another form of incidental coordination develops. She knows how to bring her hand to her mouth to suck, as we saw earlier. If she happens to have an object in her hand when it comes to her mouth, she discovers the object, rather than her hand, in her mouth (Obs. 63). She does not realize that the hand she wants to suck has anything to do with the hand that is holding an object. She wants to suck her hand, and lo and behold she gets the object instead. She still does not, of course, reach for objects she sees in order to put them in her mouth. But if her hand encounters an object, she grasps it, and once it is grasped, the hand-plus-object often finds its way to her mouth. By 4 months, 4 days, it seems clear that she is bringing directly to her mouth whatever her hand grasps, without, of course, looking at hand or object and without controlling whether it is hand or object that reaches her mouth (Obs. 63).

When she is 4 months, 9 days, Piaget has the impression for the first time that she directs a rattle—as opposed to hand-plus-rattle—to her mouth (Obs. 64). She starts accommodating her gestures so it is the object that reaches her mouth—thereby providing herself with a variety of different ways to suck.

On the same day, Piaget makes the following observation. "Lucienne makes no effort to reach for a rattle that she is looking at. But then when she is bringing the rattle to her mouth [Piaget having put it into her hand, outside her field of vision, see Obs. 64] she catches sight of it, and her visual attention has the effect of stopping the movement of her hand; her mouth was already open and ready to take the rattle—it was only a centimeter away. Lucienne then sucks the rattle, takes it out of her mouth, looks at it, sucks it again, and so on" (Obs. 67).

That evening, there is a particularly fascinating observation. Piaget again presents the rattle to her view. Again, she does not try to reach it. But as she looks at it, she starts making sucking movements with her mouth (Obs. 64)!

At 4 months, 15 days, there is further development. "She is looking at a rattle, looking as if she wants it, but again without stretching out her hand. I place the rattle near her right hand and as soon as she sees the rattle together with her hand she moves the hand near the rattle and ends up grasping it" (Obs. 79). This is the first time she will have done that. She sees her hand in the same field with the rattle, and in the same sense that seeing the rattle stimulated her to suck (above), seeing it now stimulates her to move her hand, which sometimes has held that rattle. Not knowing that it is her hand, or that moving will get her to the rattle, she does something that feels as holding the rattle feels and this moves her closer to the rattle, close enough, then, to grasp it. From now on, when her hand is in the same visual field with the rattle, she moves to grasp it.

So now, objects that are in her hand she can take to her mouth; and if she sees her hand in the same field with some object, she can grasp it, and then, of course, get it to her mouth. We are getting close.

Later the same day, she sees the rattle hanging above her head. "Her immediate reaction is to try to suck. She opens her mouth, sucks, sticks her tongue out, pants with desire," Piaget says; at which point her hands come near her mouth as if to furnish something to suck. But as it happens, her hands come within the same visual field as the rattle, and as soon as she sees them together, she reaches for the object (Obs. 80). Seeing the rattle made her want to suck; the wanting to suck made her hand come near her mouth, bringing it also into the same field of vision as the rattle, and then she reached for the rattle.

Very soon after this intermediate stage, at 4 months, 26 days, she seems no longer to need to see her hand in the same field as the object; seeing it and wanting it lead her to reach directly for it. This is consolidated, with no hesitation, at 5 months, 1 day.

This is a very different picture from the stereotype of Piaget's stages. Nothing is given. Every advance is an active accomplishment and builds on previous accomplishments. And, as I said earlier, this story all takes

place within one substage of the sensorimotor period, building from individual reflexes (at the end of substage one) to the coordination of vision
and grasping (the apotheosis of substage two and, by the same token, the
onset of substage three).

On the same day (5 months, 1 day) that she first reaches unhesitatingly
for objects that she sees, she does two other things for the first time. She
grasps an object that she happens to touch, and brings it directly to her
field of vision—rather than bringing it to her mouth to suck and catch-
ing sight of it on the way (Obs. 89). Second, when Piaget holds her hand
outside of her own visual field, she turns in the proper direction and sees
what is holding it (Obs. 90). Before this day, she would struggle, not knowing where to look or what to do; she had no realization that this feeling
of being caught had anything to do with any space that she could look at
with her eyes. But now, all at the same time, these three things happen:
She can grasp things that she sees; she can bring into her sight the things
that she grasps—and she knows how to look for her own hand when it is
held. The significance is that she has not learned tricks; she hasn't been
"conditioned"; she has developed a coordinated system of relationships,
which enables her all at once to do a variety of different things, in relation
to one another. This coordinated system now enables her to take things in
and give meaning to things in ways she has not done before.

Such a coordinated system Piaget calls a structure, and he uses that
term both for a sensorimotor organization like this and for a conceptual
organization. Children take in the world in terms of their own structures—either built-in structures, such as digestive tracts, respiratory systems, and reflexes, or structures such as these, which they construct in
interaction with the world. What makes a phenomenon or an experience
interesting and what gives it its meaning is the way that it can be taken
into (incorporated into, assimilated into) the child's structures. What the
child knows of the phenomenon is the ways it can be taken in. New encounters and new objects, for us as well as for infants, do not have their
own clear indistinguishable properties that jump out by themselves; they
do not have an inherent "meaning" that they impose on us. On the contrary, either we can assimilate them into our structures, which thus es-
tablishes what they "mean" to us; or they remain vague and nebulous
because we cannot assimilate them. This is obviously much of the world
for infants, but it is also much of the world for us; there is much that we
do not know how to take in. Sometimes we are aware of not being able to
assimilate our experience, and this creates a malaise that sooner or later
results in further differentiating and recombining our structures so that
they can also respond to these new encounters. It is a constant struggle to
incorporate more of the world into our organized systems physiological,
sensorimotor, or conceptual.

OTHER PEOPLE'S MINDS

I think it is clear how very hard it is for us to feel what it is like for an infant to know in that way. It is a good object lesson for us as teachers. A shared experience may mean something very different from one person to another, according to how each person organizes to take it in. An important part of a teacher's work is to make connections with other people's ways of giving meaning to the same experience. Trying to get into an infant's frame of mind is a good workout.

The work described in chapters 6 and 7 attempts to help teachers understand the ways they themselves construct their understanding. My approach has been to have them learn something together and pay careful attention to their own and each other's responses. The rest of this chapter goes back to that work. It is drawn from the more complete account referred to in chapter 7: "Some Depths and Perplexities of Elementary Arithmetic" (Duckworth, 1987). This arithmetic work involved 12 of the teachers and took up an hour or two in each of 10 sessions, spread over one year, from October to June. We began with chip trading, a collection of primary school activities one of whose major purposes is the understanding of place value in our number system. We used not the conventional white, green, red, and blue poker chips but paper clips, drinking straws, rubber bands, and hexagon-shaped blocks, increasing in value in that order.

The only basic rule in chip trading is that once you have agreed on an exchange rate, then any time you accumulate that number of any one value you must trade them in for one of the next higher value. The simplest game is to throw dice and take paper clips for the number of dots you throw, then trade as necessary until you reach a hexagon. With an exchange rate of three, if you throw a five, you would take five paper clips and trade three back again for a straw, so you would end the turn with one straw and two paper clips.

A different game is to start with a hexagon and *subtract* the number on the dice. That means that with an exchange rate of three you must trade in the hexagon for three rubber bands, trade in one rubber band for three straws, and trade in one straw for three paper clips before you can begin to subtract as many paper clips as the number that you threw.

By the time we came to dividing collections evenly among several people, we were having to muster all our intellectual forces. One of the sessions on dividing in various exchange rates was the intellectual high point of the year. The story of that high point itself is too complex to relate, here, but I want to tell you about what happened just after it. At the moment of the greatest excitement, we had been working with an exchange rate of five. After the excitement, we were talking about what had gone on,

Figure 8.1

and the person who had made perhaps the most significant contribution, Fern Fisher, said, "I just want to say that the thing with the hands [she had talked about hands as she was describing her insight], I started the last time we chip traded—it didn't just happen all of a sudden." Then she drew on the board a drawing she had in fact drawn in her journal after the work of the preceding session (see Figure 8.1).

After a good deal of laughter, this drawing also led to a good deal of thoughtful discussion, which is the part of the story I tell here.

WENDY: What does the drawing represent?
JOANNE: Base 5.
FERN: It's a hand. Each finger has five fingers.
RUTH: Yes, but what if you have a different base?
FERN: It's only for base 5.
WENDY: Can you show me the units, the next ones up, and the
    next ones up—which ones are which?
FERN (*pointing first to the smallest fingers and then to each bigger set of
    fingers in turn*): Paper clips, straws, rubber bands, and hexagon.

WENDY: Five paper clips equals one straw, five of the middle-sized is one thumb.

FERN: One rubber band.

WENDY: Rubber band, thumb—and five fingers. So if, let's say there were ten fingers on a hand . . . This would be a thousand. *(Wendy did very well in the world of numbers, and she had a difficult time talking about a straw or a hand when she could be talking about "ten.")*

FERN: You know what it is, it's—that is equal to . . . *(She counted the different levels of fingers, and wrote):*

$$b^4$$

FERN: I think it means that.

DUCKWORTH: Do you think you could explain that?

FERN: Well, it's like how many times you have to multiply the base times itself.

DUCKWORTH: Maybe you could write that down.

FERN: We're in base 5, so this "b" would be five . . . five times five times five times five. Twenty-five, a hundred twenty-five . . . *(She now had on the board):*

$$5 \times 5 \times 5 \times 5 \qquad \begin{array}{r} 125 \\ \times\ 5 \\ \hline 625 \end{array}$$

DUCKWORTH: What is that now, what does that mean, all those numbers?

FERN: Umm. So I think this would be the number of paper clips *(her voice suddenly becomes incredulous)* that one hexagon is worth? Is that possible? No. Can't be *(pause)*. Yeah.

WENDY: Yeah there's a way, cause if it were tens, hundreds, thousands, ten thousands. But it would be a thousand.

FERN *(marking off the levels):* It's paper clips, straws, rubber bands, and hexagon. Yeah, I guess it would.

RUTH: You keep squaring each one.

FERN: Multiplying it by itself.

RUTH: Yeah,

FERN: That means that in order to get a hexagon you have to roll the dice till you get to 625, which we all did, pretty much I had no idea it was that many.

WENDY: We rolled 625 little dots? Is that possible?

DUCKWORTH: Did anyone get to a hexagon?

WENDY: No. Only by combining.

FERN: Oh, that's right, only by combining. But still, people must have been getting hundreds.

(Many incredulous voices here, and no clarity of ideas.)

WENDY *(businesslike)*: Five times five is twenty-five.

FERN: That's straws.

WENDY: That's the first one.

FERN. Wait a minute now, it's five, twenty-five, a hundred twenty-five—

WENDY: That's right, because in tens—

SARA: But you've got ones.

Sara said this loudly, but nobody took her up on it. I even repeated it: "Sara says, 'But you've got ones.' " Still nobody noticed that it was the key to their dilemma.

Joanne was now proposing that another layer of hands was needed. In the midst of discussing why Joanne thought that, Fern said, "Oh yeah, right. Okay, so it's—" And then a sudden change of mind. "Oh, who said . . . 'Because you have ones.' . . . Right, that's the problem then. I was—Yeah, The ones aren't five to the anything."

It seemed to me then that we were close to clarity, but I was mistaken. "How many times do you multiply five by itself to reach the hexagon?" I asked. There were different answers. Some said four, and some said three, and no one was very clear about explaining why she thought it was one or the other. I thought I knew exactly how to make it clear to everybody. My definitive explanation elicited not a single sign of interest.

Nobody, including me, noticed that in fact only *three* sizes of hands are needed, even though four levels are represented. (When Joanne had talked of needing to add another layer, people had talked of adding a fifth size.) Fern came closest in her attempt at a "definitive explanation"—one that succeeded somewhat better than mine.

FERN: OK, I got it. This little tiny hand is a straw.

OTHERS: Mm-hmm. Yeah.

FERN: This hand is a rubber band.

OTHERS: Oh yeah.

FERN: And this hand is a hexagon. So you only have to multiply three times.

RUTH: So the hexagon is twenty-five times five. So where'd you get the 625?

FERN: I made a mistake.

RUTH: Oh. OK.

MARY R (*still not convinced*): Because if those fingers are straws,
    how would you indicate "one" on that drawing?

FERN: Each little tiny finger this size is a paper clip.

MARY R: OK. And then the little tiny hand as a whole is a straw.

Joanne still felt some confusion; sorting it out led to some more interesting relationships between what the fingers are and what the hands
are.

JOANNE: It's the fingers we're using . . . They're all connected by the
    hand, which holds the place . . . If each finger is a paper clip,
    then each group of five fingers makes one straw.

FERN: Mm-hmm. Little ones. See, you can't say fingers, because all
    these things are fingers—of something bigger.

JOANNE: Tiny fingers. Each one of those is a paper clip, right? OK,
    once you get five of those paper clips, you get a straw, which is
    another finger on the medium hand.

FERN: Right. Or, this is a hand, too. But it's also a finger. (*much gen-
    eral laughter.*)

JOANNE: Every little hand is worth the next finger . . . you don't
    need that big hand, then.

That was where that discussion ended. Each handful of five fingers
is also a finger, of the next level. Five paper clips are also one straw. You
don't need the big hand because the hexagon represented by its finger is
also represented by the next smaller hand.

This extended example gives a sense of the kind of exploration that
characterized the two-year project. Our leisurely exploring together and
persistence in clarifying meaning for each other laid the groundwork for
insights such as the following, which comes from a session led by my
colleague Jeanne Bamberger, a musician. In one of her sessions people
worked in groups of four, each person with a rhythm instrument, and they
were to make a "tune"—a tune of rhythms only, since none of the instruments were melodic. The tune of one group was as follows: The first person played a little figure once and then played it again as the second person joined in. The two played it once more while the third person joined
in, and the three played it again while the fourth person joined in. After
they all played it, all four of them together, the fourth person dropped
out, leaving three; then the third person dropped out, leaving two; then
the second person dropped out, leaving only one person to play it alone
once. That was their tune. Bamberger then asked the group how that tune

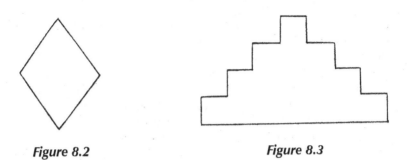

Figure 8.2   Figure 8.3

might be represented. Somebody said "It's like a diamond," and drew the shape in Figure 8.2.

It was not immediately clear to anyone how this might represent the tune. In discussing what it might mean, somebody drew the shape in Figure 8.3.

People then drew lines inside this figure, to show better what it meant to them. But some people filled them in like the version in Figure 8.4, and some people filled them in like the version in Figure 8.5.

I have given this example to a number of groups now, and it is always the case that for some people both these drawings make sense, and for some only one does—but it might be either one. Many for whom the first one is obvious simply cannot understand how the other could be taken to represent that tune, and vice versa. Why it is that some people find one obvious and some people the other, I do not know, and it is not the point of interest here. As a teacher, what is important is that they are different, valid ways of creating meaning of the same experience. The example emphasizes the point that experience is assimilated by each individual according to the nature of his or her internal structures.

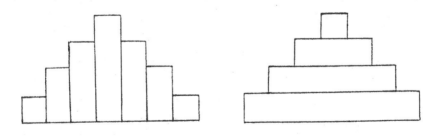

Figure 8.4   Figure 8.5

The teachers in this project became very good at watching the children in their classes, and making sense of what they were doing. A child in one class was having a difficult time learning long division. One day he invented his own way of doing it. It was quite an unusual way, which Joanne Cleary, to her credit, took time to understand. Soon after, he was finding it easy to do it her way, too, which Cleary understood like this: "It was that he understood what it was to divide, that he was moving numbers around and that once he could visualize his own way of figuring out the problem and understanding it and getting a hold on it, that he could see my way of doing it and understanding it, too. As long as I explained it to him the way he explained his to me." The mutual respect implied in that last phrase can almost alone bear the burden of this part of this chapter.

What exactly the child did, in the example above, would take too long to detail here (but see Duckworth, 1987). But there are two other examples I would like to give, which other teachers reported.

A second grader had the following subtraction problem:

$$42$$
$$-\ 27$$

Wendy Postlethwaite was able to learn that what he did was to subtract the 20 from the 40, giving him 20; then subtract the 7 from that, and add the 2.

Another second grader was adding, the following numbers:

$$1548$$
$$+\ 236$$

He gestured left to right as he explained how he did it: "Seventeen hundred and thirty-six," starting with the fifteen hundred, and adding the two hundred thirty-six. Then he added the forty, and then he added the eight. And after he had done it all in his head, he wrote down the answer.

We complicated this problem, making it:

$$1548$$
$$236$$
$$381$$
$$+\ 1682$$

And then we all looked for ways to add these numbers that did *not* call upon the conventional way of "carrying." With each person working to develop her own way, the 12 of us produced eight quite different ways. Many confessed that they never did carrying anyway when they really had to add.

In the discussion that followed, I asked what is special about the way the math series says that addition is "supposed" to be taught. Why do we insist on teaching that one way, given that there are so many possible ways? There was a long silence before one teacher said, only half in jest, that if you were ever stuck with a big addition problem to do and only a tiny piece of paper, the carrying method might be the only one you could fit on it. Many people laughed, but somehow there seemed to be a recognition that this might be the best answer they would come up with.

After some more time, the same person took her thought further: "I think there is no reason."

Joanne Cleary said, "One's *neat*, the conventional way is *neat*. So that you put down as few numbers as possible and come up with the right answer." She was implying that that was a possible source of its appeal, but that it was the very opposite of a good pedagogical basis: All the means for following the *reasons* are hidden.

Finally, Fern Fisher said, "I bet that if you look at the kids who are having trouble, they are the kids who *don't* have their own way to do it, and are trying to do it the regular way."

In my view, this remark takes us back to the first part of the chapter, Lucienne and the rattle. Meaning is not given to us in our encounters, but it is given *by* us—constructed by us, each in our own way, according to how our understanding is currently organized. As teachers, we need to respect the meaning our students are giving to the events that we share. In the interest of making connections between their understanding and ours, we must adopt an insider's view: We must seek to understand their sense as well as help them understand ours.

9

Making Sure That
Everybody Gets Home Safely

A N ADAPTATION OF THE Golden Rule—that we should strive for the security of others as we strive for our own security (Smith, 1985)—is evocative of a comment that gave rise to the title of this chapter. A number of our faculty and students were discussing the many recent national reports on schools, with their emphasis on individualism: children learning individually on computer consoles, for example, and teachers being evaluated by testing individual children. In that context, doctoral candidate Marrey Embers told us about being in heavy traffic that day, knowing she had to get where she was going by a certain time, and doing her best. She had to make one maneuver that infuriated another driver. He gave her the finger, which of course made her feel terrible. "All I wanted to do," she said, "was make sure everybody got home safely." It led us to think about the goal of driver education as "making sure that everybody gets home safely," a concrete example of the attitude of taking other people's security as seriously as you take your own.

This attitude would make a great difference, not only in driver education, but in education as a whole. But developing it is difficult. It flies in the face of most of the tenets taken for granted in our individualistic view of education. To develop that sense—that I must be responsible for others as I am for myself, in order for me to have a world in which I would like to live—is a complex job. Teachers and parents surely have a central role in that job, and that role is what I would like to discuss.

ABOUT PIAGET

I would like first to connect the view of this central role of teachers and parents with Piaget's work. Piaget began his studies by watching and listening to children in their own worlds. Many of his questions were derived from questions that his own children asked him (Piaget, 1945/1962b). Others came from long periods of watching children in their natural settings (Piaget, 1932/1965). He then found ways to ask other children to talk about the issues involved, and so to investigate them more systematically. What has come to be thought of as his "clinical method" in fact grew out of the preoccupations he had seen in children and the questions they had asked spontaneously.

If we are to learn about children's images of war and their feelings about the nuclear threat, the kind of approach we use is critical. I believe that we can best learn, not through interviewing children in accordance with preset agendas, but from the lives of children well observed by teachers and parents: in school, where children respond jointly to the diverse happenings of the day, often with a good deal of continuous concentration; at home, from their occasional comments, bedtime dream-talk, conversations in play, and spontaneous questions. These are fruitful sources of information about children's thoughts (see Engel, 1984, 1987). In my own case, what I have learned about children's thoughts and feelings in this area, I have learned from teachers.

I will say something later about this, but I would first like to say a little more about the way I think Piaget's work contributes to our thinking in this area. The basic point is how difficult it is to change what people think or feel about something simply by telling them or even showing them something different. This theme runs throughout Piaget's work.

Young children, for example, up to the age of 8 or 9 usually believe that a piece of clay will weigh more or less depending on its shape (Piaget & Inhelder, 1942/1974). Two balls are made to weigh the same on a pan balance; then one is changed into a sausage shape. A young child will estimate that the sausage now weighs more. Often, even when shown the sausage on the pan balanced with the ball on the other side, the child will convince himself or herself that the sausage *does* weigh more—"If you look real close, you can see, it's a little bit lower on this side." Other children may read the scale correctly but keep predicting that other shapes will result in a change of weight. As they see that the weight always remains unchanged, some then "give in" to the evidence (see chapter 3, p. 36), and conclude—but with no understanding—that the shape does not affect the weight. But if there then comes one last "trick" trial, where some clay is surreptitiously removed from the ball so that the sausage *does* weigh more, they accept that with relief as the "true" result, and return to their original, deeply held belief. Older children (and adults), in contrast, whose original, deeply held belief is that a change in shape will not affect the weight, reject the trick data. "There's something wrong with this scale," they'll say; or "Hey, what did you do?" In both cases what they really believe persists, in spite of evidence to the contrary (Smedslund, 1961).

Other Genevan work sheds light on what is involved in changing such deep-seated beliefs. The following example is based on two earlier experiments by Piaget. As was mentioned in chapters 1 and 3, very young children (4–5 years old) believe that the number of objects changes if their array is changed. This age group, if presented with the two arrangements shown in Figure 9.1, would say the upper set is more than the lower set, even if the two sets had first been lined up in one-to-one correspondence.

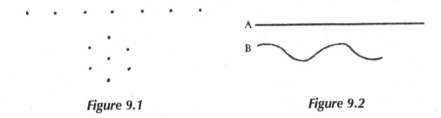

Figure 9.1	**Figure 9.2**

Slightly older children know that the number does not change with a change in display, but at 6 or 7 they still believe that lengths change if the placement of end points changes. With the lengths represented in Figure 9.2, for example, A would be judged longer than B, even if the two had first been seen to match in length.

Magali Bovet devised a beautiful set of experiments in which 5- and 6-year-olds could use either number of segments or end points as a base for their judgment of length (Inhelder, Sinclair, & Bovet, 1974). One of the most difficult problems for the children was to build a road as long as the one shown in Figure 9.3, but with shorter segments. Figure 9.4 shows three solutions, all of them being attempts to preserve both the same number *and* the same end points. In solution B, the last stick is broken into two pieces. In solution C, an extra half segment is added: "It's not very the same," this 5-year-old said, but he was unable to find a better solution.

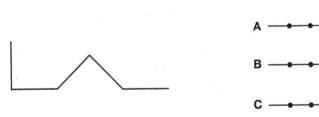

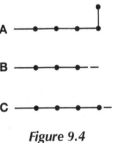

Figure 9.3	**Figure 9.4**

The general pattern here is that there are two different ways to judge the length, and these ways conflict. Looking at these lines with number of segments in mind leads to one decision; looking at them with end points in mind leads to another. The two different ways of thinking about this produce two different conclusions. In this experiment, once a child recognized that conflict, he or she always moved to a more nearly adequate solution.

That is the fundamental point. The way to move a person's thoughts and feelings is not by trying to excise them and replace them with other thoughts and feelings. Rather, it is to try to understand the person's thoughts and feelings, and to work from there. It means having the person articulate his or her own thoughts in different areas and in different ways and see where they run into conflict with themselves. That usually means *acknowledging* complexity rather than replacing one simple way of looking at things with another simple way of looking at things—acknowledging the complexity and seeing where that leads.

THE WORK OF TEACHERS

As I have described in earlier chapters, much of my work with teachers includes helping them acknowledge the complexity in what seems like simple things they thought they understood, or helping them realize the details of their own understanding and appreciate that their own ways of understanding are valid. In the course of taking seriously their own ways of understanding, the teachers also come to take seriously others' ways of understanding. Thus they come to take seriously the thinking and feelings of the children they teach.

A number of teachers who had come to respect their own, others', and the children's thoughts and feelings formed the core of a group in Cambridge, Massachusetts, who met to support one another in their attempts to ascertain and respond to children's concerns about the nuclear threat. Several nonteachers with similar concerns, including myself, met with them.*

The issues were hard. In one fourth/fifth-grade class, a parent came regularly to discuss current events. One day he brought a letter written to a newspaper by a woman living in a town in western Massachusetts to which Cambridge residents were scheduled to evacuate in the event of nuclear war. Jeanne, their teacher, told our group that the children "were

---

*The members of this group, whose work is reported in the following pages, were Larry Aronson, Joanne Cleary, Mary DiSchino, Eleanor Duckworth, Brenda Engel, Louise Grant, Isabel Hanelin, Judy Lazrus, Michael Mitchell, Linda Pratt, Mary Rizzuto, Abbie Schirmer, Peggy Schirmer, Mark Skvirsky, and Nick Wadan.

concerned about enough public bathrooms, which is one of the things the woman was writing about. Then they got more off what she was saying, and more into what they were going to do. . . . How can you breathe under all that dirt? What would happen if they were in school? How would the people in school know? Who was going to put the last shovel of dirt on top of the fall-out shelters? . . . A lot of them kept saying, 'Boy, this is really scary!' I said, 'Yes, it is.' Someone else said, 'Yes, but you have to know about it, have to think about it.'"

Robert, another teacher-member of the group, asked, "How do you answer when they say, 'What happens if the bomb takes only an hour instead of two days?'" "Well, it's obvious that there's nothing to do," Joanne answered. "It's beyond your control. They have questions that I myself have asked about the Civil Defense plan. . . . A lot of them said they were going to get in a plane and go somewhere. . . . They thought that everyone should build their own bomb shelter. . . . Someone said, 'In Hiroshima, after the bomb, no one could go near it for a month. How do they expect us to go back in a week?' They talked about the freeze and about reducing nuclear weapons. One child said, 'If I was the president, I'd just surrender and give up.' The thing that happened in the discussion was that certain kids began to fantasize, and make it into a joke . . . to laugh about it."

Jeanne realized they couldn't cope with it any more, she pointed out to the children that some people needed to turn it into a joke, because it was too scary. They ended up saying they were all very scared. There was no more giggling. "Some of them were almost turning their whole bodies around. . . . There was a lot of physical energy . . . but most of them wanted to continue. The next period was relatively quiet. . . . They seemed relaxed. There was lots of conversation in small groups. I think they had enough time to express themselves." The children then wrote letters to President Reagan expressing their fears. They did not, however, write "Dear" President Reagan.

At the next session, three weeks later, Jeanne reported, "Something strange happened in this whole business of talking about nuclear war. They became very closemouthed; it did a number on my relationship with them. It really bothered me. I didn't know if I wanted to do this any more." They compromised: The class would not talk about war any more, but about solving "our own conflicts in the classroom." Writing letters was "real scary" for the children, perhaps because "It's real scary for me. Sometimes, as a teacher you can't hide your feelings. Kids are real perceptive."

Jeanne continued, "I've always had a lot of discussions with them but recently I've felt the discussions becoming more and more one-sided, with me doing the talking, the reason being that they didn't want to talk about it." Margaret asked if they had talked at all about working for peace. "Yes, and I told them there were a lot of parents doing things . . . But I began to think these kids think they are too young. I'm beginning to think they *are* too young to talk about some of this stuff. The kids feel (and I'm beginning to feel) they have a right to be protected from this stuff by their parents and by the adults; and if we as adults are doing our best to protect these children, then there's not a lot of reason to go further than mentioning it to the kids or writing something . . . but to carry on longer than this or do more depth, more explaining about what's going on is probably not real necessary, because the kids, I think, are right, that they have a right to be protected."

Sandra said that, for our children, war is "a very far-away kind of notion," since we have never experienced it here. On the other hand, for her second- and third-graders, there is "an incredible personal fear of violence that follows my kids—having violence done to them on the street." Joanne replied that she thought her children were not thinking about violence, but that they were afraid they would not be able to grow up and fulfill their dreams. "I want to grow up and have two babies, and I want my babies to grow up. So it is real personal. A lot of these kids weren't really talking about violence."

Finally, Jeanne talked about a "real exciting thing" that her class was doing throughout this time. A volunteer in the class was going to the Soviet Union, and the children were preparing a book for her to take, on children's culture in the United States. There were 12 pages of items of importance to them—hockey, television shows, clothes; a selection of poems; a questionnaire section. One child wrote, "Russia and the United States are enemies. They might have a nuclear war. That would be awful. It would be very scary. Many people would die. You might die. I might die. Everybody might die. I'm scared, are you?" They were excited by the book—"very positive."

In another session, Helen discussed how hard it is to know what to do about your own feelings and beliefs when they are different from some children's. She talked about two children in her class who were "really pro-nuclear," in disagreement not only with her but with all the other members of the class. One child from Vietnam, she said, claimed you have to have weapons to get food; the other kept saying, "The Russians have more." "I try not to let them feel that they're wrong (although in my opinion they are wrong)." The children talked about the need for guns to protect property, and Helen tried to point out the difference between guns and nuclear weapons. The argument that the Russians have more, Helen found "real difficult to deal with." Linda asked if she couldn't say, "We have enough." "We talked about that," Helen replied, "but then that 'more' comes back. Quantity seems to be more important than the power of the missile. Ten is bigger than eight. Somehow we have to develop in kids' thinking not necessarily 'more or less' but a whole new concept."

Another oversimple idea, Helen pointed out, on the part of children who are concerned about the nuclear threat, was the nature of decision making. "For my kids, the government is President Reagan: 'How come he . . . ? It's always *he.*'"

Judith Lazrus, a teacher of second and third graders, had been particularly concerned not to introduce issues that were not the children's. She came to the fourth session delighted with a discussion that had taken place after her class had read a book recommended by another teacher at the previous meeting, *The Stranger* (Ringi, 1968). The story is about a giant that appears in town, incurring the hostility of the townspeople, who bring out their cannon. The townspeople reach only to the top of the giant's foot. Finally the giant cries, causing a flood, which raises the townspeople to the level of his face, where they become friends. "It was just wonderful. We were studying giants in the class so it didn't feel as if I was pushing things on the kids for my own purposes. We had a wonderful discussion in class about prejudice and war. It came up in a very nice, natural way. It made me think about the fact that for my age class, bringing up these issues can be very well done through books. At the end of the story, I asked, 'Now, why do you think the people wanted to fight the giant?' 'They were scared of him.' 'He was so big, they thought he was an enemy.' 'And who do you think our enemies are?' I asked. One child said, 'The Russians' and another child said, 'The Germans.' And I said to a child in our class who is German, 'Are you our enemy?' and she said, 'No.' And then somebody said, 'The Japanese,' and a kid said, 'I have a friend who's Japanese and he's not my enemy.' And then a child said, 'The Greeks' and I said, 'Well, why do you say the Greeks?'—I have three Greek children in my class—and he said, 'They fought us in a war, it's kind of embarrassing to talk about it now.' So I said, 'Are you talking about the Maccabees in the Hannukah story?' and he said 'Yes.' And I said, 'From a thousand years ago?' and he said, 'I guess it was a long time ago.' So then they said, 'The Cubans' and another child said, 'The Africans,' and I said to a child who's from South Africa, 'Are you our enemy?' and he said, 'No way.' And then another child said, 'I'm from Africa too [she meant generations before] and I'm not an enemy, either.' So I said that sometimes we think that people are our enemies because of a past war or because the people appear different in looks or customs. 'Why do you think the townspeople think the giant is an enemy?' And they said, 'Maybe a long time ago some giants hurt the people.' And then another child said, 'Maybe because he looks so different.' And I said, 'Well was he really an enemy in fact?' and they said, 'No.' So I said, What do you think the message is the author wants to convey?' and the kids had various antiwar statements. It was kind of interesting because it isn't a real war, it's just the bringing out of the cannon but that's sort of their jump to a statement about war, which I thought was very sophisticated. And then one child said, 'There's no reason ever to have a war.' He's a very quiet but very sturdy kind of child that other children look up to. So then I said, 'Now, why do you say that?' There was such a long pause that I almost couldn't wait that long, and then he said, 'Well, the people who kill each other might really be friends.' It worked out wonderfully, it was so appropriate."

Three themes come through in the notes of these sessions. The first is the teachers' excellent chance to help the rest of us understand children's thoughts and feelings about the nuclear threat. The second is the importance for teachers to be accepting and respectful of the children's thoughts and feelings. The third is how easy it is for children—and for many adults—to see things simplistically, and how important it is to try to help people see greater complexity by trying to draw out the conflicts in their own thoughts. It is this third point that relates most directly to the title of this chapter.

The tendency to oversimplify became clear to us during these sessions. The revised view of driver education requires thinking in components much more complex than we and they, good and bad, bigger and smaller, more and less, friend and enemy, winner and loser. The notion that President Reagan could simply stop the arms race tomorrow if he so decided is another example of oversimplification. Perhaps the most pernicious form is the notion of solving a conflict through a single, simple, speedy act of violence. This series of meetings took place during the Falklands war, and it became clear that, while the children were terrified by the threat of the bomb, many were fascinated by the fact of war. War seems to be different—explosive and exciting. Similarly, it seems to me, one of the great characteristics of the violence in television is its simplicity. In children's television, that is the way to solve any problem: bop the opponent on the head, and that's the end of it. And it is like the children's notions of the Falklands war: Blow up a battleship and the problem is solved. I think a critical theme to develop with children is that it is hard work to resolve conflicts. Resolutions cannot be reduced to having the good guys win and the bad guys lose. It takes hard work to manage to have no losers—to have everyone get home safely. And it takes hard work for teachers to develop the sense in children that this complex goal is feasible and desirable (see Kreidler, 1984).

What I have learned from the teachers with whom I have worked is that, just as there is no simple solution to the arms race, there is also no simple answer to how to work with children in the classroom. It is a matter of being present as a whole person, with your own thoughts and feelings, and of accepting children as whole people, with their thoughts and feelings. It is a matter of working very hard to find out what those thoughts and feelings are, as a starting point for developing a view of a world in which people are as much concerned about other people's security as they are about their own.

10

Twenty-Four, Forty-Two, and I Love You: Keeping It Complex

I N MY ENTIRE LIFE as a student, I remember only twice being given the opportunity to come up with my own ideas, a fact I consider typical and terrible. I would like to start this paper by telling how I came to realize that schooling could be different from what I had experienced.

FIGURING OUT MY OWN IDEAS

After my university studies, I joined the Elementary Science Study, a curriculum development program. I had been hired because of my background with Piaget, studying how science and math ideas develop in children, and had no formal training in either education or science. While the first of these lacks was probably a liability, the second turned out to be a great boon. I was with a highly imaginative bunch of scientists and teachers of science, all trying to put together their favorite kinds of experience to entice children. Because I was innocent in science I made a great "sample child" for my colleagues, and I spent a lot of time exploring the materials and the issues that they came up with. Of the many areas I explored, three seemingly unrelated ones came together in a way that showed me what learning could be like. I got hooked and have been an educator ever since, trying to develop learning experiences of that sort for every child and every teacher. It was the first time—with two exceptions mentioned in the opening sentence—that I got excited about my own ideas. I had been excited about ideas before, but they had always been somebody else's ideas. My struggle had always been to get in on what I thought somebody else knew and knew to be important. This was the first time that I had a sense of what it was like to pay attention to my own ideas.

It is, of course, exhilarating to find that your own ideas can lead you somewhere. Few feelings are likely to be more effective in getting you to keep on thinking about things on your own. I would like to focus here, though, not so much on my feelings as on the nature of my understanding.

One team of colleagues was developing ways to study balances. They posed problems with a simple balance that consisted of a strip of pegboard resting on a support, with metal washers as weights. In each case, they started with the balance in equilibrium, horizontal. Then, holding the balance, they moved one or more weights and asked me to adjust other weights so that when they let go, the balance arm would remain horizontal (see Elementary Science Study, 1967b).

For example, they set up a relatively easy problem with the balance, as shown in Figure 10.1. Where should I add one washer, so the board would stay balanced? My solution is shown in Figure 10.2.

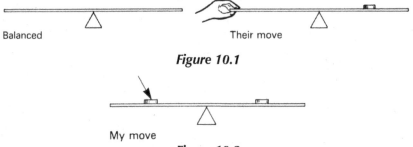

Balanced   Their move

Figure 10.1

My move

Figure 10.2

They then gave me a problem that I found more difficult: they presented me with the board balanced with one washer on one side and two washers stacked on the other side, but closer to the middle. If they moved the single washer a certain distance to the right, how could I move *just one* of the other two washers, so the board would still balance (Figure 10.3)? I found a solution that worked (Figure 10.4).

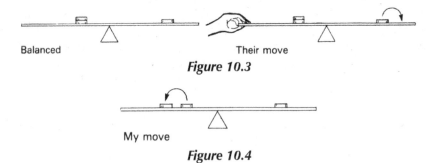

Balanced   Their move

Figure 10.3

My move

Figure 10.4

Through this example and others similar to it, I found that it did not seem to matter where the washers started; I just had to move one of them the same distance the original had been moved on the other side, but in the opposite direction.

My grand triumph was the following problem. To start with, they put three washers in a pile on one side so as to balance one on the other (Figure 10.5). Then they moved the single one a long way—practically to the center (Figure 10.6). Again, how could I move *just one* of the others so it would still balance?

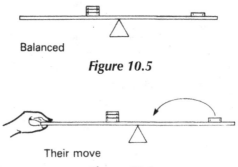

Balanced

Figure 10.5

Their move

Figure 10.6

Well, I knew by now that I should try to move it just as far in the op-posite direction. But there was no room. I ran into the middle almost right away. So what should I do? Move it in the *same* direction? That didn't seem right. Move it as far as I could towards the middle—just barely short of the middle? I thought I might try that. But the one I decided to try was my first idea—moving the washer in the opposite direction, even though it meant *crossing* the middle (Figure 10.7). It felt to me like a very daring move. And it worked! The rule worked, even across the middle. I remem-ber saying to my colleagues at the time that I felt like Helen Keller.

My move

Figure 10.7

I did not stop then. Among other things, I tried designing balances myself, and eventually even figured out what the differences were be-tween a balance and a seesaw that accounted for the fact that the balance with nothing on it is horizontal, while a seesaw with nobody on it always has one end up in the air.

A second group was working on a study of what they called *Gases and "Airs"* (Elementary Science Study, 1967a). The tight sequence of reasoning demanded by this unit turned out not to work very well with elementary school children, but the unit did entail a wonderful variety of experiences that, for me, gave substance to what gases and airs are. It started from a close and critical look at the classic school science lab demonstration of burning a candle in a tube inverted over water: the water rises, the candle goes out, and one has "proven" that the atmosphere is 20 percent oxygen. But, there are some problems, as my colleagues pointed out. For one thing, the water doesn't rise gradually as the candle burns; it rises suddenly after the flame is out. If it were gradually using up the oxygen wouldn't the water gradually rise? Another problem: the amount that it rises may indeed average about 20 percent, but it varies widely (Figure 10.8a); in contrast, when wet steel wool is wedged into a tube above water and left to rust overnight, it *does* use up all the oxygen, and the water rises exactly the same amount in each tube (Figure 10.8b).

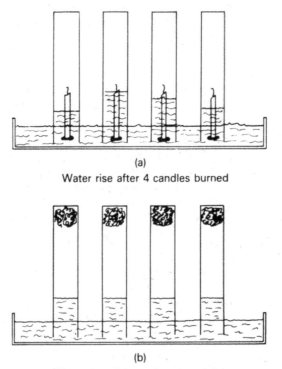

(a)

Water rise after 4 candles burned

(b)

Water rise with steelwool overnight

Figure 10.8

The "demonstration" with a burning candle turns out to be a hoax, based on a totally different phenomenon. The candle actually goes out long before all the oxygen is used up (for various reasons). While the candle burns, it heats the air so that the air expands; some of it leaves the tube, bubbling out through the water in the dish. While the remaining air cools, the water rises to take the place of the air that bubbled out. As one who had been taken in by that demonstration in my own schooling, I was fascinated to explore the more complex relationships that had been covered up by it. To begin with, I was intrigued by the idea of different kinds of "airs" easily available to us: air that a candle had burned in; air that steel wool had rusted in; lung air; room air; air that seeds had sprouted in. Could a candle burn in the steel wool air? Would another rusting steel wool ball pull up the same amount of water in steel wool air? Would seeds sprout in candle air?

I became very good at putting into a tube whatever kind of air I wanted to. Using a syringe, I could take air from any tube and put it into another tube that had no air in it (by virtue of being full of water). Bubbles came to be real things filled with some one kind of air—room air, lung air, steel wool air, or other. Putting an Alka Seltzer tablet under the lip of a water-filled tube, for example, created a tube full of Alka Seltzer air (Figure 10.9).

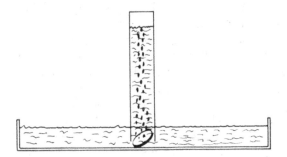

Figure 10.9

I came to imagine the inverse of filling any container with liquid. As long as your container has no other liquid in it already, you can put it straight under the dripping liquid, and you'll capture all that is falling right over the opening. In the inverse, as in the case of some escaping Alka Seltzer air, you could think of it as shown in Figure 10.10 (see next page). In a bucket of water, move a water-filled jar over the bubbles, and you will collect the escaping Alka Seltzer air.

Figure 10.10

This is not, I hasten to point out, intended as a practical example. I've never happened to be holding a water-filled jar upside down in a bucket of water when an Alka Seltzer tablet dropped into the bucket. But conceptually it helped me a lot: an "air" was for me as real as a liquid.

A third area that I explored originated in my attempts to build on my Piaget background. I thought of trying to find some situations for young children in which a certain order was maintained in spite of some striking change. It occurred to me to use the constant ordering of liquids floating on each other in a tube. Though the idea had less mileage in it for little children than I had thought it might, it did have some value (see Duckworth, 1964). More importantly for my education, however, it led me into a long series of explorations with liquids, starting with trying to make as many floating layers as I could in one tube. If I did not shake the tube, I could manage about six layers, and I experimented with dyes to keep the layers distinguishable. I expanded my horizons to include solid pieces—seeds, bits of plastic, bits of wood, bits of food. I don't recall any of these specifics, but a radish seed, say, would fall through three layers and sit on the fourth—and *every* radish seed would do that. One kind of plastic would sit on the second layer, another kind would fall through four, and so on. Some material (I do not now remember what, and it took me a long time to find this material) stopped at the top of the top surface, and floated there.

I also tried to mix alcohol and water so that the resulting liquid would have exactly the same density as the salad oil I was working with—to see what would happen when neither liquid would necessarily float on top of the other. Would I be able to make stripes with them? Or would they stand side by side, with a vertical separation? Or what? I found that the oil always formed itself into a single enormous sphere in the middle of the water–alcohol liquid; and that this sphere *always* moved slowly either to the top or to the bottom of the water–alcohol liquid. No matter how delicately I added one drop of water or of alcohol, I could never get the sphere of oil to float right in the middle—it was always either *just* heavier or *just* lighter. (These explorations came back in my own teaching more than 10 years later; see Duckworth, 2001b.)

Six or eight months after I started learning science like this, someone presented a puzzle that happened to draw on the three areas I had been exploring, and I think I was the only person around at the time who put together the right prediction. On the left-hand side of this balance is a plastic bag sealed airtight; an Alka Seltzer tablet is stuck in a piece of plasticene near the top, and some water is in the bottom. On the right-hand side is just enough weight to balance the arm (Figure 10.11). The question is, what will happen to the balance if the bag is shaken, and the tablet falls into the water?

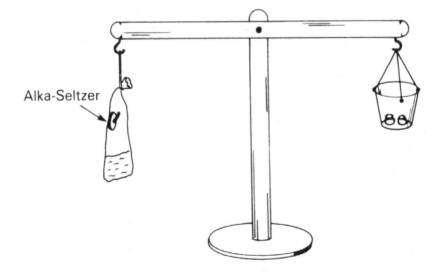

Alka-Seltzer

Figure 10.11

Most of the people present knew that when the tablet fell into the water, a lot of "Alka Seltzer air" would be formed and the bag would fill out. Some people thought that the arm would remain level, because the same matter that was in the bag to start with was still in it at the end, even if in a different form, so the weight would not change at all. Others thought that the left side would go down, because Alka Seltzer air (being, so they knew, carbon dioxide) is heavier than room air. My prediction, which turned out in fact to be the case, was that the left side would go *up*, because the filled-out bag would take up more space, while adding no more weight, thus being more buoyant in the surrounding sea of air.

I believe that it was because I started from my own ideas and found my own ways into these parts of the world that my understanding of balances, "airs," and floating belonged so thoroughly to me. Notice the difference between what usually happens in formal education—presenting the simplest, neatest explanation of "the law of moments," "the composition of the atmosphere," "density," "buoyancy," or whatever—and my experience of being enticed with the funny, frustrating, intriguing, unpredictable complexities of the world around me. Instead of disassociating myself from my own interests in my struggle to find out what whoever was supposed to "know" might have understood by the word "buoyancy," my learning was based on my own connections, within the idiosyncrasies of my own system of thoughts. The very complexities of the subject matters enabled me to connect with them, made them accessible, and the integrity of my own ideas enabled me to retrieve those connections when they could help me understand a new situation.

Lisa Schneier (1990) has put it this way, the relationship between complexity and accessibility:

> [W]e organize subject matter into a neat series of steps which assumes a profound uniformity among students. We sand away at the interesting edges of subject matter until it is so free from its natural complexities, so neat, that there is not a crevice left as an opening. All that is left is to hand it to them, scrubbed and smooth, so that they can view it as outsiders. (p. 4)

The experience of my science explorations was the exact opposite.

THE UNIVERSE IN A SENTENCE

My favorite radio show is "A Hitchhiker's Guide to the Galaxy." In one episode, a computer is built expressly for the purpose of answering the question, "What is the meaning of life, the universe, and everything?"

When it is ready, they ask it if it can answer that question. It says, yes, it can, but that it will take, as I recall, seven million years. They say, "Well, OK, go to it." Seven million years later, whoever is around goes to learn the answer. The computer says that it does have the answer, but that they might be a little disappointed. "No, no," they say, "go ahead, what is it?" "Forty-two," it says.

Who knows? Maybe forty-two *is* the answer. But such an answer is of no more help to us than no answer at all. It does not speak to our level of interaction with the mysteries of our existence.

Note the parallels with the following story from Lisa Schneier's class in an urban high school:

> It had been a lively class, with the various Juliets taking turns standing on a table and the Romeos making elaborate and often comical gestures as they stood below. . . . A group of ninth graders and I were working on a scene from *Romeo and Juliet*. They had chosen to read the balcony scene aloud and were acting it out, taking turns with the parts. They took the difficult language and its foreign style into stride, at times staying true to the text and at others replacing or skipping words and phrases. It was clear as they spoke that at points the words held meaning for them and at others they hadn't a clue as to what it was that they were reading. But we didn't stop much for discussion; the students were enjoying this kind of involvement with each other, and there was a momentum in the reading that I didn't want to interrupt.
>
> But our last Romeo of the day finally did interrupt it. We had started the scene again to give more readers a turn, and he had begun to wade through his first speech. In the midst of it, he broke off, shook his head impatiently, and turned to me. "He loves her. *That's* what he's saying. So why all that other stuff? Why not just say it? I love you! [to the current Juliet]. There!" And then in a memorable tone, a mixture of humor, frustration, and honest confusion: "Why can't he just say what he means?" (Schneier, 1990, pp. 1–2)

Why doesn't Shakespeare just say what he means? Of course that's what he *is* doing: "what he means" is complex. The words he chooses are the best he can choose to say what he wants to say. Poems and stories and paintings and dance and music are not just fancy ways of saying what could be said in a sentence. "I love you" does not quite express everything that Shakespeare meant, just as "forty-two" does not quite substitute for living our lives. There is a parallel here between a poet and a teacher: the universe is complex; science is complex; the poet's thoughts and feelings are complex. "Forty-two" doesn't do the trick. Neither does "buoyancy." Nor, in this case, does "I love you."

In this spirit, when studying a poem with a class, I start by asking students what they notice—an invitation to keep every complexity of the poem under consideration. People notice very different things, and almost every thing noticed leads to a question or another thought. Putting together what everyone notices and returning to the poem to try to look for answers to the questions leads to an understanding of the poem that is greatly expanded for each of us. Take, for instance, this Frost poem:

Design

I found a dimpled spider, fat and white,
On a white heal-all, holding up a moth
Like a white piece of rigid satin cloth—
Assorted characters of death and blight
Mixed ready to begin the morning right,
Like the ingredients of a witches' broth—
A snow-drop spider, a flower like froth,
And dead wings carried like a paper kite.

What had that flower to do with being white,
The wayside blue and innocent heal-all?
What brought the kindred spider to that height,
Then steered the white moth thither in the night?
What but design of darkness to appall?—
If design govern in a thing so small.

(Frost, 1979, p. 302)

Somebody will notice that there is a lot of white. Somebody will mention the rhyme scheme, or will imitate the rhythm. Somebody will mention that the first part of the poem seems to present a picture, and the second half seems to ask questions about it. Different people point out different possible plays on words: kindred and dreadful kin; appall and a funeral pall; a paper kite and a bird kite; morning right and morning rite; morning and mourning. Different people have different thoughts about whether the darkness is that which appalls, or that which is appalled. Arguments develop about why the flower is described as white in the first line, and blue in the ninth. This is a bare beginning. A group of adults can easily go on for more than an hour with increasing interest, and everybody's initial understanding is expanded by hearing from others.*

I have always been frightened by being asked: "What is the meaning of this poem?" My reaction is, "How could I know? I'm no good with poems!" But it is easy for me to point out something that I notice about it,

---

*For an analysis of one high school student's developing understanding of this poem, see Schneier, 1990

and in turn to listen to what other people notice about it, and to figure out whether I think that what they say makes sense, and why, and what other thoughts their ideas provoke in me. Many students have feelings similar to these. One in particular said that she had determined when we started discussing the poem that she would not say a word, knowing nothing about poems and feeling scared by them. But as she heard the various things that people were saying, her own thoughts developed, and she finally couldn't contain herself, so much did she have to say and so strongly did she feel about it. One student referred to himself as a "poem-phobe," not knowing what "the meaning" was. This prompted another student to say, "If Frost had been able to put what he had to say into a sentence, he would have. So don't worry that you can't."

I recognized that this was the same thought I had about the accessibility of science. It is in acknowledging the complexity of the poem, not "sand[ing] away at the interesting edges," to use Schneier's words, that we render it accessible. Our understanding seeks to do justice to the complexity that the poet sought to render, and by the same token it belongs to us. Just as the poet seeks to present his thoughts and feelings in all their complexity, and in so doing opens a multiplicity of paths into his meaning, likewise a teacher who presents a subject matter in all its complexity makes it more accessible by opening a multiplicity of paths into it.

"I KNOW THERE ARE TWENTY-FOUR"

I ask students to do the following: Take a fistful of four different kinds of markers (four colors of paper clips or four kinds of dried beans, for example) to represent four children who are going to the movies. Lay out the different arrangements in which they can sit in four adjacent seats. Some students ask, "Do I really have to do this? I know there are twenty-four." And I say, yes, you really have to; the question isn't how many arrangements, the question is what are the arrangements—each of them. (It happens, not infrequently, that someone who has impatiently affirmed that there will be twenty-four, because he or she knows a formula, has trouble generating the actual arrangements—which strikes me as not too different from knowing that the meaning of life is forty-two.) And the question behind that is, when you think you have laid out all the arrangements, how could you convince yourself or anybody else that you don't have any repeats, and that you are not missing any? I urge the reader to try this before continuing, and to see what system she or he comes up with.

Most people who are not yet comfortable with math start this exercise more or less randomly, but many systems emerge when they think about whether they have generated all the possible arrangements. In what follows I will present some of these systems.

Some people make diagonals, such as the P in the following arrangements:

PBLM

MPBL

LMPB

BLMP

This could be called the "revolving" system, where the last letter to the right revolves around to appear on the left and everything moves over one. This looks systematic and promising, but when they follow this rule to a fifth step it turns out to be a repeat of the first (PBLM). So they have to side-step, and think about how to find the various different possible starting points.

Another system which keeps P on the diagonal is the "squeeze between" system:

PBLM

BPLM

BLPM

BLMP

Move P to the right by squeezing it in between the next two letters. Again, the question arises about what to do after the fourth.

You could reinterpret that system to be not "squeeze between" but "exchange": Keep P moving on the diagonal by exchanging it with whatever letter is in the place where it will be moving. That explains the four above, and allows you to keep going:

PLMB

LPMB

LMPB

LMBP

PMBL

MPBL

MBPL

MBLP

At this point, after twelve arrangements, we get back to the starting point. Is that, then, all there are? Is there a reason to think that this system would have generated all we could possibly get? Is there a reason to think it is inadequate? Or can't we tell anything about it at all?

Not all approaches use diagonals. For the next ones I will limit the discussion to three children in three seats in order to write out fewer arrangements.

Many people, as a system starts to emerge, lay out something like this:

LMB

LBM

MLB

By this time they have an idea about what they will put next, and most think that their idea is the only sensible, systematic possibility. The first surprise is that there are two different, almost equally popular, next moves:

MBL or BLM

And the two completed lists would look like this:

I		II	
	LMB		LMB
	LBM		LBM
	MLB		MLB
	MBL		BLM
	BLM		MBL
	BML		BML

The system on the left started with two L's in the first position, then put two M's in the first position, and then two B's. The system on the right started with the L's in the first position, then moved the L's to the second position, and then to the last position. In both cases, people can say, "Once I have one position filled, there are only two ways to fill the other two, so these are the only possible six ways for three children to sit." They are two very different systems, and yet they end up with the same exact arrangements.

Playing this out with four children and four seats, using, for example, system I, would give this result:

PLMB

PLBM

PMLB

PMBL

PBLM

PBML

There would be six different arrangements with P in the first position. There would, therefore, be six ways to put each of the four letters in the first position; that is, four times six ways altogether. (Playing out system II above, P would end up in each position six times—again, four times six ways altogether.)

One nine-year-old—no math whiz, he—after placing a few arrangements according to no system that I could see, started to make new ones by reversing pairs in the ones he already had. (From PLBM, say, he might make PBLM; or from MLPB he might make LMPB.) He worked slowly, and for a long time he would make a new arrangement and then check to see whether he already had it rather than generate a new one from some overall system he had in his mind. After a long time, though (he worked at this for close to an hour), and as he explained to me what he was doing, a system emerged; he started to know how to look for ones that were missing and to fill in the gaps. It was a system that was totally new to me. He never articulated it as clearly as I am about to here, but essentially his system was this: Start with one block, let's say P, and pair it up with each of the other blocks in turn. Let's start with the pair PL:

Put them in the middle, and put the two remaining blocks at either end. Then reverse the two on the ends. Then reverse the originals (PL becomes LP) and repeat: then put the end-ones in the middle and the middle-ones at the ends and start over.

BPLM

MPLB

BLPM

MLPB

PBML

LBMP

PMBL

LMBP

Now we have eight. Starting with PM gives us another eight and starting with PB gives us eight more. This way you get three times eight instead of four times six. Is there any reason that this system is a convincing one? When you've started with P and each of the other letters and done all the rearrangements as described, is there any reason to think that you would necessarily hit all the possibilities?

I could go on. Looking for relationships among the systems enhances our understanding even more: What is the relationship between a system that has four variations of six positions and a system that has three variations of eight positions? The point is that the more you look at this question, the more ways there are to see it. "Twenty-four" is a sadly impoverished version of all that can be understood about it. Just as with the poem, each different way of thinking about it illuminates all of the others—a wonderful pay-off for allowing for the complexities of the matter. Note that in this math problem *as with the poem*, individuals tend to think that their way is the one way to look at it, unless they are in a social context where other possibilities are presented; then it is not a matter of replacing their point of view, but of enhancing it.

Of course, many people raise for themselves the question of arrangements of five children, and work out a formula that applies to any number—a formula which, then, *represents* their understanding instead of substituting for it.

One further comment: Another nine-year-old pointed out to me that, once he had laid out all the arrangements (and he came up with twenty-four), if he removed the first item from all of them, the twenty-four arrangements of *three* items are still all different from each other. After some thought, I can more or less understand that this must be so. But it certainly brought me up short when he raised the idea.

EXTENDED CLINICAL INTERVIEWING

Now I want to move, with one last example, to develop the idea of a kind of research that such a view of teaching and learning leads to and calls for: extended clinical interviewing. Early in my work in education I found that the Piagetian methods I used to investigate learners' understanding—that is, having them take their own understanding seriously, pursue their own questions, and struggle through their own conflicts—was at the same time a way of engaging people in pursuing their own learning. People became avid learners, even in fields which had not interested them before, and my ways of trying to follow their thoughts were, in fact, excellent ways to help them learn.

Later I came to realize that the circle is full: This way of helping people learn is at the same time an important form of research about how people's ideas develop. It really amounts to Piaget's clinical interviewing, extended in two ways: it can be extended over time, and it can be carried out with more than one person at a time.

This approach requires, however, more than just an interviewer's questions. Many of the interviews in Piaget's early books used only the interviewee's previous experience as the basis of discussion (what makes the wind; where are thoughts located). In contrast, the questions that I found most often engaged interviewees in the pursuit of their own learning grew from his later work, where children tried to explain or predict or describe relationships in something which they had before them and could transform or otherwise keep returning to (the last example above is based on an investigation in Piaget and Inhelder, 1951/1975). The more surprises people encountered, and the more possibilities they became aware of, the more they wanted to continue to do and to think.

Extended clinical interviewing as a research approach requires just as much resourcefulness in finding appropriate materials, questions, and activities as any good curriculum development does. Whether it be poems, mathematical situations, historical documents, liquids, or music, our offerings must provide some accessible entry points, must present the subject matter from different angles, elicit different responses from different learners, open a variety of paths for exploration, engender conflicts, and provide surprises; we must encourage learners to open out beyond themselves, and help them realize that there are other points of view yet to be uncovered—that they have not yet exhausted the thoughts they might have about this matter.

Only if people *are* interested in expanding their views does one learn anything about how people's ideas actually develop. Curriculum development goes hand in hand with following the intricacies of the development of ideas. (This intertwined relationship led me first to refer to this research as "teaching-research," a phrase I retain in the last chapter.)

Once we are willing to accept the real complexities of subject matter, we find that they lurk even in the most unlikely places. One of the abilities I seek to develop in teachers is the ability to recognize unsuspected complexities in what seems like straightforward, even elementary, material. (David Hawkins, 1978, has pointed out how mistaken it is to think that "elementary" ideas are necessarily simple.) It is always in confronting such complexities that one develops real understanding.

"AND THAT'S HOW THEY DID THE LATITUDE LINES" . . .
"IT MAKES ME DIZZY"

I want to close with one detailed example of extended clinical interviewing that shows what can happen when learners confront, rather than cover, complexities. I want to show the process as it actually takes place in a group over time. I hope to be able to convey the relationships—both interpersonal and ideational—that this approach to learning entails. I hope to reveal the interplay of thoughts and feelings, the tantalizing confusions, the tortuous development of new insights, and the crowning accomplishment possible when people struggle honestly with their own ideas. I think it is a rare picture of minds at work.

The account involves some of the teachers from the MIT Project (Bamberger, Duckworth, & Lampert, 1991) mentioned in the previous four chapters. After the official end of the two-year project, about 10 of the original 15 teachers wanted to keep going. We met periodically through a third year, as we tried to decide which strands of our work together we wanted to continue. For six of the teachers, moon-watching was really the most passionate interest. This was the experience that they felt had given them the greatest insights into themselves and their students as learners, and thus into themselves as teachers. (For more on moon-watching, see DiSchino, 1987.) So for thirteen more years, seven of us* continued to meet with a focus on moon-watching. (Now, almost 30 years later, six of us still work in schools, and we still meet, though less regularly.) For some time now I have been a learner like everybody else. This, in fact, does not change my role very much. In all of my extended clinical interviewing I keep asking people to say what they mean again, please, more clearly. In this group I have no special standing in asking for such clarification.

I did not set up the conflict described below. It emerged on its own as we continued to try to understand the motions of the bodies in our solar system. I may have played a role in keeping the conflict on the floor as an issue worth trying to resolve, and in refusing to believe too readily that we had resolved it. The discussion presented here is about what "east" means, which at first blush seems like a pretty simple idea. Let me first try to present two different views, and then give some sense of the discussion that took place.

Both views put east in the general direction of the rising sun. ("Orient"ing literally means taking a bearing to the east, heading for the rising sun.) The first view is relatively simple: east is along a latitude, in

---

*The members of the group besides myself are: Jinny Chalmers, Joanne Cleary, Mary DiSchino, Fern Fisher, Wendy Postlethwaite, and Mary Rizzuto.

the general direction of where the sun rises. The second view is more difficult to convey, and for us it came from two different sets of thoughts. The
simpler of *these* is the following. East lies 90 degrees from north, in the
general direction of the rising sun. If you look at the North Star (or to the
earth underneath the North Star) and put your right arm out at a right angle, you'll point east. If you cut a 90-degree L-shape from a piece of paper,
and lay it on a globe so that one tip of it is at the North Pole and the bend
in the L is at Boston, then the arm that is heading east does *not* go along a
latitude; it goes on a gentle slant from the latitude, so it ends up crossing
the equator (Figure 10.12).

Figure 10.12

Our second way of getting to this view is the following. In September
you may find the sun rising in a certain position, relative to your house,
for instance, or to the end of your street. As the months go by, the sunrise point changes. In the northern hemisphere it moves to the right along
the horizon until about Christmas. By mid-January it has started to move
back, until some time in March it is again where it was in September; it
then continues to move to the left for a couple of months. In June it begins
to move to the right again, and by September it is back where it started.
So where, in all this, is east? This group thought of the one in the middle
of those extremes as a reasonable candidate—the place where it started in
September and that it reached again in March. That is also the time when

the sunrise and sunset divide the twenty-four hour period into exactly half. Everywhere in the world, that day, the twenty-four hour period is going to be divided exactly in half. Everyone in the world, that day, will look to the sunrise to find where the exact east is. And here's what that led us to think. If everyone on one north-south line from the North Pole to the South Pole is looking toward the sun at the same sunrise moment, they are all looking at the same place at the same moment. On that day, the sun is actually rising so as to keep going directly overhead *at the equator*, which means that we must all be looking, not directly along a latitude, but in a direction gently sloping towards the equator.

We had these two reasons to think of east as tending toward the equator, rather than along a latitude parallel to the equator. And, of course, we also had common sense and pragmatic reasons to think of east as heading along a latitude. In order to proceed with an investigation that we were engaged in, we needed to know which of these easts to deal with.

This discussion lasted three long sessions, which are the essence of the following account. The first took place at one of our two-day summer retreats, in June 1987. It refers back to a conversation at a retreat three years earlier, when one central idea first emerged and left us perplexed. The second session took place in December at an all-day meeting, and then there is a follow-up to that. *Much* material has been cut, but I still hope to convey a sense of the nature of what can happen when complexity is accepted as a pedagogical resource, rather than avoided.

> FERN: [one major protagonist in this discussion; always willing to take on a seemingly unlikely idea if it expands her/our understanding] . . . [T]here's always east, even if the sun isn't rising there. There's still due east . . . it's down there, because it's towards the equator.
>
> WENDY: [another major protagonist] No. I'm not happy with that sentence, I'm sorry. Due east is *not* towards the equator. . . .
>
> FERN: Where is due east, even if the sun isn't there? It's towards where the sun rises on the equinox, which is . . . towards the equator. . . .
>
> WENDY: What makes you think that it tips towards the equator? . . .
>
> ELEANOR: [altogether quite unsure of myself in the discussion] It's the 90 degree thing [the L-shape, which we had discussed earlier]—the latitudes are not 90 degrees to the longitudes. . . .
>
> WENDY: I think I see what you're saying. You're saying that if I look due east eventually my eyes will . . . touch the equator . . . if I could look around the corner.

FERN: You know what it is? There's always due east. Whether or not the sun rises there. And what due east is, the definition of it is, where the sun rises on the equinox.

WENDY: I think of it very differently. I think of due east as, I drew a line from the North Pole to the South Pole and then went 90 degrees off . . . from that.

ELEANOR: OK, that would come to the same thing. . . .

WENDY: But I don't like it. . . . I don't like it ending up on the equator. . . . It really makes me nervous. . . .

WENDY: [taking a styrofoam ball] Well if I draw a line from there [the North Pole] to there [Boston] and go at a right angle [she starts to draw a line like a latitude] (Figure 10.13).

Figure 10.13

FERN: Nope, that's not a right angle, your right angle's going to go like that [tending toward the equator, as in Figure 10.12].

WENDY: Yeah, but I don't like that right angle. I'm having serious problems with that right angle.... Well how come the latitudes don't tilt down? How come they don't bump into the equator?

FERN: Latitudes are latitudes, they're not east.

WENDY: You say Spain is due east from of us, and—

ELEANOR: That's a good point. . . .

WENDY: If I get into a boat and I drive due east and I keep the compass on due east, I bump into Spain.

FERN: [stretching things a bit] You say Spain is on the same latitude, you don't say Spain is due east.

ELEANOR: [quite uncertain] Although we do say that. . . .

FERN: They're not east–west lines, they're latitudes. If they were east–west lines we wouldn't need latitudes.

ELEANOR: Huh?

MARY RIZZUTO: Why? Why [then] do you have longitudes? They're [after all] north–south lines.

JINNY: [laughing] That *was* a little—cryptic! Go on!

MARY R.: Go on, we need to hear this.

[We all recognized that she had made a far-out comment, but had confidence that Fern would say something interesting about it.]

FERN: OK, here we go. [Fern thought silently for a while, but, to our great disappointment, she decided she did not, after all, have something clear to say.] No. . . .

WENDY: Alright, hang on. You're saying that if I got a compass, and I started walking in California, and I followed that compass wherever it said east, I would end up on the equator.

FERN: Right. . . .

WENDY: You're saying that if I were a sailor, and my compass told me to sail due east, I would end up on the equator no matter what I did.

FERN: Right. . . .

MARY R.: So which way would you have to go to get to Spain?

JINNY: You'd have to go—

MARY DISCHINO: North of east. . . .

[with hilarity] So north isn't north and east isn't east. . . . So if you want to stay in the Northern Hemisphere you have to keep going north. . . .

WENDY: [arm around Fern's shoulder] This is the first time in eight years that I don't understand what you're saying. In eight years you're the only person who I've always, always understood. . . . If I'm driving [east] . . . am I driving [on a latitude]?

JINNY: Probably if it's short enough. Because, right? It's going to take you a long time to get down to the equator. [This was the first inkling of a resolution—but nobody noticed.]

MARY R.: It's incredible. Well it's interesting, one of the kids last year in mapping asked me why there was an Eastern and a Western Hemisphere. Why did one get named one and the other one get named something else [given that they each get their turn at sunrise]. [She laughs.] I said, "I have no idea." I had no idea. I mean, why? . . .

MARY D.: What would happen if we took the crust off the earth and then started walking due east? . . . Lie it flat . . . It would be like the orange peels [another reference to an earlier session] (Figure 10.14). . . .

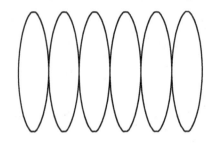

Figure 10.14

WENDY: Do you mean to say you don't believe that compasses tell you where due east is?

FERN: No, I do.

WENDY: So you think that if I were a sailor and I sailed whatever number of degrees due east is, 90 or whatever, that I would end up on the equator? [We acknowledge the need to adjust a compass for magnetic north, and proceed on the assumption that is done.] . . .

FERN: I think you'd go due east.

WENDY: And would you end up on the equator?

FERN: Yeah.

ELEANOR: Instead of Spain.

WENDY: Instead of Spain. If Kevin who has sailed and navigated said that doesn't happen, would you say your due east is different from the compass due east? I don't know what he's gonna say, he might say, yes, you have to correct—...

FERN: This is the thing. This is the thing. I *think* maybe this is the thing. If you *start*—

[Now here, Fern *is* able to articulate her insight, and it is related to Jinny's partially formed thought above. She comes to it, alas, just as the men and children arrive back for lunch, so the tape is stopped! I wrote down the following, in which Fern refers to an example we had used of walking along the 49th parallel.]

FERN: If you *walk* east, you walk along the [US–Canadian] border; if you *look* east, you look into the United States.

[We get a brief respite from the children, to finish our discussion, and the tape is back on. I had not understood what Fern had said, and Jinny tries to recapture it for me.]

JINNY: . . . Where were we. We were on the border. If you're going to walk, umm, if they, if you continue to adjust . . . 90 degrees, so you stay consistently 90 degrees east of north, you know, 90 degrees in relationship to north, you'll stay on that border, and . . . [a new thought she has here now] and that's the definition of a latitude. . . .

ELEANOR: But I want to know, I just want to know the thing you said, about it keeps pushing up, could you say that part again?

MARY R.: Well it, it keeps, if you're just walking, [Eleanor: Yeah.] then you're just, you're constantly straying down. [Eleanor: Yeah.] But if, if you, if you keep yourself on the compass, and you constantly push the compass, then you're constantly keeping yourself at 90 degrees. . . .

ELEANOR: And what's the pushing up? . . .

JINNY: You have to adjust. You have to keep the adjustment happening. Because of . . . the sphere. That's what the pushing up is. . . .

ELEANOR: Yeah. I haven't quite got that. I'll keep thinking about it.

[In December, we started by watching some of the summer's videotape, and then the conversation went on this way.]

JOANNE: [who had been running the videocamera in the summer session] The last thing you said there, [on the tape] do you know what it is? "There's always due east." [laughter]. . . .

FERN: [reflecting her insight at the end of the last session] I think where we ended up was if you navigate, if you're a sailor and you navigate and you're heading due east you don't go to the equator. You go to Spain or whatever—

ELEANOR: Any step is headed toward the equator, but the next step—. . .

MARY D.: It's due east from that step. Due east is due east from each step that you take. That's how you get across [to Spain]. As opposed to due east from your starting point. [Jinny: Mmhmm.] If you look at a compass when you begin, and you go due east, if that compass froze there at that moment, then you'd get to the equator, but the compass is heading due east even when you're ten steps ahead of where you started. . . .

MARY R.: It corrects it sort of.

[I still do not follow the line of argument, and keep asking for more clarification.]....

[Fern starts drawing a picture.]

WENDY: If you were walking around a circle, around the top of the globe.... It's telling you to go, like, due east is this way [she steps slightly outside the circle]. But really it's saying take a step this way and then it says, OK, now, north is over there. [Wendy essentially outlines the argument that I finally understand a little later. I shall present it more clearly at that point.]

JINNY: It's like making a circle in Logo....

WENDY: East is pointing off the circle, down.

ELEANOR: Yeah.

WENDY: But I don't believe it.

ELEANOR: I believe it but I don't get it. You get it and you don't believe it....

JINNY: Well the only thing I said, just when Wendy just did that, is it's like making a circle in Logo....

MARY R.: With straight lines. You make a circle with straight lines.

WENDY: That's lovely.

[I try but fail to understand this analogy.]....

MARY D.: ... [Y]ou keep moving, also. That's part of it.

FERN: [Fern finishes her drawing] Something like that picture....

(Figure 10.15)

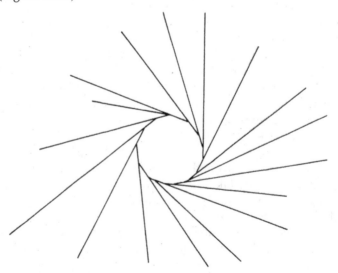

Figure 10.15

ELEANOR: How come I go there [around the circle] when the compass says to go off into space, I don't know. How come I go there, that's my question. [Jinny and Eleanor laugh.]

WENDY: 'Cause the circle is big enough that you can take a step this w—I mean, if you think of, like, octagons, but with, like hundredsagons . . . You walk a little bit this way, and then you look and say, oh, north has moved from here to here, 'cause I've gone a little bit around. . . .

ELEANOR: 'Cause *north* moves.

MARY R.: It doesn't.

ELEANOR: No, it does, with respect to *me*.

WENDY: Perhaps you move with respect to it.

MARY R.: Yeah.

ELEANOR: Yeah. [I start walking with my left arm out to the side, supposedly pointing at the North Pole, and my right arm straight ahead of me, supposedly in the direction that my compass would indicate is east.] So I take this step now . . . (Figure 10.16) [ahead of me, essentially down one of Fern's lines, as shown in Figure 10.15] but I can't have . . . kept my hands like that, . . . 'cause I have to stay like this. . . . (Figure 10.17, see next page)

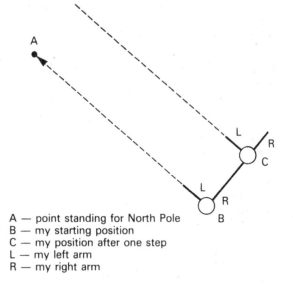

A — point standing for North Pole
B — my starting position
C — my position after one step
L — my left arm
R — my right arm

Figure 10.16

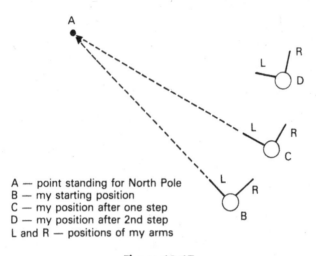

A — point standing for North Pole
B — my starting position
C — my position after one step
D — my position after 2nd step
L and R — positions of my arms

Figure 10.17

[I shift slightly left, so my left arm still points to a supposed North Pole.] So then I take this step here, [down another of Fern's lines] and then I have to move back [to the left] like that, [Mary R.: Right, right.] and then I take this step here [down another line]. [The others break out in applause.]. . . . And then I follow that one [another line], but if I take my left arm with me, it's left the North Pole, and it has to correct back again. . . .

MARY R.: It keeps adjusting you. It's really neat. . . .

WENDY: But if you glued, if you could clamp the compass so it wouldn't move when you walk a little bit, suddenly north would be at a totally different place. . . .

FERN: . . . . [T]his line that you're going around here [the circular part of Figure 10.15] is the latitude . . . that would bring you to Spain, as opposed to down there [down one of the lines], to the equator. . . . This shape, when you put this shape onto the globe [her drawing, with the North Pole at the center], this line [the circle] would set at a certain latitude. . . . (Figure 10.18)

MARY R.: Everything else would go down. . . .

FERN: 'Course then they would keep going past the equator, I don't know about that.

[This introduces the third idea of east, which we did not resolve with the other two. The going-to-the-equator view of what east is had, as you recall, two sources. The L-shape *crosses* the equator, while in the other version, Fern's lines would wrap around the equator. I include a short bit of discussion of that idea.]. . . .

FERN: [T]here's something wrong about the L, maybe . . . maybe it's not really an L. . . .

ELEANOR: Wouldn't it stay on the equator once it got to the equator? . . .

MARY D.: Because then if you're in the Southern Hemisphere, you'd do the opposite. . . .

JOANNE: What kind of a shape is that?

ELEANOR: That is an amazing shape, though . . . a spiral that then reaches a circle, and stops getting bigger. . . .

FERN: The only way you'd get this line [the one that would wrap around the equator] is if you had a laser beam, and you shot your laser beam from where you were standing, due east, and in an instant, the laser beam burns a trail on that line. . . .

JOANNE: This line is a continuation of one of those lines up there [in Fern's drawing], which eventually reaches the equator. . . .

WENDY: If you could stand on the earth, on the equinox, and shoot one of those pistols that has a string with a sucker, and you could shoot it right at the sun . . . and have it "blip" on the sun, so you had this lovely string from you to the sun. And then the earth began to turn, that day, and the string would be wound—

Figure 10.18

MARY D.: You could be putting this dot on the earth, as every point on the earth passes through sunrise. This is sunrise. As it passes through sunrise, if there were something spitting at the planet, making points on it, . . . when you went through, when the day was over, you'd have an equator on your planet . . . I see how the equator is made. Now the equator has a different meaning for me.

[We return to a discussion of our other two easts.]. . . .

WENDY: I will not agree that that's due east, toward the equator. . . . I want another word than due east for that. . . .

WENDY: [If Fern's east is east] how can you say Spain is east of us? Spain is north of us [since the compass reading is corrected to the north].

MARY R.: No it's not! . . .

WENDY: But you have to constantly correct, after each step.

MARY R.: You don't have to correct, because your constant corrects for you. Either the north star, or the compass—one of those changes for you. They keep you going in the direction, and that's how you, and that's how they did the latitude lines.

WENDY: But then, why—Then there are two easts.

MARY D.: Yes! We said that. There's Fern's east, and there's the latitude east.

WENDY: Right. But I don't—, I can't—, I don't feel comfortable with it . . . it makes me dizzy. . . .

WENDY: What I would like to do is . . . I'd like to present that kind of information to somebody who deals with east and west. . . .

FERN: I'm thinking, if he came in here right now, and said, you're right and I'm wrong, I would think he hadn't thought about this problem long enough. . . .

WENDY: . . . Now we have two different words for east.

ELEANOR: Different meanings for east.

WENDY: Right. And one word.

JINNY: In two different lang—I mean it's like two different worlds, it's a flat world and a spherical world. . . .

ELEANOR: You'd like a map-maker.

WENDY: Yeah, or somebody who sails. . . .

FERN: I don't think any of those people would have had to resolve this issue in order to be able to do what they do. . . .

WENDY: . . . What I understood today doesn't fit with what I've understood from all of that learning and all the things that I understand about east so far. Or believe about east, have read

about east, hold about east . . . I'm trying to think if there's another way to resolve it that wouldn't have two easts. . . .

FERN: The two views that we have right now are not, one, that east
is Spain and the other one that east is something else. We have
two views. One is that east is Spain. And the other is that east is
both Spain and something else. . . .They're not two conflicting
things. One is part of the other. . . . Do you know what I mean?
Like one has more parts to the explanation . . .

WENDY: I don't think that anyone will agree—

MARY D.: Then why aren't we the experts?

We did go off to see Philip and Phylis Morrison, creators of PBS's *The
Ring of Truth*, which included one episode on map-making. And there
we learned, to our extraordinary satisfaction, how Charles Mason, astronomer, and Jeremiah Dixon, mathematician and surveyor, laid out the
Mason–Dixon line. At night they fixed north, by the stars. By day they
cut through the trees at 90 degrees from north. At night, they fixed north
again, and when they started each new day, returning, in Jinny's terms, to
the "flat world," they had to adjust their continuing swath slightly to the
north. It was just like Wendy's walking circle. As Mary R. had said, "And
that's how they did the latitude lines."

CONCLUSION

This is an exceptional group, admittedly; not in its make-up at the outset, but in its history of learning together. That is one reason I wanted to
present an impression of their work together. They know it pays off to
stick with a complex issue. They know the value to each person of starting from her own set of ideas and points of engagement and relating new
ideas to that base—Piaget's fundamental point, but so rarely really acted
on in formal education. And they know the value of paying attention to
each other's ideas, to see how they can expand their own through making
the accommodations necessary to assimilate other points of view—classic
Piaget again.

Any one of us in this group might have dismissed the discussion by
saying that, of course, Spain is east, so let's get on with it. Or, well, we
know that east is where the sun rises, so let's get on with it. Instead, by
recognizing that this was a complex issue, we pushed our ideas into a
construction of a fairly sophisticated understanding of relationships between a flat world and a round world. This took us into map-making,

surveying, history, geography (as we talked about this issue with various people we learned that the east–west highways in the Canadian prairies have periodic small-angle turns—like Wendy's hundredsagons—having been set out in a fashion similar to the Mason–Dixon line), and math (what is the mathematical nature of that third version of east, a curve which approaches the equator and wraps around it?).

Our delving into these areas grew out of the simple question of what east is, which itself grew out of the simple question of what can we see the moon do in the sky—a question that has engaged this group for fifteen years. This exaggerated example is the strongest way to make my point: most areas of study that are at all worth our attention entail far more complexity than is acknowledged in our curriculum; and, further, people's intellectual engagement, when they are given the chance to pursue these complexities according to their own lights, is extraordinary. Our challenge as curriculum developers is to find the ways to engage learners, young or old, in the complexities of the areas we think it is important for them to know about. As researchers who are interested in how ideas actually develop, I think we have exactly the same challenge. I hope I have made clear how intertwined these challenges are.

I am under no illusion that, in the current climate of oversimplification, curriculum activity that celebrates the complexities of subject matter will be readily received. The point of this article is to rail against that climate, and to offer an idea of what our schools, our teachers, and our students may be missing by being subjected to that oversimplified view of the nature of teaching and learning.

I would like to end with some high school students' points of view, that poignantly express their awareness of how they are short-changed by current curriculum. With Candace Julyan (1988), they studied trees changing color in the fall. They were watching the trees themselves, in all their complexity, and trying to relate what they saw to their textbook course on chlorophyll and photosynthesis. The quotes exemplify their feelings about details that make a complex study accessible; about being able to figure out complex things in their own ways; and about the futility of trying to over-simplify curriculum.

> "It took me a while to get it . . . [to get] all my ideas together and see what I think. Once I got it was good. . . . This is fun. I like it. It's neat that I figured all this out."

> "I was thinking how the wind takes the tree and the leaves . . . and when the tree bends, it stops feeding the leaves. Did you ever think of that?"

"I love this project. . . . I can never come up with ideas like this during labs. . . .But *this*, it seems like I can come up with ideas really well. I don't know. I like this so much. I love it. . . ."

"You have to think. I don't think a lot of people like to think. . . . [This study takes] a lot of figuring out. It's fun, but it's hard."

"They throw something new at me and I can't stand it, and I have to do it their way. That's what I don't like about science, everything has already been figured out ahead of time. But if you find something different it's wrong."

"I don't know why we *read* about trees in science class. It seems stupid not to come outside and really study 'em, don'tcha think?"

11

Critical Exploration
in the Classroom

A COLLEAGUE TOLD ME about a meeting she attended some years ago with Michael Huberman and some doctoral students. She never forgot it, she said. I was interested because I was about to go to a symposium in honor of Huberman, so I asked her for whatever she could remember. A few days later she sent me these recollections:

> I remember the conversation so vividly. . . . He spoke about the importance of doing research that is both methodologically rigorous and educationally relevant. Specifically, he argued that the research we do is only as effective as it is accessible to those whose lives have been the subjects of our learning and investigation. He was very concerned that we spend so much time learning the "trade" of research and getting to "findings," and we too often forget, or worse, ignore, our responsibility to engage the subjects of the field—the teachers, the students, the parents, the communities, as opposed to the "research" audience of the field—in our on-going findings. This oversight he felt was indicative of a field that had grown larger than its own life—larger than the people who make it what it is. "How arrogant and how dangerous," he said. These were among his closing remarks and they are the words that have been lodged in my head since. (Mary Casey, personal correspondence, October, 2002)

A related statement comes from Claryce Evans (1981), urging recognition of the importance of teachers' knowledge as a basis for research in education. She refers to "the separation of those who practice from those who study practice" (p. 13).

Educational practice *is* what teachers do: . . . If research is to affect practice, it must be through what teachers do, how they do it, and what it means to them. It must address central concerns and must be accessible to them. Yet by and large . . . even those researchers whose main interest is the improvement of practice do not consider teachers the primary audience for their work. . . . The assumption is that teachers can act on the basis of information schematically conveyed to them, without making it a part of their personal knowledge and relating it to that central set of concerns.

Teachers for their part are also too willing to let this happen. . . . Many teachers pay no attention to research even in those areas in which that attention would be rewarded. This is largely in response to the fact that research is not written for their consideration. Researchers ignore teachers; teachers ignore researchers right back (p. 11, emphasis in original).

Evans offered teachers a seminar in which they could formulate researchable questions about their teaching concerns, and then develop research methods that would provide answers that were usable to themselves. She used her funding to offer doctoral students as research assistants to the teachers.

In this paper, I will take Huberman's position that the audience for research needs to be the people involved in the practice; I will focus particularly on teachers; I will take up Evans' point about the centrality of teachers' own knowledge; and I will make the case for involving teachers in the front lines of research in the development of human understanding.

CRITICAL EXPLORATION

My own background, before moving into education, was my work in Geneva with Jean Piaget and Bärbel Inhelder. For my own part, it has not been Piaget and Inhelder's research on the specifics of the development of certain foundational ideas (like volume and proportion) that have shaped my work, although that research has been exceedingly useful. Two more general aspects of their research have been important to me. One is the basic idea of assimilation: that a person takes any experience into her own previous understanding (schemes, structures); that we cannot assume that an experience whose meaning seems clear to us will have the same meaning to someone else. A teacher must be constantly striving to understand the meaning any particular experience (a reading, an explanation, an observation) holds for his students. As strong as this theoretical influence has been, the second influence has been equally great: their method. It is their method that I think is having an impact in schools, and that can have an even greater one. The Piaget/Inhelder method is where I would like to focus this chapter.

Let us first look at the method as researchers use it. Piaget first called it clinical interviewing, or "the clinical method," and it consisted, essentially, of engaging children in talking about their ideas, and following where those ideas might go. Later, in 1974, Inhelder, in her book *Learning and the Development of Cognition* (with Sinclair & Bovet), used the term "critical exploration," which recognizes that this method involves more than interviewing—more than talking. Clinical interviewing is combined with devising a way to present subject matter to children, and with watching the children's exploration of the subject matter as an indication of their thinking about a problem. This reflects Inhelder's interest in learning, and in how the theory helps us understand children's progression from one understanding to another (its "functional" aspects), in addition to describing the nature of what a child is capable of at a given moment (its "structural aspects"), which Piaget pursued. Inhelder was drawn to seeing the evolution of the thoughts of individual children, as much as to seeing the evolution of Piaget's theoretical "epistemic knower."

"Critical exploration" seems to me to be a better name for this method than "clinical interviewing," because it gives value to the work of devising the situations in which the children are called upon to think, and to talk about what they think. And it has two levels of meaning: exploration of the subject matter by the child (the "subject" or the learner), and also exploration of the child's thinking by the adult (the researcher or the teacher). (Note the two uses of "subject" in the first part of the preceding sentence—which in fact reflects the two levels at which this exploring takes place: There is "subject" matter, and there are what research psychologists call their "subjects," whom they would like to come to understand.)

In chapter 3, I mentioned Alex Blanchet's 1977 paper about developing a method for an exploration where children were asked to build mobiles, as a way of studying their understanding of equilibrium. He describes several different forms of posing this problem to the children. He settles on one, showing that a good experimental situation "must permit the child to establish plans to reach a distant goal, while leaving him wide freedom to follow his own routing." The question must be clear; it must be broad enough to invite a response of more than yes or no; it must be appealing enough to invite the child to do something immediately; and the materials must be adequate to respond to further questions the subject may ask of them.

Critical exploration, then, as a research method, has two aspects: 1) developing a good project for the child to work on; and 2) succeeding in inviting the child to talk about her ideas: putting her at ease; being receptive to all answers; being neutral to the substance of the answer while being encouraging about the fact that the child is thinking and talking; getting the child to keep thinking about the problem, beyond the first thought that comes to her; getting her to take her thinking seriously.

These two aspects of critical exploration have their parallels in school teaching—and in teaching learners of all ages. One can think of curriculum as the domain of the first, and pedagogy as the domain of the second.

IN THE CLASSROOM

As an intermediary step between discussing the researcher's use of this method and what classroom teachers can do, let us look at some work that Androula Henriques has done in classrooms (Henriques, 1990). A Piaget-trained researcher, she describes how she and her assistants went about doing research in Genevan elementary school classrooms of 20 to 25 children.

While the children were working with materials in small groups, Henriques tried to make sure that she heard from each child, going from group to group saying things like, "Tell me what you're doing," or "Tell me something about this," or "I didn't understand that; could you explain it to me again?" Sometimes, in order to get a different child in the group to talk, she would say, "Perhaps you can help me understand what Joan is telling me." "Very often," she reported, "the children called out to us without awaiting their turn in order to share their findings or a problem with us" (p. 157).

Then in the class discussions, after the children had been working with materials in small groups, she would ask a general question about which all the children would have something to say, given what they had just been doing.

> Whenever the children asked the question "Why . . . ?" we refrained from giving them any information and even less an explanation. We would simply say, "What do you think?" We realized that when children asked "Why?" they always had their own thoughts about the question and were only too pleased to express them (p. 157).

Henriques found that a classroom was a good place to be a researcher into children's thinking. And she learned that the very process of doing the research was a teaching process as well.

Teachers have discovered this relationship from the other end. Listening to students' thoughts is a good way to teach. And that very process of teaching is a research process as well.

A classic work by a teacher is Lucy Sprague Mitchell's *The Young Geographers*. This was published in the days when it was not surprising for teachers to publish significant contributions to the field of children's thinking. In 1934 Mitchell published her study of young children coming to understand geography. It included a two-page table entitled, "Notes towards a chart of the development of geographic thinking and tools: Each stage may include some or all of the preceding stages" (Mitchell, 1934/1963, pp. 18–20). Her stages are much more loosely determined than Piaget's and less theoretically developed. But they are given life in her descriptions of the activities, drawings, and words of the children—a treasure for researchers and/or teachers who would want to pursue further these observations or activities.

These days it is far rarer for teachers to write about what they learn. There is, however, some such writing, and some of that writing grows from teachers' attending to their pupils' thinking, as Ramsey (2002) has discussed in an unpublished study. The teachers' work calls to mind both Huberman and Evans.

Citing teachers of both young children and adolescents, Ramsey points out that, as these teachers attend to students' thinking, it is difficult to say which comes first: They teach in such a way as to make their students' thoughts visible to them, and seeing their students' thoughts affects how they teach. The burden is as much on their curriculum—their planning how to engage their students' minds with the subject matter—as on their ways of inviting the students to express their thoughts, their understandings. Though they do not call it critical exploration, it has the same characteristics: The curriculum is explorable, and the pedagogy asks the students to express their thoughts about it.

Ramsey finds that confusion is acknowledged by these teachers as a valuable phase of learning, and students' expressions of confusion are encouraged, as conflicting ideas work their way out. Relationships are developed with students, building trust so that they are willing to express themselves openly, even when they are not sure, or feel confused.

She also points out that attending to children's thinking requires a change in the kind of question that is asked. After children have been working on a problem, Strachota asks, not "What is your answer?" but "Tell us how you are thinking about it" (1996, p. 34). Lampert asks, "Okay, who has something to say about [this one]?" (2001, p. 145). Other teachers ask, "What do you notice about [these numbers, this scene from our story, these two trees—or any number of other well-chosen phenomena]?"

What I want to emphasize is how the work of these teachers resembles a researcher's stance. It is what I would call *neutral*. I do not mean to say that the teachers are neutral in their relationships with the children (on the contrary, as Ramsey observed above) nor that they are neutral about the children's efforts to understand, nor in any other dimension of their interaction with the pupil. I mean only that the teachers do not indicate whether the youngsters have said what the adult would like them to say. This is, of course, crucial to the work of a researcher. We cannot learn anything about what children think if we signal to them what we hope they will say. This should and can be crucial for teachers, too. Teachers cannot know what learners have understood, and what needs more and different attention, unless they listen genuinely, without trying to influence what learners say.

Further, when I use the word *neutral*, I do not mean to say that the teacher is indifferent to the response. Within her own mind and thoughts, each response calls for difficult and complex work to be done (see Duckworth, 2001b; Lampert, 2001; Strachota, 1996). What lies behind this response? How may the others in the class be responding to it? What question shall I ask next, or what experience shall I offer next, or where shall I direct their attention next? Although the teachers accept equally all learners' serious responses, they know that each thought can be deepened, and they are always attuned to that possibility. All thoughts offered seriously are productive—are the basis of further thoughts.

Rather than being concerned with telling his students what he knows, then, a teacher involved in critical exploration must find something else to do with his knowledge. Just as a researcher's knowledge guides her further questioning, and gives rise to the next problem she asks them to consider, so a teacher, convinced that he cannot put his own understanding into the learners' heads, uses that understanding to help the learners take their own thoughts further. His own understanding determines what he sees and hears in the students' responses, and suggests further questions to ask, further resources to offer, further stories to tell.

Proceeding in this way, teachers in fact have access to far more powerful insights than laboratory researchers do, into understanding of the growth of human thinking. Teachers are witness to, and can encourage, the interaction of many minds—what I have called the "collective creation of knowledge" (Duckworth, 2001a, p. 1).

It was always Piaget's belief that discussion among peers was the most likely means of moving learners beyond their current understanding (contrary to the widespread misunderstanding that the role of social interaction is more Vygotskian than Piagetian; see, for example, "Social Factors in Intellectual Development" in *The Psychology of Intelligence*, Piaget, 1947/1981, pp. 156–163). This belief both supports and is supported by critical exploration in classrooms. A teacher in a classroom is not likely to learn as much detail about one learner as is a researcher in conversation with one child at a time. But when people talk seriously about their ideas, they excite and build on one another's, so the ideas keep coming—more happens. Delaney (2001) writes:

> As I brought these ways of listening and talking into classrooms, I have noticed that students are interested in one another's thinking; extended conversations with one or three students in a classroom can happen without my losing the rest of the class. This practice challenges some current notions about classroom engagement. Sometimes extended conversations with a few students can in fact engage everyone and push an entire class to think more deeply. (p. 145)

And a teacher is there to keep it going, to witness, and—if the research community can develop in this direction and consider teachers as legitimate researchers, deserving of the support that university faculty receive—to record and write.

SOME EXAMPLES

Four different classroom teachers have collaborated with Constance Kamii, Piaget-based researcher and educator, in writing four books on primary school arithmetic teaching (Kamii & DeClark, 1985; Kamii & Housman, 2000; Kamii & Joseph, 1989; Kamii & Livingstone, 1994). The curriculum— the problems designed for the children to explore critically—was first proposed by Kamii, and then developed by the teachers as they became more familiar with the approach. As for the pedagogy, the teachers developed a researcher's attitude: For them, the important thing was to find out how the children were thinking.

These four books are laden with examples of teachers listening to children's ideas as they put their minds to arithmetic, many of them presented in great detail. Here is a brief one. Georgia DeClark, teaching a class of 25 6-year-olds, wrote:

> Class attendance was an important topic, particularly since we did so much voting. . . . I found that if I said, "I see that only 21 people have checked in today. How many people are absent?" almost all the children could figure it out. However, if I reversed the question by saying, "Wow, there are four people out today. How many are here?" it was more difficult to figure out the answer (Kamii & DeClark, 1985, pp. 125, 126).

In this teaching, the assumption is that it is the children's work to figure out how to do the problem; the teacher's work is to present engaging problems, and to attend to how the children figure them out. These teachers see convincing evidence that having children develop their own approaches to arithmetic is the best way for them to learn to do it. And listening to them also provides these particular teachers with information about what to do next, in order to take their students' arithmetic further. In doing what she sees as the best teaching job she can, DeClark, like Kamii's other co-authors, contributes to our understanding of young mathematics learners. This often provides material of interest to other teachers and researchers, even though that is not the main purpose.

Bob Strachota, another teacher influenced by the work of Kamii, writes about coming to realize that, in pursuing critical exploration (not his term) in the classroom, "the teacher must be fascinated by the intersection made by the content and the learner" and, in his example, must be "intrigued by what the numbers could do . . . [and] curious about how the children might think about what the numbers could do" (Strachota, 1996, p. 39). He writes this as a teacher. But it is the quintessence of a researcher's attitude.

Vivian Paley (1986) has also drawn attention to the importance of a teacher's curiosity, and has shown us how following that curiosity constitutes marvelous research into the nature of childhood.

One thing that both researchers and teachers are in a position to note is the way conflicts nourish youngsters' minds. Lisa Schneier (1986) demonstrates this from both points of view. As a Boston high school teacher, she writes about an episode with Mary, a 14-year-old in a remedial class who was going through the multiplication tables.

> There were points at which she would count wrong or get mixed up, but I did not intervene until she got to 7 × 6, saying it equaled 41. She had said a few moments before that 6 × 7 = 42, and I asked her if the different orders of the numbers should lead to different answers. She said that the two answers should be the same, but insisted that 7 × 6 = 41 because 7 × 5 = 35 "and then you add six more." . . . She knew that there was a problem with having two answers, but I am not sure what she thought the problem was. She didn't know what to do about it, saying quietly, "They aren't the same—but they have to be . . . but they aren't—but they have to be—" (1986, pp. 11–12)

Schneier had studied Piaget and Inhelder's work, and she refers to that work in this account:

> I was reminded, hearing [Mary's] quiet, rhythmic chant, of a [younger] child, Jenny, whom I had once worked with on the questions of how a person would see an object that Jenny was seeing if that person was in a different position than Jenny in the room. She, like Mary, was trying to bring

together seemingly conflicting ideas, and a rhythm came from her also as, thinking deeply, she said, "The same—but different—the same—but different—the same . . . but different—he would see it the same but different as me." She was trying to reconcile the ideas that the object was the same, the viewpoint different. Mary's rhythm impressed me as also coming from careful thought (1986, p. 12).

Neither child resolved the conflict in that moment. But we see the power of the conflict to hold their minds to the problem. And we come to see potential conflicts that can enlighten the work of other teachers and researchers.

Fiona Hughes-McDonnell (2000) documented work by Kris Newton, who was teaching high school students in an exploratory study of electricity in which a large part of the work consisted in following the students' own ideas, and helping them to think them through with one another. The students had the following comments:

I like that whole idea of inviting our ideas about things and combining everything gives me a better understanding. . . . At the end I just knew so much more. (p. 312)

I would advise a mixture of student involvement in the curriculum, in the development of experiments, and a component for students to have the time to answer their own questions (that they have no doubt been stewing over). And I think that it's really important for the students to have discussions amongst themselves. (p. 320)

Hughes-McDonnell noted, "One student reflected that it was the confusion and uncertainty about the materials and phenomena that 'pulled [him] in'" (p. 312).

In addition to learning about ways the students came to their understanding—ways that are not in the canon—she found, more generally:

As I complete [this writing] I am struck by the energy that these students put into working through an idea, both alone and together, and how they worked to maintain coherence within and among all of their different thoughts. I am struck, too, at how these students saw each situation through their own ways of understanding and how they resisted interpretations imposed from the outside that seemed to "make no sense at all," given those understandings. I am struck by how activities that intended to support ideas that the students had not yet considered largely failed in that effort. And I am struck by how within structured tasks these students found crevices to explore because that is how people learn. (p. 276)

Deborah Ball (Ball & Wilson, 1996) writes of coming to the end of a school year with her 10-year-old students in disagreement about whether 4/4 and 5/5 are the same amount. After having spent considerable time on this matter, she finally decided to tell them that they are, demonstrating by cutting similar circles, one into quarters, and one into fifths. In this case, a researcher temporarily abandons her research stance, in an effort to teach by "telling."

Here are two representative student comments (from after the demonstration), followed by Ball's own:

> LUCY: I think they both have the same. Because . . . it's the same size and you're cutting it—and it doesn't matter if—'cause [one] has less papers, they're both the same size.
> DANIEL: I disagree because that one [4/4] has lots less . . . 'cause it gots four, and it gots five (p. 171).

Ball writes, "I was humbled to see that, even when I do choose to tell students something there are no guarantees . . ." (p. 171). She recalled that this was one of the reasons she focused on explorations in the first place!

Lynn Strieb (1985) was studying trees with her class of 1st-graders in inner-city Philadelphia. "I asked the children to move into the shade of the tree. For the third time we talked about what makes a shadow. They know you need light, but it's hard for them to think of the object (tree) as being in between. Between the sun and what?" (p. 118). What a great insight into what the children were struggling with!

Rhoda Kanevsky (in preparation), a kindergarten teacher in Philadelphia, describes how she engages her students in studying silkworms and their lifecycle.

> I bring a clear plastic container with a few samples of the eggs. . . . I direct the children to look closely, say what they notice, and then pass the container to the next child. . . . I say, "What do you notice? Say what you are seeing." At this point the new caterpillars, no longer than a quarter-inch, are climbing (wriggling) out of their egg cases over the yet unhatched eggs and onto the tiny mulberry leaves. The following discussion on April 11 begins the story.

> JORDYN: I see baby caterpillars and some eggs.
> DERRICK: Little black babies. It's laying in the egg.
> KIERRA: Some already came out because some are white. The ones that are black didn't hatch yet.
> [. . .]

JASMINE: Some are all on different places.

ALEX: They're really long eggs. A tiny bit longer than the eggs. The eggs are tiny. They [the caterpillars] look a tiny bit like long eggs.

TYLER: They're very small. The eggs are soft.

WESLEY: How do you tell the difference between which eggs have already hatched?

NAWAR: That the ones that are hatched, those eggs are white.

BRITTANY: How come the eggs can attach to the paper?

GAGE: That's where they laid them.

TYLER: They made of silk.

What are the children noticing? They witness the baby caterpillars, visible as black masses one moment "laying in the egg;" the next moment "some already came out" leaving behind their white egg cases. The caterpillars seem to be "a tiny bit longer than the eggs."

The children listen to one another, add particular details, build a picture of the whole. Questions and wonder are part of their seeing and knowing. (pp. 7, 8)

They spend the necessary weeks to observe, with continuing astuteness and wonder, the life of the silkworms, until the worms emerge as moths. On the day the moths emerged, one 6-year-old asked this remarkable question: "Does the moth remember when it was a silkworm?" (Kanevsky, personal communication, June, 2002) How could a one-interview researcher uncover thinking of this depth, or trace its origins?

Most of the examples above have come from math, science, and nature study. I close with an extensive example from literature.

Lisa Schneier (2001) did this work with six students in a Boston public high school. For four of the students English was their second or third language. They were all inexperienced readers of poetry. Four of the students were 15 years old; one was 14, one was 16. She asked them to read "miss rosie," by Lucille Clifton.

miss rosie

when i watch you
wrapped up like garbage
sitting, surrounded by the smell
of too old potato peels
or
when i watch you
in your old man's shoes

with the little toe cut out
sitting, waiting for your mind
like next week's grocery
i say
when i watch you
you wet brown bag of a woman
who used to be the best looking gal in georgia
used to be called the Georgia Rose
i stand up
through your destruction
i stand up

The students' first responses were as follows:

NILDO: I don't get this.
JAMES: It don't rhyme.
JUANA: It don't make sense.
MADDIE: It's silly.
MARCO: It doesn't make sense.
JAMES: It's stupid. It's exaggerating too much. I mean, it can exaggerate, but it's got to make sense.
L.S.: You said, too much exaggeration. What do you mean by "too much?"
JAMES: It's stupid. I don't know. I just don't like it. (p. 47)

This is a beginning that might have discouraged most teachers! But Schneier—experienced in accepting all student comments that were offered seriously—knew that this was the only way she could learn enough about their thoughts to take them further. Schneier's account of the youngsters' coming to know this poem—and thereby coming to know something about the poetic use of language—is almost 40 pages long. It entails more than a week of daily discussion. I can give only the slightest suggestion of its nature.

In the early exasperation, a number of the students remark that the poem doesn't hang together: "It's supposed to be one main thing." Schneier follows up on that remark.

L.S.: Can you show me what the different pieces are?
NILDO: Oh, yeah.
JAMES: [looking at the poem] Like around the end, the starting, the middle, like everywhere. I don't know.
L.S.: So just show me one piece and then what another piece is that doesn't seem to go with it. (p. 50)

In responding to that request, James actually finds more pieces that go together than pieces that don't.

> JAMES: [still studying the text]. Um, the garbage, the garbage and the shoes go together, right?
> L.S.: OK, how do they go together, the garbage and the shoes?
> JAMES: I mean, they are talking about shoes that are torn up. That's what garbage is too, so.
> L.S.: OK, I see. And then which part doesn't go with it?
> JAMES: The bottom one. I don't get it. Even after he [Nildo] explained it, I still don't get it.
> L.S.: OK, point to where you start not to get it. Where are the lines where you start not to get it?
> JAMES: Like around where she starts talking about Georgia, "the best looking gal in—"
> L.S.: "Who used to be the best looking girl in Georgia"? That one? Or the one before, "you wet brown bag of a woman"?
> JAMES: That goes.
> L.S.: That goes? How does that go?
> JAMES: That's just like the garbage. I mean, you know, it's almost the same. She's just saying she's garbage.
> MARCO: They're still saying that she's garbage. (p. 50)

With this careful work, Schneier gets the students finding some of the ways the poem can be seen to be holding together.

Several sessions later, Marco starts to develop an extraordinary insight: "It doesn't have to be a woman or a man, it could be the destruction of our forests or something. Something torn down. Or a farm or something." Schneier comments that the other students "paused and turned to stare at Marco. Thus began one of the loudest and most animated discussions of this poem, a discussion that often consisted of escalating voices as several students talked at once" (p. 57).

> JUANA: Yeah, but she didn't say "farm" or anything.
> MARCO: She says "potato peels."
> JUANA: No, because right here it says—
> NILDO: [now understanding what Marco is saying] It's a woman!
> MARCO: It doesn't *have* to be a woman!
> JUANA: Yeah, Marco says it could be forests or something.

Nildo and Juana, speaking at the same time, refer emphatically to the poem in order to persuade Marco that his idea couldn't hold true:

NILDO: It couldn't because when it says, "When I watch *you*—,"
   you can't refer to a forest as like that, as if it would be a person.
   That's too much exaggeration.
JUANA: [laughing] They're "watching" the trees? And it says "wait-
   ing for your mind."
MADDIE: [referring to Nildo's statement about "too much exaggera-
   tion"] I know.
MARCO: No!
L.S.: Go ahead. "No" what?
MARCO: It still doesn't have to be a woman, man! (p. 57)

Schneier says:

> I was confused by what he was trying to put forth, and also perhaps by his
> very steadfastness, which seemed much more than stubbornness or an ar-
> bitrary holding on. I wondered what had given rise to this "It doesn't have
> to be a woman" idea in the first place. His tone when he first broached it
> was . . . experimental. There was something that he was thinking through.
> Not yet being able to articulate what that was, his "No!" seemed a kind of
> placeholder . . . of something as yet inarticulate. (p. 58)

With a little more study of the poem, Marco begins to articulate his
ideas in greater detail through references to the poem's text.

> "About the grocery part [line 10], it could be a farm or something they don't
> get to and the potatoes. It's not gonna be used any more so it's garbage . . .
> and the groceries, yeah, it's like this, this, this [pause] garbage, whatever it
> was that was the groceries, the potatoes were growing from it, it could be
> torn up and they call it garbage, whatever it was, the potato peels and the
> groceries and stuff is garbage."

> He constructs the poem's images into a scene that stays true to the feeling
> of decay that the poem gives him. The other students listened to this in si-
> lence. James made an "Mhmm" noise that seemed to indicate understand-
> ing, and Juana nodded. Nildo responded most forcefully: "I see what he's
> saying. He's making it more—ah—simple now." (pp. 58, 59)

In the next exchange, one of the other students teases him (kindly) and
Nildo, who has said something in Marco's support, replies, "I'm serious,
because you could be exaggerating in a poem," and Marco adds. "Yeah! It
could be anything" (p. 59).

> It took this last statement, with its emphatic "could" to make me realize the
> enormity of the question Marco was raising. . . . On the one hand, to say that

the "you" of the poem could be anything is absurd; if it meant anything, it would really mean nothing. But Marco is not saying that the "you" in this poem does mean anything; he's saying that it *could*. The question is that of the boundaries of language. He's focusing on the nature of the figurative language, in which the possibilities of meaning are exponentially increased by the movement beyond the boundaries of the literal. His assertions about the "you" in the poem are as much assertions about the figurative possibilities that he knows the language to contain. . . . These possibilities, named "exaggeration" by the students in our first moments together, are implicit in all of our work with the poem. It must be so, since the poem embodies them. But Marco has forced an explicit study of them, because he needs these possibilities, to make sense of the poem in front of us. As he and the other students struggle with his ideas, he making statements that the others then counter, each with reference to the text, they are exploring, even dramatizing, the very boundaries that secure the poem's meaning, that make it mean something rather than anything. I interpreted Marco's main question as follows: Once language moves beyond the boundaries of direct referring, once it becomes figurative, how do we secure its meaning? If it *could* mean anything, since it is no longer bound by the rules of ordinary prose, how do we determine what it does mean? (Schneier, 2001, pp. 59, 60)

This lengthy example embodies everything that I have attempted to say: Young minds struggling with complex problems are exciting to witness, for both researchers and teachers. It behooves a teacher to be curious about the learners' ways of understanding. A teacher's extensive knowledge of the subject matter is put to work, even if nothing is "told." So is the ability to keep the students' minds on the matter at hand. Learning in a group is powerful. There are ideas that seem to be beyond a student's grasp at some given moment. And there are powerful ideas that students come up with, ideas that astonish us. Taking a stance that combines that of a teacher (in bearing the responsibility for continued engagement with the subject matter) and that of a researcher (in being dedicated to finding out what the learners really do think), advances the understanding of the subject matter, by these particular students, and at the same time is a window into the development of human minds.

"How do we determine what it does mean?" This question that emerges from the work of Schneier's students ranks with the 6-year-old's "Does the moth remember when it was a silkworm?" In both cases, it is because of the depth of connection between the learners, the teacher and the subject matter that these insights become available to us. It is really only a teacher who could get to these depths, by engaging the students' thoughts, and attending to them with the neutrality of a researcher.

When teachers take a researcher's stance in the classroom—engaging learners' minds and hearing what they have to say—the students are not the only ones who learn. It is a kind of work that, to my mind, responds to Evans' call to take advantage of teachers' knowledge, and fulfills Michael Huberman's urgent demand for research that is responsible to teachers, students, parents, school communities. And further, it illuminates our understanding of human understanding.

12

Teaching as Research

W HAT I LOVE TO DO is to teach teachers. I love to stir up their thoughts about how they learn; about how on earth anyone can help anyone else learn; and about what it means to know something. I love to help them feel that any aspect of human endeavor is accessible to them and that they can make it accessible to any person they teach. I love to try to find ways into a subject that will catch everybody's interest; to find out what people think about things and to find ways to get them talking about what they think; to shake up things they thought they knew; to get people wrapped up in figuring something out together without needing anything from me; to help build their fascination with what everybody else thinks, and with the light that other people's thinking might shed on their own. I love to see the most productive of questions be born out of laughter, and the most frustrating of brick walls give way to an idea that has been there all along.

But there are two main reasons that I love to teach teachers in particular. One is that teachers are as interested as I am in how people learn, so the dialogue is deeply felt. The second is that I always learn from them in return, when I see the endless variations on how they use what they learn in their own teaching. This chapter is about how I teach, how teachers respond to it, and what one can learn through teaching in such a way.

It was a conviction about learning that got me started teaching the way that I do. As a student of Piaget, I was convinced that people must construct their own knowledge and must assimilate new experiences in ways that make sense to them. I knew that, more often than not, simply telling students what we want them to know leaves them cold.

So what is the role of teaching, if knowledge must be constructed by each individual? In my view, there are two aspects to teaching. The first is to put students into contact with phenomena related to the area to be studied—the real thing, not books or lectures about it—and to help them notice what is interesting; to engage them so they will continue to think and wonder about it. The second is to have the students try to explain the sense they are making, and, instead of explaining things to students, to try to understand their sense. These two aspects are, of course, interdependent: When people are engaged in the matter, they try to explain it and in order to explain it they seek out more phenomena that will shed light on it.

ENGAGING WITH PHENOMENA: THE FIRST ASPECT OF TEACHING

Since I am teaching about teaching and learning, the phenomena with which I must engage my students must entail teaching and learning.* Rather than reading and hearing lectures, the students must learn and teach or watch people learn and teach, and somehow I must make these phenomena interesting and different enough to intrigue them and raise questions they had not thought of before.

There are three major kinds of teaching and learning phenomena with which I try to engage the students. This account is complicated, though, by the fact that within each of these three—circles within circles—we find both of the aspects of teaching mentioned above: Since I am teaching about teaching, the phenomena I present are themselves composed of the two aspects.

The first kind of phenomenon in which I try to engage these students is demonstrations with one or two children or adolescents. In these demonstrations, I attempt to engage the children with some problem or activity (first aspect), and to understand their explanations (second aspect). I try to capture the students' interest in the children's ideas and their enjoyment of this intellectual work. I also try to show that the children have reasons for thinking what they think, and that it is possible to find out what these reasons are.

The second kind of phenomenon consists of the students' own attempts to carry out a similar inquiry with one or two people at a time, outside class. They are invited to present some phenomenon (for example, a particular reflection in a mirror, see Duckworth, 1990) in a manner that engages people, and to try to understand their explanations of it. This is

---

*In the course referred to in this chapter, I usually have about 45 students in a class, including experienced classroom teachers, undergraduates seeking teacher certification, and professionals from other careers who have chosen to switch into teaching. Their teaching interests cover all subject matters, dramatic arts through geography, and all ages, preschool through adult. I have done similar work with urban public school teachers, with undergraduates, with university faculty—and on many continents.

quite a new and difficult experience for people whose idea of teaching is to do the explaining.

The third kind of phenomenon for the students in this course is to learn as a group about a particular subject other than teaching and learning, for example, about pendulums, or floating and sinking, or mathematical permutations. Again we find the two aspects. I try to engage the students in the subject and encourage them to explain how they are thinking about it. My challenge is to engage the students in such a way that they are intrigued not only by the subject we are studying—which I shall call the secondary subject—but by the nature of the teaching and learning phenomena they experience as they learn (and I teach) this secondary subject. We proceed on both these levels at once. It is this third activity, learning a secondary subject together as a group, that I would like to discuss at greater length in this chapter.

Both the subject of teaching and learning and the secondary subjects present the difficulty, in my classes, of a great range in what people know, or think they know. As far as teaching and learning are concerned, I can at least count on the fact that they are interested in the topic, and everybody is prepared to think that they can learn more. The secondary subject, by contrast, is something they have not bargained for and do not particularly care to learn about. Furthermore, a number of them believe they know all about it already, while many think that they are incapable ever of learning about it. Engaging students in the secondary subject is a considerable challenge.

I go about engaging the students in the secondary topic in about the same way as I go about engaging them in the topic of teaching and learning. I look for some phenomenon to draw their attention to, counting on it to do the work of engaging them. I make sure there is always something to do or to watch and make sense of so that everybody can have something to say, even if it is only to say what they saw. My focus on what they themselves see and how they make sense of it goes a long way toward providing a common ground. Part of what I have learned to do is to find phenomena that, familiar as they are and simple as they seem, do not lend themselves to satisfactory explanations by distant theories.

Of the many different secondary subjects I have used to engage teachers, the example I will use here is the study of the habits of the moon.* Before we start, I usually ask them when they last saw the moon, what it looked like, when they think they'll see it next, and what it will look like then. Sometimes this preliminary discussion gives rise to conflicting

---

*Engaging students in moon watching as a way into astronomy is an approach I learned from Donald Ford, a fellow staff member at the Elementary Science Study, in 1965, when he was preparing a moon-watching teacher's guide (Elementary Science Study, 1968).

Figure 12.1   *Figure 12.2*

ideas, so some students find themselves immediately engaged. Once, for example, one person said that the previous night she had seen the moon as illustrated in Figure 12.1 and another said she saw it as shown in Figure 12.2. The class was about evenly divided among those who thought they both could have seen what they said they saw, those who thought at least one person must be mistaken, and those who had no idea whether it was possible or not.

More often, there is no discord at the start, nothing particular to talk about. Some people accept this as a rather flaky assignment that they will do because it does not seem too complicated, and why not seize the chance to be flaky in the midst of graduate school. Some accept it solemnly because they have been asked to do it. Some resist it as an imposition and a waste of time. Some like the idea right from the start.

I ask the students to keep and bring to each class a separate notebook in which they make an entry every time they see the moon—when and where they see it and what it looks like. By the first week's reporting time, at least some people have something specific they want to look for in the following week. Little by little, the assignment changes from one that is flaky, arbitrary, or easy to one that is absorbing and serious.

The following excerpts from retrospective accounts that students wrote late in the term exemplify this range of responses. Some of the writers include quotes from their daily moon notebooks.

Student One

I guess the major question I had going into this experiment was, "Is she serious?" In fact the requirement almost stopped me from taking this class—I really thought it was silly. I also thought it would be a lot of tedious work. I was wrong.

I keep [my notebook] on my bedside table and every night it's there to remind me to look out the window. . . . It only takes 2 or 3 minutes to write down my observations and draw my pictures, but later, when I sit down and read several weeks' notes all together, I can spend 15 to 20 minutes just generating questions and checking answers. I get excited when the moon moves across the sky just the way I thought it would, and I'm so disbelieving when it does something unexpected that I check my notes again and again. . . .

My observations formed my questions, which caused the focus of my observations to change. I'm now concentrating on the path of the moon each night, not on its color or shape, although I'm still shaky enough to always note those, too. . . . Everything . . . is expanding—my questions and observations are getting broader. . . .

My biggest problem in this class [is] forgetting about being a teacher and relearning how to be a learner. This [notebook] is a big help. I can make hypotheses, and they can be wrong—that's OK. . . . I can share observations and theories and be proud when someone says, "Ah, that's good. Tell me how it turns out." I can move at my own pace and ask my own questions. I like it.

Student Two

My knowledge of the moon has become internalized. It is not what someone is trying to "teach" me. Rather, it is an area of interest I choose to explore. . . . As such . . . moon knowledge represents the way in which I have come to understand learning.

I have come to see the unknown as available and optional areas of exploration rather than as required and restrictive areas of study. I am not bound by my lack of knowledge. I am free to explore in my own time, at my own pace. That change has not occurred suddenly. The following excerpts from my journal may help to illustrate the transformation.

9/25   Moon watching is proving difficult. I am never in the same place at the same time and in any event, I can't see it from my house. Irritating.

9/29   I'm finally succeeding at my moon watching. I was looking too early in the evening and in the wrong direction. . . . Now that I've found it, I can watch it. (Little did I realize that once found is not always found!)

10/7   Even though being able to watch the moon is the most difficult part, I know I've already learned some things. (1) It isn't always the same color. (2) It goes from A to B [see Figure 12.3 on next page]. (3) It rises and sets at different times. (4) It comes up in different places.

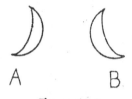

A   B

Figure 12.3

10/8   Learning about the moon is . . . like I have a bunch of unconnected facts–a puzzle. It's fun to think about it without being punished.

10/20 I have found the moon again. Yea!! It shines mostly during the day right now. Before this, even though I saw it sometimes during the day, I really thought it only shone at night.

10/22 I thought the moon had changed tilt and now I know it does. . . .

10/26 I am having a wonderful time learning about the moon. I can't believe how much it changes in just two days. . . .

The evolution from student to learner occurred over time as a change of perspective. In September, I saw the moon and its habits as external pieces of knowledge which were somehow requirements of the course. I now see them as orienting devices, a way of looking at learning.

Student Three

At the beginning I didn't want to watch the moon, I felt that being required to do so was an imposition without any sense. Why did I have to watch the moon? Why did I have to write about it? I felt that in doing so I was being conducted to a new relationship with nature, that I was being told to relate with nature, in a predetermined way. . . . During the first weeks of classes, I looked at the moon without allowing myself to get too much involved. I was trying to understand the course, trying to grasp what was really happening. Little by little things were getting clarified. But there was still one piece missing. The moon . . . I was still resisting to watch it. I wanted to understand, but I couldn't. I hadn't yet realized that in order to really learn about the moon . . . I had to watch it.

I must say that during this period, I did look at the moon more frequently than before. The discussions in class, my thoughts about the course, and mirrors [another secondary subject] led me to an increasing curiosity: "There must be something in this moon watching." And then I began to catch myself looking at it, thinking about it. . . .

Then, questions began to arise from this "casual watching." The questions led to new questions, to new curiosities and, also, to new surprises. I'm still a beginner as a moon-watcher and I have thousands of questions: How do changes in shape occur? Why do I see it sometimes "here" and sometimes "there"? Does it move always at the same pace? Where does it go when I don't see it?

Student Four

During my first observations of the moon was when I realized that my understanding of the moon had nothing to do with the theory, and that in fact I am very ignorant about the movement of it. I thought that the moon was sufficiently high and for that reason you could see it from every angle. I also thought that the moon was at the same place every night. This was my first discovery (to understand that my understanding of the moon was wrong).

Student Five

October 10: The Morning Moon

6:00 A.M. What! The moon is where it was at 7:30 P.M. last time I saw it. It's early morning. What time did it rise? Why? Is there a connection between its waning and its rising time?

October 11–16: The Moon Turns Around (or seems to)

During this five-day period, I am intent upon systematically measuring the angle of the moon in the sky. I am also checking whether or not I can see it well into the morning. I record the moon on the 11th as shaped like this . . . [See Figure 12.4.] Then, between the 13th and 15th I lose it, don't see it at all.

One evening coming out of Longfellow Hall, 6:15 P.M., I see it right up Appian Way toward the Charles. As if that's not astonishing enough, I notice and record (thank goodness) that the *direction of the horns has changed.* [See Figure 12.5.] I commented on it in my diary, but had thought little more of it until right now.

7:00 A.M.

Figure 12.4

6:15 P.M.

Figure 12.5

Student Six

I like a lot of things about the moon watching. I seem to connect with other things in the sky. I look up and observe the stars. I also watch the sun—especially when it sets.

I also like the idea that friends of mine are getting interested in the moon-watching idea and discuss things with me. One friend called me up two weeks ago at 4:15 A.M. and told me to look at the huge moon in the western sky!

Student Seven

I felt that I knew a great deal about the moon (I'd thought about the moon as part of a unit in astronomy with six graders [I thought I had]). I knew things about orbits and distance and reflected light and was very comfortable that my familiarity with my friend the moon was an intimate one. . . . The first class discussion . . . clued me in to the fact that my knowledge of the moon falls far short of an understanding. My knowledge was one from a perspective way out in space looking in. It was always easy to think about these three objects in space and their interactions (sun, moon, earth). With this new perspective I had many questions without answers. . . .

Not knowing can be so much more fun than knowing. It's opened my eyes to look for understanding. I curse whatever it was that led me to believe this puzzle was solved.

THE STUDENTS EXPLAIN: THE SECOND ASPECT OF TEACHING

Having the students watch the moon corresponds to the first of the two aspects of teaching that I mentioned: It engages them with phenomena. It serves this purpose at two levels. With regard to engaging with the solar system, it puts them in touch with the motions of the moon (and, it always turns out, of other heavenly bodies). With regard to engaging with teaching and learning, it puts them in touch with themselves and each other as learners, and with what I am doing as a teacher.

Similarly, the second aspect is brought into play at both of these levels. With regard to the motions of the moon, I continually ask them what they notice and what they make of it, and I encourage them to do the same with each other. The questions that we ask over and over again in class are. "What do you mean?" "Why do you think that?" "I don't quite get it." "Is that the same as what (someone else) thought they saw?" We also talk about what sense they are making of the primary subject of teaching and learning—what do they notice about this experience as learners and what do they make of that?

At both levels, although much more often in the secondary subject, more knowledgeable class members sometimes get impatient. I invite them then to put their efforts into trying to elicit and understand someone else's explanation—to join me in practicing teaching by listening rather than by explaining. I also point out that it serves nobody's purpose to declare something if you are sure of it. It does serve a purpose to propose a tentative idea—because then people can help you think it through.

The students also keep journals of their thoughts, their reactions, and the sense they are making of the discussions.

In some ways, it is easier to understand how this works with respect to teaching and learning than with respect to the solar system. After all, what one believes about teaching and learning is complicated, large-scale, hard to define, and close to the soul. If one stops to think about it, it is hard to imagine students learning about teaching and learning *other than* by working out for themselves what they think. Of course, when I say "working out for themselves" I do not rule out presenting people with material for them to make sense of, as I try to describe here—experiences in which they learn, try to explain what they are learning, watch others learn, try to help other people explain, and hear other people's ideas. But it is the *students* who make sense of all of this. It could not be otherwise. And they make sense by trying out their own ideas, by explaining what they think and why, and seeing how this holds up in other people's eyes, in their own eyes, and in the light of the phenomena they are trying to understand.

In other matters less close to the soul I believe that it works the same way. Whatever it is that a person believes and understands, it *is that person* who believes and understands it. Paley (1986), engaged in a very similar exercise in her teaching of 3-year-olds, observed, "Why not just tell Frederick the truth: 'Of course your mother has a birthday; everybody has a birthday.' Tempting as it might be to set the record straight, I have discovered that I can't seem to teach the children that which they don't already know" (p. 126). The best Paley can do is to accept the children's perspectives and to draw attention to some aspects they might think about at the same time. When older children or adults are struggling to make sense, they might be more inclined than Frederick to repeat what I have told them, but I have found that they are no more likely to have integrated it, I have not "set the record straight." Evidence to this effect comes up time and time again, whether the subject is the habits of the moon, a foreign language, fractions, photosynthesis, reading, or poetry.

Instead of explaining to the students, then, I ask them to explain what they think and why. I find the following results. First, in trying to make their thoughts clear for other people, students achieve greater clarity for themselves. Much of the learning is in the explaining. (Why should the teacher monopolize occasions for trying to make herself clear?) Second, the students themselves determine what it is they want to understand. It is not only the explanations that come from them, but also the questions. Third, people come to depend on themselves: They are the judges of what they know and believe. They know why they believe it, what questions they still have about it, their degree of uncertainty about it, what they want to know next about it, how it relates to what other people think. Any other "explanation" they encounter must establish its place within what they know. Fourth, students recognize the powerful experience of having their ideas taken seriously, rather than simply screened for correspondence to what the teacher wanted. One student, an elementary school principal, speaks to these third and fourth points:

> Moon watching has been a profound experience for me. From the beginning, I was thoroughly engaged by the activity. . . . I wrote in my journal, "One of the things I love about moon watching is this—as a nonscientific person, I have finally been afforded the opportunity to learn about a phenomenon without feeling dumb and unscientific because I don't know the scientific answers. Hurray . . . !"
>
> Here was a profound difference from my previous experience with science, Why? In this case, no premium was placed on "quick right answers." Instead, totally mistaken notions were not only accepted, but honored. . . . How could I feel dumb when whatever I was thinking was accepted with respect?
>
> Do I understand the moon now? I understand a great deal more than I did four months ago, but I feel fairly certain that some of what I "know" is probably wrong, and there's still a lot I don't begin to understand. Why doesn't that bother me? I no longer think I'm dumb if I don't know the "quick right answer." . . . What I do know about the moon is mine forever.

Fifth, students learn an enormous amount from each other:

> Class discussions have helped out a lot. Often people see the moon at different times than I do, and they can tentatively fill in some of my gaps in knowledge (the gaps won't really be filled in until *I* see things for myself). I also like to hear other people's hypotheses,

because they give me other avenues and ideas to check out. I especially like it when I can't believe what someone else has seen—it makes me slow down and reevaluate my own notes and theories.

Finally, learners come to recognize knowledge as a human construction, since they have constructed their own knowledge and they know that they have. What is written in a book is viewed as somebody else's creation, a creation produced just as they produced their own. Its origin is not of another order. (By contrast, most students—adults and children—believe "knowledge" to be an absolute, which some people have caught on to, and which they, if they are smart enough, will be able to learn from someone who has caught on.) The following excerpt speaks to this point.

> I had seen the moon changing shape in regular ways, but I never thought of trying to make sense of this, to see it in connection to how the moon and sun and earth work. It's this connection that's been so exciting, this realizing that the moon that we see in our visible world can tell us about a larger world which I thought before was only to be found in classrooms and libraries, that we can watch the world and begin to understand how it works. . . .
>   There's so much I don't understand, and trying to understand means giving things up, at least partially trading part of a familiar way of seeing for the beginnings of another. But I also have this terrific feeling of an *opening* of things—that's the word that goes around inside my head when I think about moon watching. It's exciting! It's opened up a way of thinking and learning about the world, a potential to slowly make sense of what I see and know and for this visible, familiar world to teach me about things I don't see or understand.

While the major burden is on the students to explain what they think, I actually do try to say much of what I myself believe on the subject of teaching and learning. I often remark on what I see in our work together and I try to say what I think about issues that students raise. (After all, I too am grateful for the occasion to learn from trying to say clearly what I think.) I do not take much air time, though. And I have no illusions that what I say will mean the same thing to others as it does to me, nor that the students will, in general, give credence to what I say. But what I say does add to the assortment of things they have to think about. It is partly because of the complicated nature of teaching and learning, where people cannot possibly understand everything that anyone else means by what they say, and partly because these students are likely to have convictions

with what they understand me to be saying, rath-
at face value, that I feel it may be helpful rather
I think.

f the secondary subject in which they have as
bout which they have few ideas of their own (the
ance), I do not usually say what I think. My efforts are
abling people to see that their own ideas are perfectly rea-
d, in fact, are the best starting points. It would be all too easy, if I
e to give my account, for people to sit back, stop thinking, and assume
that they understand what I am saying and that what I say is right—not
to mention the likelihood that the topic will cease to hold any interest for
them if they are simply listening to what I think. I do, though, offer ideas
for consideration if I can see a different point of view that no one else has
mentioned. Sometimes such an idea is one I believe in, and sometimes it
is not. In either case, I do not present it as a "right" idea, but simply as
another one that should be considered. (I usually introduce it by saying,
"Some people say . . .") If the discussion gets to a point where I am not at
all sure what I think, then I might enter with my own tentative thoughts,
acknowledged as mine, as in chapter 10.

The essential element of having the students do the explaining is not
the withholding of all the teacher's own thoughts. It is, rather, that the
teacher not consider herself or himself the final arbiter of what the learner
should think, nor the creator of what that learner does think. The important job for the teacher is to keep trying to find out what sense the students
are making. This sometimes involves what has come to be called in my
classes "monkey wrenches"—some idea or evidence that raises a question
about what a learner has just said, even if that might be something I agree
with. "Throwing a monkey wrench," instead of "reinforcing the right answer" (as the common wisdom of the trade goes), at first seems a perverse
teaching practice. Yet it is because of the basic concerns of a teacher—because of wanting to be sure that students understand—that one remains
noncommittal, resists early acceptance of a student's understanding, and
searches for any soft spots that require more thinking.

There is one other important aspect to having students do the explaining. I try to have all the students share with me the responsibility of making sure they understand each other. This is tough for many people. For
one thing, it is often hard to admit to oneself that one does not understand.
Second, many (in fact, most) of the adults I have taught assume that if
they have not understood what has been said, the shortcoming is their
own. Few think that the speaker said it unclearly, and even fewer that the
speaker might not have been clear in his or her own mind.

The following excerpt indicates how significant it is even for competent adults to take this step.

> [We paid] careful attention . . . to the understanding of each other's understanding, as well as our own. . . . For the first time in my life, I heard myself say to a fellow classmate, in front of approximately 50 others, "I don't think I understand what you mean. Could you please say that again?" Never before had I experienced the self-confidence, the freedom, and, perhaps, the comfort necessary to do such a thing. What is significant, however is that such an honest statement on my part was able to lead to further explanation and exploration of the other's thoughts, thereby raising issues in his own mind to be shared with the others as he experienced them, himself. In a journal entry . . . I wrote the following:
>
>> For the first time, I was able to examine another's thoughts at work. Simultaneously, it seemed, I could examine my own. Excitement! I feel like a supercharged machine, discovering realms of my own capacities which I'd never know were there! What other worlds within worlds within me exist?
>
> Such euphoria was certainly not the norm, but what joy to experience! I felt as though my eyes and ears were operating at heights never before reached—certainly not within a classroom.

TEACHING-RESEARCH

My view of teaching suggests an analogy to the work of a psychotherapist with a research interest. She is both a practitioner and a researcher. She could not possibly learn anything significant about psychodynamics if she were not genuinely engaged in the therapeutic process. It is only because she knows how to do her job as a practitioner that she is in a position to pursue her questions as researcher. I would like to propose that, similarly, one is in a position through teaching to pursue questions about the development of understanding that one could not pursue in any other way. If as a researcher one is interested in how people build their understanding, then the way to gain insight is to watch them do it, and try to make sense of it as it happens (to paraphrase Armstrong, in Engel, 1984).

When I speak of "teaching," I do not necessarily mean schoolteaching. I am not, myself, a school teacher, for example. By "teacher" I mean someone who engages learners, who seeks to involve each person wholly—mind, sense of self, sense of humor, range of interests, interactions with other people—in learning. And, having engaged the learners, a teacher finds his questions to be the same as those that a researcher into the nature of human learning wants to ask: What do you think and why? While the students learn, the teacher learns, too. And it helps if, like Paley (1986), he is curious about the students' thoughts. How do other people really think about these matters? Which ideas build on which others and how? Which interests build on other interests? Which ideas get in the way of other ideas? What seem to be, in Hawkins's (2000) phrase, the "critical barriers" in this field? How is an idea modified? How does a firmly held conviction influence how a person reads an experience? What is the range of conceptions covered by a "right-sounding" word or phrase? In what circumstances is a person confused by/deaf to/helped by another person's thoughts? What factors keep interest high? How does a specific representation of one's thoughts influence how the thoughts develop further? How does a new idea lead to a new question, and vice versa?*

This kind of research need not take place in a classroom. But it does require, as a researcher, someone who knows ways into a subject matter well enough to engage a great variety of learners, and to keep them going as they ask and answer further questions—that is, it requires someone who is a good teacher.**

After her experience in the course just described, Delaney (1986a), a high school teacher of government, on leave from her classroom, did some pilot research of this kind. As she stated in the project proposal,

> I am attempting to understand how two high school students [Mark and Tim] . . . make sense of the presidency. In so doing, I would like to be able to identify questions and problems that interest people and prompt them to take notice of their own understanding and to elaborate on it. I am especially interested in . . . four aspects of the presidency: the powers of the president, the restrictions on these powers, the relationship between the president and other government institutions (particularly Congress), and the relationship between the president and the electorate. These four

---

*In addition to the works cited elsewhere in this volume, see the following sources listed in the References for a variety of approaches to such work: Apelman, 1982; Armstrong, 1980, 2006; Bamberger, 1991, 2006a, 2006b; Carini, 1987; Cavicchi, 1999, 2005, 2006a, 2006b; Cavicchi et al, 2001; Chittenden & Salinger, 2001; Chiu, 2003; Cirino, 2001; Davis, 2000; Delaney, 2001; Dominick, 1988; Doris, 1991; Duckworth, 1987, 1990, 2001b, 2005; Gill, 2004; Goldberg, 1990; Hart, 1979; Himley, 2000; Hooper, 1998; Hooper & Auger, 2006; Hsueh, 1997, 2005; Hughes-McDonnell, 2000, 2006; Jones, 1997; Julyan, 1988; Julyan & Duckworth, 2005; Kamii & Devries, 1980, 1993; Knox, 2001; Lerea, 2004; Lowry, 2006; Magau, 2001; Mayer, 2004, 2006; McKinney, 2004; Moise, 1965; Paley, 1986; Quintero, 2001; Ramsey, 2006; Rauchwerk, 2005; Rowe 1987; Schneier, 1990; Seidel, 1995; Shorr, 2006; Tierney, 1988. Also see the *Inventions!* curriculum written by Naomi Mulvihill (Intercultural Center for Research in Education [IN-CRE], 1998).

**For a related view of teachers as researchers, see Cobb and Steffe, 1983.

aspects of the presidency seem to be sufficiently broad so that I might be able to glimpse how the national government is understood. Yet they are sufficiently focused so that we have specific problems and issues to explore. (p. 1)

Each of her students kept a notebook in which they recorded each day at least one observation of the president, taken from news broadcasts, papers, or magazines.

Even though she was "attempting to understand," her primary interest in the project was in being a teacher. "The most important goal of this project for me was that [they] learn to think about some aspect of the president in some new way" (Delaney, 1986a, p. 4). She did succeed in "engaging" the students, the first aspect of teaching described above. At the end of the study, she wrote, "The most amazing aspect of this project . . . has been how engaged both Mark and Tim stayed. Every time I called them [to confirm their meetings], they wanted to tell me what they thought of some event and ask what I thought." The following excerpts from one of her field reports further show how the two, research and teaching, are one. Tim was sick this day, and the session took place with Mark alone.

> Mark rarely hesitates in stating his opinions or thoughts. If his statements seem contradictory to me and I ask him to explain, he calmly states each statement again, not bothering to reconcile the contradiction (Delaney, 1986a, p. 20).

> In our last session, when I asked Mark if a person is disloyal to the country when he or she disagrees with the president, he replied: "No. You have to distinguish between two things. A president is gonna base his decision on two things: either on what the majority of the people like *or* on what he knows best. . . . If he decides to rule by his feelings on a subject on which he knows more than the public then you can't say those people are un-American. Not every American knows in-depth."
>
> Because I did not understand this explanation, I asked Mark about it again [in this session]. I read to him what he had said. He said, "Yeah, I know you didn't really understand all that. . . ." He explained: "People that do [know] as much as Reagan, they still disagree. Because on a particular subject, if they didn't agree . . . Now you got me stuck." "Good. . . ." Mark was truly stuck. He was hesitant from "particular subject" on. He does not like being stuck. When I replied "good," we both laughed. I could see him relax. (Delaney, 1986b, pp. 1–2)

Delaney chose to back off from that question for the time being, in order to put him at ease. Later she returned to it. This passage is particularly interesting in enabling us to see the kinds of decisions Delaney is making throughout this work.

I asked him to explain once again his notions of the two ways presidents can make decisions. He said, "Well, first of all, it's not just the president. All politicians have that choice. . . . It would be good if politicians in order to get into office tell people what they want to hear, but once they're in just do what they think is best. . . . [I]f what they're doing is right that's OK."

My mind went in two different but related directions: (1) What if what the politicians do is wrong? and (2) who determines what is right and wrong, and how . . . ? For some time I had suspected that Mark's view of decision making rested on an assumption that decisions could be classified into either right or wrong decisions. . . . [I asked him:]

"How do you determine if a decision is right?"

"What would benefit overall the people."

"How do you decide what would benefit the people overall?"

"I'm not sure."

"Let's look at an example that we've talked about."

"Okay."

"Contra aid. In the public opinion polls, the majority of the American people seem to oppose aid to the contras. Yet the president supports it. How does he decide that the majority is wrong and he is right?"

". . . You don't know that. The majority could be people who just don't like it. Some people know. Some don't."

From this statement I realized that Mark probably thought of the "majority" as one huge chunk—a monolithic entity holding the same views for these same reasons. . . . I suggested that we make up a poll. . . . I asked: "This 52% represents 624 individuals and this 48% represents 576 individuals. Had you thought of that?"

"Yes. "

"Okay, how do you know if these 624 individuals know or do not know about the contra aid issue?"

He responded: "I could say the majority don't know or I could say the minority don't know. You would have to do a very in-depth study."

"Knowing" to Mark seems to be directly linked to "right" and "not knowing" to wrong. In this session and the last . . . he uses "right" and "knowing" interchangeably. To know is to be right. . . . I asked if it might be possible that some people in the majority be misinformed and some be informed? "It's hard to say . . . because some people just base it on what they saw in the news and not on what's real."

In this last statement we have plenty of questions for another [session]. . . . What's the difference between the news and "what's real"? Bypassing this for a moment I decided to rephrase my question using his terminology. "Is it possible that some people in the majority base their decisions on the news and others on what's real?" Silence. Mark was thinking—*hard*. I could practically hear his brain working when he said, "Wow, I never thought of that before."

"What?"

"That a majority could have different reasons why they're on that side." (Delaney, 1986b, pp. 4–6)

Here was confirmation of her hunch about how Mark was thinking (Delaney as researcher) and, at the same time, a great new idea on his part (Delaney as teacher). The session had to come to an end shortly after this. Delaney asked Mark to watch the news "for examples of how people on the same side of an issue . . . may agree for different reasons," and for "more data on how the president decides."

Among her several comments on the session is this one, where she uses the insight gained into Mark's thinking to help her understand something that had puzzled her since the first session:

> From our last session, I had suspected that Mark's notion of decision-making rested on a belief that absolutely right and absolutely wrong decisions were possible, and that part of the president's job was to identify *the* right decision. He said in our first session, "It's wrong to change your opinion. You can't just change it like that." This seems a curious statement at first glance, and the juxtaposition of the statements seems even more curious. However, if you believe that your opinion is right then both statements and their relationship begin to make sense: If you *are* right then changing your opinion *is* wrong. (Delaney, 1986b, p. 9)

What, then, has Delaney learned as a researcher? On the face of it, it might look as if what she learned were particulars about Tim and Mark. Of course that is what she learned, and at one level we could say that what she learned helped her make specific decisions about how to go further with them. In this, she is being a "reflective practitioner," in Schön's (1983) sense. But there are other levels where her learning goes far beyond her work with Tim and Mark. She contributes to our knowledge of what is involved in an understanding of how the American government works, and how such understanding can evolve. For readers with no interactions at all with Tim and Mark, her field reports are fascinating. So that's what you have to think about as you try to help someone understand the workings of government!

In her final report, she uses Hawkins's (2000) notion of "critical barriers" in discussing two factors she found to characterize Tim and Mark's ideas about the workings of the government. One factor was what she called "single-group nouns"—"majority," "public," and also "White House" (in referring vaguely to the president and/or his staff)—which the boys used, as she put it, to "communicate a single entity and obscure the diversity inherent in them" (Delaney, 1986a, p. 31). The second factor is their tendency to view the presidency in what she called "bipolar terms"—characterized by making "right" and "wrong" decisions. She points out that the first of these barriers makes it difficult, for example, to appreciate the central importance of diversity in a democracy. The second makes it difficult, for example, to appreciate why a democracy limits the powers of its leaders.

Even from this exceedingly small-scale study there seem to be countless questions for further teaching-research into what is involved in order for people to come to understand the workings of a democratic government. That is one kind of contribution this approach to research makes.

Furthermore, in shedding light on the growth of understanding about a democratic government, such research also sheds light on the growth of understanding in general. Oversimplifying single-group nouns and viewing situations as bipolar are both widespread characteristics of human thinking and a lively concern of psychologists (see Basseches, 1984). Just as specifics can be understood only through generalities, so generalities can be understood only through specifics: It is helpful to think of bipolar thinking as a critical barrier; at the same time, it is only possible to understand what critical barriers are when we see instances of them.

I believe there is yet another kind of knowledge to which this research contributes—namely, knowledge of curriculum possibilities. Delaney's attempts to learn how these youngsters understand government seem to me to indicate ways to *teach* youngsters about government. This almost seems like a tautology—the procedures that result in people's getting involved enough to want to talk about what they think are the very procedures that result in people's getting involved enough to learn. But if it is a tautology, it certainly has not been much recognized. In any event, Delaney has also learned and written about how to approach the teaching of government in a way that I think would certainly be helpful to other classroom teachers. If we take "curriculum" to be ways of engaging students in giving thought to those matters we think important, then she has started to develop curriculum.

SCHOOLTEACHING

Delaney did not carry out this research while working as a schoolteacher. She used her capacities as a teacher, but in a less pressured situation. It is a rare schoolteacher who has either the freedom or the time to think of her teaching as research, since much of her autonomy has been withdrawn in favor of the policies set by anonymous standard setters and test givers.

But even given the terrible constraints, and even if no resources are available to make known what they learn, there is some opportunity—and I think great need—for teachers to listen to their students explain what they think (for more on this point, see chapter 11 and Ramsey, 2002, 2006).

Another student in this course, who was at the same time teaching science in a middle school, did a project with small groups of students from her class (Young, 1986). The following are some of her comments about this work and her regular teaching job.

> I chose to center my field work around the topic of pulse as an
> avenue to understanding the . . . circulatory system (a curriculum
> which I was supposed to "cover"). Initially, I was doubtful about
> how far we could get with our investigation. I had never given
> pulse much thought and imagined that it offered a few tactile ex-
> periences but might not turn out leading the students on to more
> questions. . . . I was amazed to discover how much investigation
> was generated from the pulse work.
>
> My research on students' understanding of pulse is entwined
> with my teaching. . . . The teacher is researching the student and
> his understanding and then trying to help that student move on
> to more unknown territory. My bent is to apply my small group
> work to my classes . . . ! This is the ultimate challenge. The task
> appears so immense and fragile with one or two people, that the
> prospect of applying the same concentration to a large group is
> overwhelming. I do think that it is possible though with some
> modifications.
>
> If nothing else . . . the teacher would be more sensitive to listen-
> ing, observing, and then talking with her students rather than at
> them. Although I did not initially link my research with what I do
> in room 126 at the Middle School, I now see a crucial relationship.
> . . . My research has become and hopefully will remain a vital ele-
> ment in my teaching. I realize that my understanding of myself as
> a learner weighs heavily on how I perceive the understanding of
> other learners. So, we in room 126 are all learners.

CONCLUSION

I am not proposing that schoolteachers single-handedly become published researchers in the development of human learning. Rather, I am proposing that teaching, understood as engaging learners in phenomena and working to understand the sense they are making, might be the sine qua non of such research.

This kind of researcher would be a teacher in the sense of caring about some part of the world and how it works enough to want to make it accessible to others; he or she would be fascinated by the questions of how to engage people in it and how people make sense of it; would have time and resources to pursue these questions to the depth of his or her interest, to write what he or she learned, and to contribute to the theoretical and pedagogical discussions on the nature and development of human learning.

And then, I wonder—why should this be a separate research profession? There is no reason I can think of not to rearrange the resources available for education so that this description defines the job of a public school teacher.

So this essay ends with a romance. But then, it began with passion.

References

Ackermann-Valladao, E. (1977). Analyse de procédures de résolution d'un problème de composition de hauteurs [Analysis of solution procedures in a problem of composition of heights]. *Archives de Psychologie, 45*, 101–125.

Ackermann-Valladao, E. (1981). *Statut fonctionnel de la représentation dans la conduite finalisée chez l'enfant* [Functional status of representation in children's goal-oriented conduct]. Unpublished doctoral dissertation, University of Geneva.

African Primary Science Program. (circa 1967). *Ask the ant lion* [Prepared by Joseph Elstgeist]. Newton, MA: Education Development Center.

African Primary Science Program. (1970). *Making things look bigger* [Prepared by W. U. Walton & M. B. R. Savage]. Newton, MA: Education Development Center.

Apelman, M. (1982). On size and scale: Learning with David Hawkins. *Outlook, 45*, 18–51.

Apostel, L., Jonckheere, A. R., & Matalon, B. (1959). *Logique, apprentissage, et probabilité* [Logic, learning, and probability]. Paris: Presses Universitaires de France.

Armstrong, M. (1980). *Closely observed children*. London: Writers and Readers Publishing.

Armstrong, M. (2006). *Children writing stories*. London: Open University Press.

Ball, D., & Wilson, S. (1996). Integrity in teaching: Recognizing the fusion of the moral and intellectual. *American Educational Research Journal, 33*(1), 155–192.

Bamberger, J. (2006a). "Changing musical perception through reflective conversation." In R. Horowitz (Ed.), *Talking texts: How speech and writing interact in school learning*. Mahwah, NJ: Erlbaum.

Bamberger, J. (2006b). Restructuring conceptual intuitions through invented notations: From path-making to map-making. In E. Teubal, J. Dockrell, & L. Tolchinsky (Eds.), *Notational knowledge: Developmental and historical perspectives*. Rotterdam: Sense Publishers.

Bamberger, J., Duckworth, E., & Lampert, M. (1981). *An experiment in teacher development: Final report* (Contract No. G-78–0219). Washington, DC: National Institute of Education.

Basseches, M. (1984). *Dialectical thinking and adult development.* Norwood, NJ: Ablex.

Bereiter, C., & Engelmann, S. (1966). *Teaching disadvantaged children in the preschool.* Englewood Cliffs, NJ: Prentice-Hall.

Blanchet, A. (1977). La construction et l'équilibre du mobile, problèmes méthodologiques [The construction and balancing of mobiles, methodological problems]. *Archives de Psychologie, 45,* 29–52.

Blanchet, A., Ackermann-Valladao, E., Karmiloff-Smith, A., Kilchner, H., & Robert, M. (1976). *Présentation des termes et des hypothèses directrices* [Presentation of terms and of guiding hypotheses]. Unpublished manuscript, University of Geneva.

Bruner, J. (1960). *The process* of *education.* Cambridge, MA: Harvard University Press.

Carini, P. (1987). Another way of looking. In K. Jervis & A. Tobier (Eds.), *Education for democracy* (pp. 10–28). Proceedings from The Cambridge School Conference on Progressive Education.

Carini, P. (2001). *Starting strong: A different look at children, schools and standards.* New York: Teachers College Press.

Cavicchi, E. (1999). *Experimenting with wires, batteries, bulbs, and the induction coil: Narratives of teaching and learning physics in the electrical investigations of Laura, David, Jamie, myself and the nineteenth century experimenters—our developments and instruments.* Unpublished Doctoral Dissertation, Harvard University.

Cavicchi, E. (2005). Exploring water: Art and physics in teaching and learning with water. In R. France (Ed.), *Facilitating watershed management: Fostering awareness and stewardship* (pp. 173–194). Lanham MD: Rowman & Littlefield.

Cavicchi, E. (2006a, June). *Science experimenting with old and new things.* Paper presented at the annual meeting of the Jean Piaget Society, Baltimore.

Cavicchi, E. (2006b). Historical experiments in students' hands: Unfragmenting science through action and history. *Science and Education.*

Cavicchi, E., Hughes-McDonnell, F., & Lucht, P. (2001). Playing with light. *Educational Action Research, 9,* 25–49.

Christofedes-Papert, A. (1965). *Construction des intersections* [Construction of intersections]. Unpublished manuscript, University of Geneva.

Chittenden, E., & Salinger, T. (2001). *Inquiry into meaning: an investigation of learning to read.* New York: Teachers College Press.

Chiu, S. (2003). *Exploring traditional Chinese painting: A case study of a group of five U.S. students.* Unpublished Doctoral Dissertation, Harvard University.

Cirino, H. (2001). Journal journeys: An exploration with young writers. In E. Duckworth (Ed.), *"Tell me more": Listening to learners explain* (pp. 79–92). New York: Teachers College Press.

Cobb, P., & Steffe, L. (1983). The constructivist researcher as teacher and model builder. *Journal for Research in Mathematics Education, 14*, 83–94.

Davis, B. (2000). *Skills mania: Snake oil in our schools.* Toronto: Between the Lines.

Delaney, M. K. (1986a). *Understanding the presidency: Final report.* Unpublished manuscript, Harvard Graduate School of Education.

Delaney, M. K. (1986b). *Protocol 5.* Unpublished manuscript, Harvard Graduate School of Education.

Delaney, M. (2001). Understanding the presidency. In E. Duckworth (Ed.), *"Tell me more": Listening to learners explain* (pp. 125–146). New York: Teachers College Press.

DiSchino, M. (1987). The many phases of growth. *Journal of Teaching and Learning, 1*(3), 12–28.

Dominick, A. (1988). Games as a tool for evaluation. *Arithmetic Teacher, 35*, p. 5.

Doris, E. (1991). *Doing what scientists do: Children learn to investigate their world.* Portsmouth, NH: Heinemenn.

Duckworth, E. (1964). Floating color tubes. *Nature and Children, 1*(2), 6–7.

Duckworth, E. (1978). *The African primary science program: An evaluation and extended thoughts.* Grand Forks: North Dakota Study Group on Evaluation.

Duckworth, E. (1983). Teachers as learners. *Archives de Psychologie, 51*, 171–175.

Duckworth, E. (1987). Some depths and perplexities of elementary arithmetic. *Journal of Mathematical Behavior, 6*, 43–94.

Duckworth, E. (1990). Opening the world. In E. Duckworth, J. Easley, D. Hawkins, & A. Henriques, *Science education: A minds-on approach for the elementary years* (pp. 21–59). Hillsdale, NJ: Erlbaum.

Duckworth, E. (2001a). Inventing density. In E. Duckworth (Ed.), *"Tell me more:" Listening to learners explain* (pp. 1–41). New York: Teachers College Press.

Duckworth, E. (2001b). *"Tell me more": Listening to learners explain.* New York: Teachers College Press.

Duckworth, E. (2005). A reality to which each belongs. In B. Engel (Ed.), *Holding values: What we mean by progressive education* (pp. 142–147). Portsmouth, NH: Heinemann.

Elementary Science Study. (1967a). *Gases and "airs."* St. Louis: McGraw-Hill.

Elementary Science Study. (1967b). *Senior balancing.* St. Louis: McGraw-Hill.

Elementary Science Study. (1968). *Where is the moon?* [Prepared by D. Ford]. New York: Webster Division, McGraw-Hill.

Elementary Science Study. (1969). *Batteries and bulbs.* New York: Webster Division, McGraw-Hill.

Engel, B. (1984). Interview with Michael Armstrong. *Elementary School Journal, 84*, 350–356.

Engel, B. (1987). *Between feeling and fact.* Grand Forks: North Dakota Study Group on Evaluation.

Engelmann, S. E. (1971). Does the Piagetian approach imply instruction? In D. R. Green, M. P. Ford, & G. P. Flamer (Eds.), *Measurement and Piaget* (pp. 118–126). New York: McGraw-Hill.

Evans, C. (1981). *Teacher-initiated research: Professional development for teachers and a method for designing research based on practice.* Cambridge, MA: Technical Education Research Centers.

Ferreiro, E., & Teberosky, A. (1983). *Literacy before schooling.* Exeter, NH: Heinemann.

Frost, R. (1979). *The poetry of Robert Frost* (E. C. Lathem, Ed.). New York: Holt, Rinehart & Winston.

Furth, H. (1966). *Thinking without language: Psychological implications of deafness.* New York: Free Press.

Gill, K. (2004). *At Cezanne's table: Exploring content-based instruction in the English language in an art museum.* Unpublished Doctoral Qualifying Paper, Harvard University.

Goldberg, M. (1990). Teaching and learning: A collaborative process. *Music Educator's Journal, 76,* 38–41.

Goustard, M., Greco, P., Matalon, B., & Piaget, J. (1959). *La logique des apprentissages* [The logic of learning]. Paris: Presses Universitaires de France.

Greco, P. (1959). L'apprentissage dans une situation à structure opératoire concrète: Les inversions successives de l'ordre linéaire par des rotations de 180° [Learning in a situation of concrete operational structure: Successive inversions of linear order by 180° rotations]. In P. Greco & J. Piaget (Eds.), *Apprentissage et connaissance* [Learning and knowledge] (pp. 68–87). Paris: Presses Universitaires de France.

Greco, P., & Piaget, J. (1959). *Apprentissage et connaissance* [Learning and knowledge]. Paris: Presses Universitaires de France.

Gruber, H. (1981). *Darwin on man: A study of scientific creativity.* Chicago: University of Chicago Press.

Gruber, H. E., Girgus, J. S., & Banuazizi, A. (1971). The development of object permanence in cats. *Developmental Psychology, 4,* 9–15.

Hart, R. (1979). *Children's experience of place.* New York: Irvington Publishers.

Hawkins, D. (2000). *The roots of literacy.* Boulder: University of Colorado Press.

Hawkins, D. (2003). *The informed vision: Essays on learning and human nature.* New York: Agora Publishing.

Hawkins, F. (1986). *The logic of action.* Boulder: Colorado Associated Universities Press.

Henriques, A. (1990). Experiments in teaching. In E. Duckworth, J. Easley, D. Hawkins, & A. Henriques, *Science education: A minds-on approach for the elementary years* (pp. 141–186). Hillsdale, NJ: Erlbaum.

Himley, M., with Carini, P. (2000). *From another angle: Children's strengths and school standards.* New York: Teachers College Press.

Hooper, P. (1998). *They have their own thoughts: Children's learning of computational ideas from a cultural constructionist perspective.* Unpublished dissertation, Massachusetts Institute of Technology.

Hooper, P., & Auger, J. (2006, April). *The involvement of critical exploration in supporting children from underserved communities in mathematical inquiry with programmable media.* Paper presented at the annual meeting of the American Education Research Association, San Francisco.

Hsueh, Y. (1997). *Jean Piaget, spontaneous development and constructivist teaching.* Unpublished doctoral dissertation, Harvard University.

Hsueh, Y. (2005). The lost and found experience: Piaget rediscovered. *The Constructivist, 16,* 1–11.

Hudson, L. (1968). *Frames of mind: Ability, pereption and self-perception in the arts and sciences.* London: Methuen.

Hughes-McDonnell, F. (2000). *Circuits and pathways of understanding: "I can't believe we're actually figuring out some of this stuff."* Unpublished dissertation, Harvard University.

Hughes-McDonnell, F. (2006, June). *Learning as a creative act.* Paper presented at the annual meeting of the Jean Piaget Society, Baltimore.

Inhelder, B., & Piaget, J. (1958). *The growth of logical thinking* (A. Parsons & S. Milgram, Trans.). New York: Basic Books. (Original work published 1955)

Inhelder, B., Sinclair, H., & Bovet, M. (1974). *Learning and the development of cognition* (S. Wedgewood, Trans.). Cambridge, MA: Harvard University Press.

Intercultural Center for Research in Education (INCRE). (1998). *Inventions! A social studies and technology curriculum.* Arlington, MA: Author.

Jones, F. B. (1977). The Moore method. *American Mathematical Monthly, 84,* 273–278.

Julyan, C. (1988). *Understanding trees: Four case studies.* Unpublished doctoral dissertation, Harvard University.

Julyan, C., & Duckworth, E. (2005). A constructivist perspective on teaching and learning science. In C. Fosnot, (Ed.), *Constructivism: Theory, perspectives, and practice* (2nd ed., pp. 61–79). New York: Teachers College Press.

Kamii, C., & DeClark, G. (1985). *Young children reinvent arithmetic: Implications of Piaget's theory.* New York: Teachers College Press.

Kamii, C., & Derman, L. (1971). Comments on Engelmann's paper. In D. R. Green, M. P. Ford, & G. P. Flamer (Eds.), *Measurement and Piaget* (pp. 127–147). New York: McGraw-Hill.

Kamii, C., & DeVries, R. (1980). *Group games in early education.* Washington, DC: National Association for the Education of Young Children.

Kamii, C., & DeVries, R. (1993). *Physical knowledge in pre-school education: Implications of Piaget's theory.* New York: Teachers College Press.

Kamii, C., & Housman, L. (2000). *Young children reinvent arithmetic: Implications of Piaget's theory* (2nd ed.). New York: Teachers College Press.

Kamii, C., & Joseph, L. (1989). *Young children continue to reinvent arithmetic, 2nd grade: Implications of Piaget's theory.* New York: Teachers College Press.

Kamii, C., & Livingston, S. (1994). *Young children continue to reinvent arithmetic, 3rd grade: Implications of Piaget's theory.* New York: Teachers College Press.

Kanevsky, R. (in press). Ways of knowing: Children observing and describing. In A. Martin & E. Schwartz (Eds.), *Making sense.* North Bennington: Prospect.

Karmiloff-Smith, A., & Inhelder, B. (1975). If you want to get ahead, get a theory. *Cognition, 3*, 192–212.

Kilcher, H., & Robert, M. (1977). Procédures d'actions lors de construction de ponts et d'escaliers [Action procedures in the construction of bridges and stairs]. *Archives de Psychologie, 45*, 53–83.

Knox, I. (2001). Newborn developments. In E. Duckworth (Ed.), *"Tell me more:" Listening to learners explain* (pp. 147–165). New York: Teachers College Press.

Kreidler, W. (1984). *Creative conflict resolution.* Chicago: Scott, Foresman.

Kuhn, T. (1962). *The structure of scientific revolutions.* Chicago: University of Chicago Press.

Labov, W. (1970). *The study of nonstandard English.* Champaign, IL: National Council of Teachers of English.

Langer, S. (1967). *Mind: An essay on human feeling.* Baltimore: Johns Hopkins Press.

Lerea, D. (2004). *"They have so much to say!" A dynamic approach to Jewish religious education.* Unpublished Doctoral Qualifying Paper, Harvard University.

Lowry, C. (2006) *An inquiry into parents learning a Piagetian perspective on how their babies learn.* Unpublished Doctoral Dissertation, Harvard University.

Magau, N. (2001). Looking at learning to understand teaching: A South African case study. In E. Duckworth (Ed.), *"Tell me more": Listening to learners explain* (pp. 166–180). New York: Teachers College Press.

Mayer, S. (2004). Apprehending the thought of (all) others in classrooms. In *Democratic responses in an era of standardization* (pp. 179-196). Troy, NY: Educator's International Press.

Mayer, S. (2006). *Analyzing agency and authority in the discourse of six high school English classrooms.* Unpublished Doctoral Dissertation, Harvard University.

McKinney, M. (2004). *Shaping history: Five students, three artifacts, and the material, social and economic lives of late nineteenth-century butter makers.* Unpublished Doctoral Dissertation, Harvard University.

Mitchell, L. S. (1963). *The young geographers.* New York: Basic Books. (Original work published 1934)

Moise, E. E. (1965). Activity and motivation in mathematics. *American Mathematical Monthly, 72*, 407–412.

Montangéro, J. (1977). Expérimentation, réussite, et compréhension chez l'enfant, dans trois taches d'élévation d'un niveau d'eau par immersion d'objets [Experimentation, success, and understanding in the child, in three tasks of raising water level by immersing objects]. *Archives de Psychologie, 45*, 127–148.

Morf, A., Smedslund, J., Vinh-Bang, & Wohlwill, J. F. (1959). *L'apprentissage des structures logiques* [Learning logical structures]. Paris: Presses Universitaires de France.

Nussbaum, J., & Novich, S. (1982). Alternative frameworks, conceptual conflict and accommodations: Toward a principled teaching strategy. *Instructional Science, 11*, 183–200.

Oléron, P. (1957). *Recherches sur le développement mental des sourdsmuets* [Research on the mental development of deaf-mutes]. Paris: Centre National de Recherche Scientifique.

Paley, V. (1986). On listening to what the children say. *Harvard Educational Review, 56*, 122–131.

Pettigrew, N. (2006, February 6). *A listening pedagogy.* Paper presented at the College Board New England Regional Forum, Boston.

Piaget, J. (1921). Essai sur quelques aspects du développement de la notion de partie chez l'enfant [Essay on some aspects of the development of the notion of part in the child]. *Journal de Psychologie Normale et Pathologique, 18*, 449–480.

Piaget, J. (1959). Introduction: La troisième année du Centre et le troisième Symposium International d'Epistémologie Génétique [Introduction: The third year of the Center and the third International Symposium of Genetic Epistemology]. In P. Greco & J. Piaget (Eds.), *Apprentissage et connaissance* [Learning and knowledge] (pp. 1–20). Paris: Presses Universitaires de France.

Piaget, J. (1962a). *The language and thought of the child* (M. Warden, Trans.). New York: The Humanities Press. (Original work published 1923)

Piaget, J. (1962b). *Play, dreams, and imitation in childhood* (C. Gattegno & F. Mary Hodgson, Trans.). New York: Norton. (Original work published 1945)

Piaget, J. (1965). *The moral judgment of the child* (M. Gabain, Trans.). New York: The Free Press. (Original work published 1932)

Piaget, J. (1966). *The origins of intelligence in children* (Margaret Cook, Trans.). New York: International Universities Press. (Original work published 1936)

Piaget, J. (1970). *The child's conception of movement and speed.* (G. E. T Holloway & M. J. Mackenzie, Trans.). New York: Basic Books. (Original work published 1946)

Piaget, J. (1976). *Judgment and reasoning in the child* (M. Warden, Trans.). Totowa, NJ: Littlefield, Adams & Co. (Original work published 1924)

Piaget, J. (1981). *The psychology of intelligence.* Totowa, NJ: Littlefield, Adams and Co. (Original work published 1947)

Piaget, J. (1986). *The construction of reality in the child* (M. Cook, Trans.). New York: Ballantine. (Original work published 1937)

Piaget, J., & Inhelder, B. (1967). *The child's conception of space* (F. J. Langdon & J. L. Lunzer, Trans.). New York: Norton. (Original work published 1948)

Piaget, J., & Inhelder, B. (1974). *The child's construction of quantities: Conservation and atomism* (A. Pomerans, Trans.). London: Routledge and Kegan Paul. (Original work published 1942)

Piaget, J., & Inhelder, B. (1975). *The origin of the idea of chance in children* (L. Leake, Jr., P. Burrell, & H. Fishbein, Trans.). New York: Norton. (Original work published 1951)

Piaget, J., Inhelder, B., & Szeminska, A. (1981). *The child's conception of geometry* (E. A. Lunzer, Trans.). New York: Basic Books. (Original work published 1948)

Quintero, I. (2001). Children map their neighborhoods. In E. Duckworth (Ed.), *"Tell me more": Listening to learners explain* (pp. 93–124). New York: Teachers College Press.

Ramsey, L. (2002). *Developing curriculum in light of close attention to student thinking: An examination of selected narrative research literature by classroom teachers.* Unpublished Qualifying Paper, Harvard University.

Ramsey, L. (2006). *"And then she changed herself": Engaging and giving close attention to student thinking in elementary classrooms.* Unpublished Doctoral Dissertation, Harvard University.

Rauchwerk, S. (2005). *Incubating knowledge: A critical exploration with teachers studying live chickens.* Unpublished Doctoral Dissertation, Harvard University.

Ringi, K. (1968). *The stranger: A modern fable.* New York: Random House.

Robert, M. (1978). *Les modifications du déroulement de l'activité observable, comme indices d'un changement de significations fonctionnelles* [Modifications of observable activity, as indicators of changes in functional meaning]. Unpublished doctoral dissertation, University of Geneva.

Robert, M., & Sinclair, H. (1974). Réglages actifs et actions de transformations [Active regulations and transformation actions]. *Archives de Psychologie, 45,* 425–456.

Rowe, T. (1987). *Using introspective methods to investigate the learning strategies of adult foreign-language learners: Four case studies.* Unpublished doctoral thesis, Harvard University.

Schneier, L. (1986). *Dancing in the hall.* Unpublished manuscript, Harvard Graduate School of Education.

Schneier, L. (1990). *Why not just say it?* Unpublished manuscript, Harvard Graduate School of Education.

Schneier, L. (2001). Apprehending poetry. In E. Duckworth (Ed.), *"Tell me more": Listening to learners explain* (pp. 42–78). New York: Teachers College Press.

Schön, D. (1983). *The reflective practitioner.* New York: Basic Books.

Shorr, W. (2006). *Coordinating conceptions of peace: A critical exploration in social studies curriculum development.* Unpublished Doctoral Dissertation, Harvard University.

Seidel, S. (1995). *"To be the complete thing": A case study of teachers reading children's writing.* Unpublished doctoral dissertation, Harvard University.

Sinclair, H. (1967). *Langage et opérations: Sous-systèmes linguistiques et opérations concrètes* [Language and operations: Linguistic sub-systems and concrete operations]. Paris: Dunod.

Smedslund, J. (1961). The acquisition of conservation of substance and weight in children: Extinction of conservation of weight acquired "normally" and by means of empirical controls on a balance. *Scandinavian Journal of Psychology, 2,* 85–87.

Smith, G. (1985). Arms control in history: What lessons for the present? What prospects for the future? *The Connecticut Scholar, 7,* 5–14

Strachota, B. (1996). *On their side.* Greenfield, MA: Northeast Foundation for Children.

Strauss, S., Stavy, R., & Orpag, N. (1981). The child's development of the concept of temperature. Cited in S. Strauss (Ed.), (1982), *U-shaped behavioral growth.* New York: Academic Press.

Strieb, L. (1985). *A Philadelphia teacher's journal.* Grand Forks: North Dakota Study Group on Evaluation.

Tierney, C. (1988). *Construction of fraction knowledge: Two case studies.* Unpublished Doctoral Dissertation, Harvard University.

Young, L. (1986). *Teacher as learner in research and the classroom.* Unpublished manuscript, Harvard Graduate School of Education.

Index

About the Author

Eleanor Duckworth grew up in Montreal and Halifax, Canada, and spends all available time in Quebec or Nova Scotia.

A former student and translator of Jean Piaget, Duckworth grounds her work in Piaget and Inhelder's insights into the nature and development of intelligence and in their research method, which she has developed as a teaching/research approach, Critical Exploration in the Classroom. She seeks to bring a Freirean approach to any classroom, valuing the learners' experience and insights. Her interest is in the experiences of teaching and learning of people of all ages, both in and out of schools.

Duckworth is a former elementary school teacher and has worked in curriculum development, teacher education, and program evaluation in Canada, the United States, Switzerland, Latin America, Africa, and Asia.

She is a community coordinator with the Greater Boston Coalition United for Justice with Peace; she is also a performing modern dancer.